THE MOTHERHOOD AFFIDAVITS

THE MOTHERHOOD AFFIDAVITS

A Memoir

LAURA JEAN BAKER

THE EXPERIMENT

NEW YORK

The Experiment, LLC
220 East 23rd Street, Suite 600
New York, NY 10010-4658
theexperimentpublishing.com

Many of the designations used by manufacturers and sellers to distinguish their products are claimed as trademarks. Where those designations appear in this book and The Experiment was aware of a trademark claim, the designations have been capitalized.

The Experiment's books are available at special discounts when purchased in bulk for premiums and sales promotions as well as for fund-raising or educational use. For details, contact us at info@theexperimentpublishing.com.

Library of Congress Cataloging-in-Publication Data available on request

ISBN 978-1-61519-439-1
Ebook ISBN 978-1-61519-440-7

Cover and text design by Sarah Smith
Cover illustration by CSA Images/Printstock Collection
Author photograph by Kim Thiel

Manufactured in the United States of America

First printing April 2018
10 9 8 7 6 5 4 3 2 1

For Ryan, my steadfast supplier

AUTHOR'S NOTE

This memoir blends public and private lives. Our family story is carefully constructed from personal archives, including but not limited to journals and other writings, photographs, videos, and firsthand accounts.

Stories of Ryan's work in criminal defense have been corroborated through Open Records (Wisconsin Public Record Law, enacted 1982), an abundance of discoverable evidence, court proceedings I personally attended, and news coverage of high-profile cases.

Ryan used these theories, themes, and client details when presenting openly to district attorneys, judges, and juries, as a means to frame his clients' defenses. Although Ryan's clients were not afforded anonymity in court, I changed their names and (in some cases) identifying details to protect their privacy. I also took modest artistic liberties in developing scenes, such as reframing reported speech as dialogue and using my own descriptive language, but I have preserved the facts of all cases. Everybody appears as him- or herself throughout the book. I have created no composite characters or events.

As Thomas Larson writes in *The Memoir and the Memoirist*, "To write a memoir is to be selective." This story covers an eight-year span of time, from 2008 to 2016, such that I excluded facets of our lives for efficiency and thematic cohesion. Through a meticulous writing and editing process, I have attempted to render our story in as true a fashion as artistically possible.

There was an old woman who lived in a shoe.
She had so many children, she didn't know what to do.

She gave them some broth without any bread;
And whipped them all soundly and put them to bed.

—Unknown

High Waters

June 2008 in Oshkosh, Wisconsin—birthplace of OshKosh B'gosh; birthplace of us—would end up the wettest on record since 1897. Playgrounds were muck pits at best, cesspits at worst. A University of Wisconsin–Madison entomologist advised residents to pump or siphon standing water. At this rate of rainfall, rotting lawns were predicted to breed March flies, fungus, gnats, and mosquito eggs into critical excess.

Ryan and I had just embarked on our new lives as outnumbered parents: two adults divided by three children. The sunshine season lay un-calendared before me, liquid and lustrous like a gasoline rainbow. No essays or quizzes to grade. No paycheck either. Just a four-year-old daughter, a two-year-old son, their baby sister, and a used minivan with windows that worked and air-conditioning that didn't. Ryan was grinding away for a small law firm in Milwaukee, commuting 160 miles per day.

My kids and I needed free, dry entertainment. The ominous incubation of bug babies seemed an extension of our ongoing negotiations with the out-of-doors. On several instances in summers past, we'd been shooed away from our Lake Winnebago beach for *E. coli* warnings, and today's forecast predicted more rain. We'd already been to the YMCA once. We were costumed out. Our firstborn, Irie, had dressed her little brother in a faux-fur kitty-cat ascot—one of her many whims—and forced him to crawl around in it, though by now he could run upright.

The best I mustered in my one-mother brainstorming session was the McDonald's PlayPlace. By baby number three, eager to keep the children occupied, I didn't cringe at indoor germs. Never mind *Staphylococcus* or fecal matter. Parenting does not afford us the luxury of puritanism. *What's the big deal about leaky diapers in those fast-food crawl spaces?*

Instead, I worried over money. How meager a purchase would justify admission for two? Was that little box of McDonaldland Cookies stamped into the shape of the Hamburglar still on the menu for less than a dollar? On top of our refrigerator we kept "the coin jar," actually a wedding gift, a hand-sculpted clay pot with two lovebirds on a chipped lid. In need of amusement, we'd often count pennies and dimes into snack-size baggies.

The sky looked thunderously purple as we left on our outing, clouds swollen—pregnant with rain—though I didn't bother to pack umbrellas.

As soon as we arrived and spent $1.05, a deluge of rain began hammering the floor-to-ceiling PlayPlace windows. Irie and Leo clambered up the slide against one-way traffic, creating a pileup of squealing bodies with instant friends. A smattering of grandparents, mothers, and other caretakers slurped milkshakes and sodas, listening to pandemonium reverberate off the big red plastic tube.

As with Irie and Leo, I breastfed Fern on demand—everywhere, including the plastic swivel chair at McDonald's. Midwives had identified me as a likely candidate for postpartum depression, given my medical history. Instead of contracting the baby blues, though, I'd been struck with a serious case of the baby yellows, one long, exhilarating trip I hoped would never end.

Since Irie's birth in 2004, I'd come closer to solving the mystery of why motherhood pumped me up with such joy. The intimacy, the purposefulness, and the promise of a blank slate were among the plausible explanations, but most important was my new chemical makeup. Oxytocin, the "love drug," had compensated for my lifelong serotonin deficits. Oxy au naturel was better than anything the pharmaceutical companies had invented—and, for me, equally addictive. Proven to counteract adrenaline, the baby-making hormone had completely rebooted my mental health. I felt electrified and tranquilized simultaneously; I lulled my babies, and they lulled me.

Perhaps that was why I watched in wonderment as rain surged up under the door between the playland and the parking lot with remarkable force, a sudden high tide urged on by gravity. Within seconds, the McDonald's PlayPlace was a wading pool. I thought I was watching a movie. I unlatched my breastfeeding baby calmly, as if a bathroom sink had simply overflowed. But a server rushed toward us, insisting we evacuate. With two children in soggy socks, another in a portable carrier, I huddled at the main entrance alongside fellow patrons, calculating how fast we could sprint if I goaded Irie and Leo with fun, games, and merriment. But by the time we reached the car, we were soaked to the bone. Fern, at least, was damp but not waterlogged beneath the gingham canopy of her hand-me-down car cradle. I called Ryan at work.

"We were at the McDonald's on the frontage road, and the playland flooded."

"You're exaggerating," Ryan said, and I was forced to reiterate the melodramatic truth. "Shit, OK. I'll leave right now." We quickly clicked good-bye. If Ryan didn't act fast enough and the deluge continued, Ryan worried we'd be separated in the coming days.

As the children and I drained into the upholstery, Irie said, "It's like being at the car wash!"

"Yes," I said. "Or Niagara Falls." Ryan and I had honeymooned seven years earlier in a cheesy motel with a heart-shaped Jacuzzi a few blocks from the famous cascades of water, eating cheap food we paid for on credit, blessing our marriage on *Maid of the Mist*, but this water plummeted from the sky instead of over the Niagara Escarpment. Clouds clenched, groaned, and broke historic floodwaters as if from a bottomless amniotic sac.

I tried turning from McDonald's onto the frontage road through a cataclysm of water where the asphalt dropped. Other vehicles, mostly cars, forged through depths up to their hubcaps, headlights submerged like alligators' eyes. I maneuvered through crisis as my brain dispensed oxytocin in calm, liquid surges, along-side a quarry where the road was high, but every time we reached a T intersection, our minivan careened again into the floodwaters. On Ninth and Ohio, a bar owner stood knee-deep in waders, as if fishing.

"Stop the car!" he screamed. "You're making waves!" Water billowed against the breakwater of his establishment, Andy's Pub & Grub, sloshing and smacking. I called Ryan again, and he warned me of being swept away in a current. It seemed possible: we stalled and bobbed in a truck's wake. The rain pelted the windshield as I revved through the churning brown vortex onto a side street. An auto body shop, cutely labeled Automobile Hospital, dark and seemingly defunct but nevertheless like a beacon of light, appeared. Nestled alongside the south entrance was a measly ramp—an incline of no more than twelve inches. We coasted up onto that wedge of gravel like a boat up onto the shoreline.

The lagoon at South Park, retention ponds, and creeks were overflowing, making a dirty bath of the entire city. Yards, gardens, and sidewalks blurred indistinguishable from our natural boundaries—the Fox River and Lake Winnebago, which literally means "people of the filthy water." Locals affectionately refer to it as Lake Winne-septic, and today we were all swimming in it. As Ryan neared Winnebago County from Milwaukee on Highway 41, his was one of the last vehicles allowed to pass before police closed all four lanes. Water sluiced up from the ditches over the road like schools of river eels. When he gained on Oshkosh, he took his chances at the first exit. Lane markers refracted beneath the water.

"I felt like I was in one of those mazes on a kids' restaurant menu," he said. "Every drowned car was a dead end."

White-knuckled and gritting his teeth, Ryan wondered if driving his Nissan Sentra and its $325-per-month payment into the floodwaters might be a blessed setback. Our comprehensive plus gap insurance policies would cover the loss. The Oshkosh city manager and governor of Wisconsin declared a state of emergency. Half of Oshkosh homes would be pronounced variably damaged; three-quarters of the streets were impassable. A Canadian National train derailed at a washed-out bridge, and the accident led to an oil spill. Our house on Hazel Street, one block from Lake Winnebago, built in 1888, suffered only a dainty rivulet of water in the basement, which flowed right back into a hole on the concrete floor. Every small stroke of luck buoyed our spirits.

A year earlier, we'd escaped our short life in Milwaukee, one of the most dangerous and *the* most segregated city in America, according to census reports. In Bay View, where we'd rented an apartment, businesses were robbed at gunpoint, Irie's Radio Flyer trike was swiped in broad daylight, and the skittish driver of an armored car, replenishing cash at our nearest ATM, once pulled his gun on me and my stroller of babies. Everybody in Milwaukee lived on the brink of hysteria. Life in Oshkosh would be different—a good, wholesome place to raise a family.

Ryan killed his long commutes talking to colleagues on his cell phone. Fellow lawyers in other states convinced him that if he started his own law firm in Oshkosh and lasted two years, he'd be self-employed forever. "It's Wisconsin," a friend told him. "You can be the OWI guy." Just about everybody was known to operate a vehicle while intoxicated.

By the Fourth of July, a month after the flood, gasoline prices had vaulted to $4.18 per gallon. Between the car payment and the price of fuel, we were spending more than $1,000 per month on Ryan's transportation. A truck driver once chased him down Highway 41 in a fit of road rage. What if he'd been murdered? Would he have minded? "I'll make sure to set you up with a nice life insurance policy," he always joked. But mileage became his stock answer as to why he was quitting his job, and the June flood was another good justification for leaving Milwaukee. Fathers should be near at hand, in case of emergencies. Ryan resigned from his first law job in July and left officially in September.

The day after the flood, the *Oshkosh Northwestern* headline read WASHED OUT. Better that than washed up. I wonder now, on those arduous drives, how many times Ryan conjured up the worst solutions—burning our house down, running away and changing his identity, if not simply jumping from his office window—to our already looming money problems. "Poor at the bank; rich in love" remained my naive philosophy. Ryan and I seemed to have boarded little rescue boats coasting in opposite directions. I cast my anchor toward Ryan's unrelenting hopelessness, and he cast his toward me, as we worked hard to remain compatible. At the end of each day, though, the burden of family morale fell heavily upon me, the idealist and dreamer.

So much damage was yet to be uncovered after the flood—warped infrastructures, rust, mold, mildew, and all the chemical breakdowns inside our houses and schools. The *Northwestern* reporters tried to keep up: WINNEBAGO COUNTY'S CLEANING TAB AT $13M AND CLIMBING. In that same issue, editors printed a cartoon of a man and woman in a raft labeled OSHKOSH FLOODING. She is smiling, and her thought bubble reads, "All through bailing. Looks like we'll stay afloat after all." The man, however, is looking up at a tsunami labeled CONTINUED STORMS, eyes bulging, mouth agape. I might have taken this for a sign, but I could not have dreamed how Ryan's impending career in criminal defense would alter the trajectory of our lives.

Casework in criminal law was readily available in 2008—the least lucrative but most efficient way to start a legal practice, especially for a family man with a mortgage. On September 17 of that year, Ulrich Law Office would be inaugurated in suite 812 of the First National Bank Building on Main Street in Oshkosh. Ryan accepted work like a beggar, taking up alms, welcoming into our lives not just town drunks but drug dealers, heroin and meth addicts, thieves, violent men on the brink of homicide, and mothers who birthed their babies but failed their real-world maternity tests.

As the onslaught of rain turned to drizzle, I opened the sliding doors of our van. Ryan had enlisted his parents to retrieve us in their all-terrain truck. We were waiting.

Fern, though no feline, mewed for milk. Hunkered on the rear bumper, I cradled and breastfed my baby girl again, as Irie and Leo saluted strangers in kayaks and canoes paddling up Michigan Street. As a child, I'd visited *Wetlands and Waterways*, a permanent exhibit at the Oshkosh Public Museum, dozens of times and often wished I could see Oshkosh at the end of its Ice Age, a wish that seemed to have come true. We applauded passersby in their make-shift dinghies. In the summer of 2008 and forever after, floods were earmarked as our meteorological frames of reference.

"Can we swim?" Irie asked in that moment, perched above the first flood of her short lifetime, and I almost said yes. Fern at my breast, I was buzzing with the thrill of motherhood, recklessly invincible and wide-eyed. Later that night, I'd breastfeed Leo and Fern together, one "baby" per breast, worth the double shot of oxytocin. If I had traversed this historic flood, I could do anything. Jacked up on survival, I felt ready to baptize all of us by plunging headfirst into the floodwaters of euphoria or oblivion—whichever came first.

CHAPTER 1

The Walmart Heist

Derek Green and Allison Shaffer engineered their first Walmart shopping heist by hiring a babysitter for their newborn daughter, Destiny; borrowing the babysitter's Chevy Astro minivan as their getaway vehicle; and looting, along with the rest of their spoils, a case of Milwaukee's Best Ice—the Cadillac of Wisconsin beers—to pay the babysitter, fair and generous compensation, depending, arguably, on how many beers she would drink per hour.

Unfortunately, their babysitter must have been on duty elsewhere the night Green and Shaffer planned their encore caper. Destiny, fledgling conspirator, accompanied her parents, Daddy at the helm of her hand-me-down Cosco stroller. Along the dark frontage road, cars seethed and snow flurries churned a full mile until the family arrived at their destination. Inside the whirlwind beyond the sliding doors, where hot met cold, Shaffer selected a cart, gripped the handles, and ambled into the superstore, followed by Green, the baby, and the baby carriage.

Did they wave to Walmart greeters or clerks as they maneuvered toward Baby & Toddler, a slow-motion shopping spree, which Shaffer had expertly rehearsed, hands like soft paddle wheels? She propelled the cart forward, pulling baby clothes—Gerber

Onesies, fleece leggings, and Garanimals hoodies—into the belly of the shopping trolley. This cart could hold eighteen thousand cubic inches of merchandise. Maximizing the space, not minimizing the cost, was the object of Mama's concern. With each little stocking cap, Shaffer's heart pumped frantic hyper-oxidized blood to her brain. She felt awakened, even as baby Destiny snored beneath her frayed canopy.

Green then suggested a tour of Electronics, where he laid eyes immediately upon a Sony Home Theater. He realized they might have a problem. If Shaffer was pushing the cart, and Green was pushing Destiny, who would carry the fifteen-pound box? He knew from experience, as all parents do, that baby strollers are sturdy machines. He finagled the entertainment system so it teetered evenly over the handlebars like a little roof. Baby remained safely snuggled in her bottom bunk, and Daddy resumed pushing the stroller. Green's stunt, alongside Shaffer's filled-to-bursting cart, raised no suspicions. The couple wandered toward the storefront, chatting halfheartedly, dawdling with nonchalance, and then dillydallying their way into the Walmart parking lot with $1,231.91 worth of stolen goods, including the shopping cart, its own kind of getaway vehicle.

Green and Shaffer were surprised by how quickly December flurries had accumulated and seemed to be smoldering in the parking lot like a widespread scattering of ash. The snow was pinkish gray where kicked-up gravel poked holes, crystals spinning velvet and crinoline layers, as the temperature fluctuated. Shaffer followed Green's tire treads. He was pushing the cart now, wheels spinning like electric beaters, the Sony system box newly fastened to the shopping cart as they headed uphill. Shaffer pushed Destiny's stroller into the white wind, knuckles wet and red. I wondered, later, had they considered snagging gloves, warm winter jackets, or shoes without holes for themselves?

Halfway home—they had almost made it—a police officer spied Green, Shaffer, and all their baggage, including their infant child. He pulled over, offered assistance, and discovered, as backup arrived on the scene, evidence, or lack thereof—no receipt, no bags—that would be used against both parents in a court of law. Ryan and I were out celebrating; he turned thirty-one that very day in 2008, a momentous epoch—the year Fern was born and also the year he had opened Ulrich Law Office. Fittingly, we would mark Derek Green and Allison Shaffer's Walmart theft as the exact moment in time when Ryan's work in criminal defense truly began.

From the outside looking in, Oshkosh appears innocent, known worldwide for its children's clothing and overalls, but having both been raised here, we ridiculed our city with nicknames like Oshburg, Osh Vegas, and the Big Zero. Initially when Ryan gained VIP access to our hometown underbelly, we were dazzled, instead of distressed, to learn that our hamlet possessed an alter ego characterized by offbeat, sometimes Hollywood-like hijinks and crime. One of the first mothers Ryan defended, Renee Dubois, was charged with a felony crime known as uttering—distribution of forged checks. I could not help but imagine this devious woman "udder-ing," or milking that quintessentially female organ. The judge showed no sympathy as Dubois cried about a daughter awaiting her return in Florida.

Another mother, Imani Butler, was accused of stabbing her boyfriend in the back with a paring knife while her daughter watched TV in an adjoining room, an incident humorous only because the guy avoided hospitalization, and we never knew whether to take the story figuratively, as a metaphor for betrayal, or literally. Violence registered on a sliding scale, but where crimes landed was never clear, such as when a guy named Malik Turner pointed the muzzle of an unloaded gun at his girlfriend's stomach. She quickly chased him from the apartment, hurled a twenty-pound cinder block onto his windshield from her second-story window, and screamed till he burned rubber up the street, brick still wedged into the spray of broken glass. He craned his head out the driver's side window, a preposterous spectacle that made it easy for the police officers to track and arrest him. Facing up to twenty-five years in prison for battery and recklessly endangering safety, Turner almost rejected the deal of the century in favor of a trial but came to his senses after a jury had been selected.

"That guy scared the shit out of me," Ryan said of this first on a list of truly dangerous clients. Of course, the women—victims, "victims," or perpetrators—interested me most, immersed as I was in motherhood, temporarily relieved of a depression I'd suffered since childhood. I had always imagined myself derailing like a freight train. When I was only six years old, at the babysitter's house, I'd wear plastic bags over my head, plotting my death. "You've got to do more than just breathe into a bag, moron," older children would tell me. My backup plan was to suffocate beneath a kid pileup, and I begged them to sit on me. Often my depression manifested as anger, and I'd chase my full brother, Christopher, through our house with a chef's knife as if hunting an animal, ready to skin him alive. When he called me ugly or stupid, I'd snap and scream, "I'm going to kill you!" I'd run brandishing the blade, my urge insatiable. He usually locked himself in our parents' home office, but once (or twice) I forced the butcher blade into the opening between the sliding wood doors, hoping to cut my brother open.

Two of my own three children, during our first full winter in Oshkosh, were daughters, and I studied them just as closely as I did Ryan's clients, wishing away my brand of madness. Fern was born the same month and year as Green and Shaffer's daughter,

Destiny—a potential playmate, had our social circles overlapped—and we also struggled to afford the high cost of raising a family. Even though quitting his daily ninety-mile commute to Milwaukee to hang his own shingle in Oshkosh was a good decision family-wise, those transitional years would prove financially deadly. Starting a business sounded dreamy in June, nerve-racking in December.

Even before Fern, Ryan had worried himself sick over money. Throughout our childbearing years, his most repeated utterances were variations on the same theme: "Let's wait another year." "Enough babies already." "How can we afford to feed all these mouths?" "Jesus Christ, we're robbing Peter to pay Paul." Wisconsin's payment to private attorneys taking public defender cases was the lowest in the nation, frozen since 1995, when the per-hour rate was lowered from $50.00 to $40.00 per hour, a rate that seemed almost feasible, until a report by the Sixth Amendment Center ascertained that the average overhead rate for running a law office in Wisconsin was $41.79. The State Public Defender's Assigned Counsel Division began contracting with freelance private defense attorneys in 1978, the year I was born, when the pay rate was $35 per hour. Adjusting the 1978 rate for inflation, the 2008 rate should have been $118 per hour. With three children in day care now, and a new auto-pay requirement at the Children's Center, we'd somehow need to stretch our monies to cover $2,600 a month just to clock normal work hours, me at my campus office and Ryan at his downtown.

Also aggravating Ryan's financial unease was the troubling reality that private retainers, as he sought to balance out his practice with independent clients, came straight from the hands of criminals, and his clients—especially the Derek Greens of the world—committed crimes precisely because they were poor. We wondered, often, where the money to pay Ryan for his legal services had circulated before dropping anchor in the rock bottom of our hands.

Dirty money was the mother's milk that sustained Ulrich Law Office from early on. Ryan referred to the dirty money in slang, as in "bones," "simoleons," maybe "Benjamins" on a good day, all in lighthearted denial. The cash payments replenishing his empty wallet were laced with the sad and sordid stories of his defendants' lives. If scientists can link thousands of micro-organisms on dollar bills to gastric ulcers, staph infections, and acne, the money we used to pay for diapers, breastfeeding bras, a lifetime supply of Dole fruit cups, winter boots and replacement mittens, school supplies, library fines, and out-of-pocket expenses at the pediatrician's office could be linked to thefts, batteries, burglaries, heroin deals, and worse.

The origin of our money was an ongoing joke, like when a "dancer" paid Ryan three hundred dollars entirely in singles. Another time, on the eve of a preliminary hearing, a client charged with armed robbery delivered a three-thousand-dollar cash wad, rolled into the kind of greenback boutonniere one might find instructions for on Pinterest. Ryan tucked it into his shirt pocket and wore it to parent-teacher conferences. Afterward, when he purchased a few books at the Scholastic Book Fair, we joked about laundering our dirty banknotes, passing them into the PTO's hands, cotton-blossom clean.

Many of Ryan's clients "did not have a pot to piss in," as he liked to say, and they paid for legal representation in excuses, bartering their services—housecleaning, painting, auto repairs. Some scofflaws sacrificed their most prized possessions, like an autographed Green Bay Packers helmet and a pair of two-carat diamond earrings, while others offered fresh produce, donuts, and handmade key chains as unsolicited trade-ins for discounts unheard of elsewhere in the legal community. Ryan wondered if he spent more time chasing clients for money than any doing real legal work, relying upon the most destitute people to make their payments. If only the wealthy committed these kinds of conspicuous crimes. Every deposit at our bank was a sacrilege, and I wondered, how much did we forgive the burglars, thieves, and addicts we came to know as a way to exonerate ourselves from the crimes that helped to finance our family as we teetered on the threshold of a middle-class existence?

Maybe we offered up forgiveness because the state didn't. One of many ways Ryan justified his daily grind in criminal defense was to consider it a reformist effort. "In a courtroom, the only people less respected than criminal-defense attorneys," Ryan said, "are my clients." The district attorney's office, on behalf of the state, sometimes sought higher penalties for crimes, without rhyme or reason, or to a degree that seemed malicious to Ryan and his clients. One of Ryan's roles was to mitigate oftentimes disproportionate sentences. As a repeat player in the judicial game, he tried advocating for fairness, comparing sentences for defendants from diverse socioeconomic and racial groups accused of similar crimes. The system was neither class-blind nor color-blind. Once, a judge lost his temper, threw up his fists, and called the entire system racist. That day, by his own words, he gave Ryan's black defendant "the white man's deal."

Ryan's give-a-shit meter pointed to full in his first years. He was youthful, doused in freckles, still, sort of, a boy. "You my lawyer?" his clients asked, expecting the overweight, aged version of an attorney Ryan would later become. Calls to action for social and criminal justice vied with less exalted and more practical concerns for his energy and attention, often winning out. However, like so many undercompensated defense attorneys in Wisconsin, Ryan spent much of his brain power testing algorithms for family sustenance, desperate to earn a steady and reliable paycheck and to prevent our homelessness.

Before becoming a criminal-defense attorney, Ryan appeared regularly in Milwaukee County Small Claims Court suing uninsured motorists. He marveled at the picket fence separating paupers in the gallery from lawyers in the well, their newspapers and Victor Allen's coffee sleeves murmuring secrets. Ryan could barely work magic of our funds, but thanks to his education, he flashed a courtroom VIP pass. How on earth, he wondered, could these defendants, on the wrong side of the bar, scrounge up enough scratch to pay? He found himself balancing the duties of his job to get as much money as possible for the insurance companies, his rich clients, while making sure poorer defendants might still provide for their families.

"I'd make a shitty businessman," he said. He was more minister than attorney, and sadly but truly, his social awareness and bleeding-heart compassion were incompatible with the detached attitude he'd ultimately need to adopt in order to run Ulrich Law Office like a business instead of an outreach program.

Our beloved Badger State was no help. With limited funds to provide constitutionally guaranteed representation to poor defendants, Wisconsin paid its freelance attorneys erratically, anywhere from two weeks to several months after a case was completed. To make matters worse, the biennial allotment to the State Public Defender's Assigned Counsel Division experienced regular shortfalls. One year, when he billed the state in January, monies arrived in July. The delays exacerbated our money woes, and Ryan defaulted on his student loans within two years of graduating.

Ryan reminds me often of our Pick 'n Savings and Loan Crisis, named for our local grocery store, Pick 'n Save, and for the poorest period in our early parenting. Ryan was a first-year associate making $40,000 for our family of four. I was not teaching, as the cost of day care canceled out my earnings. As we struggled to pay down debt and survive on Ryan's wages, he wrote checks at our grocery store, Pick 'n Save, every other Wednesday night, to replenish our bare cupboards, knowing a thirty-six-hour delay in the transaction would coincide with payday. For months we kited checks, our private payday loan operation, a so-called victimless crime that helped to sustain our diet of eggs and toast. Pick 'n Savings and Loan was a compound problem, having been primed by our yet earlier financial mistakes.

When Ryan was still a law student, in fact, we'd preemptively bought our modest Oshkosh house, assessed by the city at only $139,000, with what is known today in the mortgage industry as a "liar's loan." I was sole breadwinner at the time. In addition to teaching adjunct at the local university, making $25,000 a year, our only real source of income, I agreed to our mortgage broker's suggestion that I exaggerate additional earnings from odds-and-ends tutoring, and signed off on my falsely inflated bankroll. If we could stretch thin without snapping until Ryan graduated from law school, we could make our little saltbox work, or so we deceived ourselves. To make ends meet, we avoided paying property taxes while Ryan earned his JD, and this debt matured quickly, our tax backlog ultimately generating a Notice to Delinquent Parcel Owners from some computer system in Winnebago County shortly after Ryan opened Ulrich Law Office in 2008.

We needed to pay $1,837.18 of a more than $8,000 debt by the New Year to prevent foreclosure. By the time our hens came to roost, we lived permanently in our house on Hazel Street with three small children under the age of five. Irelyn, nicknamed Irie, was four; Leo was two. They both still adored their baby sister, Fern, not yet aware of the bleeding-heart knockoff she'd grow into by the age of four, jotting down 1-800 numbers off infomercials about starving children or abused dogs. "She's so annoying," they'd quickly learn to say. "She tries too hard to be nice." Fern collected pennies in envelopes and donated them to a hospital.

Her heart hemorrhaged for people in need, as she became family mediator and defender, any outsider guessing correctly which child's birth coincided with Ryan's criminal advocacy work. If Irie or Leo were sent to their bedrooms for bullying Fern, she'd lobby for their immediate liberation.

As Fern offered to post bond for her siblings, we kept our own financial woes a secret; nothing was more embarrassing for us, supposed middle-class professionals, than practicing the etiquette of deadbeats. By skimping on groceries and eluding debt collectors seeking past-due balances from Children's Hospital of Wisconsin in Milwaukee, we paid our delinquent taxes, but we remained in a deep, dark hole. The next September, I'd returned to teach, and as we awaited my first paycheck of the new academic year, Wisconsin Public Service cut our power for failure to make regular payments. As our refrigerator warmed and our beds grew cold, we cursed our house and our educations, which were not yet paying off, beginning to wonder if childbirth and childrearing were upper-class luxuries we couldn't afford and didn't deserve.

Our house ripened into our biggest regret when Irie began kindergarten at our neighborhood school, and Ryan realized his clients and their children lived a stone's throw from us. At the kindergarten open house, an entourage of hard-bitten women—a mother, a grandmother, and a couple of aunts, perhaps—ushered one of Irie's classmates into the classroom, her face iridescent blue, glinting like metal. "She ran into a flagpole at the park yesterday," the oldest caretaker said. The girl began to vomit and was rushed outside. Later in the year, Ryan pulled up at school to drop off Irie's lunch, only to discover a used hypodermic needle alongside the curb, in plain view of the front entrance. The secretary, unfazed, made a routine call to the custodian for cleanup.

For months, while on campus at UW Oshkosh teaching, grading, or enduring meetings, I'd agonize about my children's safety, imagine them hanging upside down from monkey bars over infected syringes. We hated ourselves for buying our house on the old side of town. The historic sweetness of our character home did nothing to mitigate our anguish. The size of our domicile could be calculated as the inverse of its growing number of occupants—it was the incredible shrinking house. We referred to our basement as "the laundry project," heaps upon heaps of stinky clothes mounded on concrete. The most critical part of washing clothes was the return trip, scaling the steep stairs and latching the basement door. Irie once fell down the breakneck steps and landed forehead-first with a goose egg. Afterward, I developed the habit of slapping and locking the door as soon as I emerged, but one morning Ryan stood guard over the precarious ledge as I muscled up with a full load of clean clothes. When I ripped the door shut, Ryan yowled. I'd slammed his fingers in the hinged side of the door. Miraculously his hand was bruised, not broken, but our frustration deepened. Why should everyday tasks be so treacherous?

Broken squares of glass on our multipaned windows were time-consuming to fix; glass needed to be cut to variable size and then caulked. Lead paint bubbled up and flaked off in chunks we'd vacuum away before they were optioned as candy. We lived literally on the wrong side of the tracks—an ambulance might wait ten minutes at the railroad crossing on Broad Street. When a police officer stopped by, late one night, to introduce himself, we grew suspicious of his intent. Was this *before* the standoff between a resident with a loaded gun and the police, just around the corner, or was it *after* a car plowed through the four-way stop and crashed into our neighbor's front porch?

One morning at breakfast, the kids noticed a lady staggering up our sidewalk, pushing a swanky new barbeque grill. They called us to the window, and together we watched her zigzag along Hazel

Street. Ryan called the police, and on our way to school thirty minutes later, we spied the Char-Broil thief locked in a squad car.

Our biggest financial mistake was also our biggest miscalculation in safekeeping. Attorneys and writers explain the world in analogies, I've learned, and Ryan elucidated the relationship between work and family like this: "It's like I pump PCBs into the river, only to trawl fish from those same waters to feed my family." Nothing better described our quandary, especially considering that the Fox River, long contaminated by the lumber and paper industries, bisects Oshkosh into socioeconomically distinct plots of land.

Ryan was the bona fide great-grandson, seven generations removed, of Jacques Porlier, fur trader and later first judge in Wisconsin, which gave him a certain kind of confidence. We still drove our beat-up van embossed with a BOOKS NOT BOMBS sticker, later adding TFYQA (Think for yourself. Question authority). Ryan was a first-generation college student. His years in mock trial combined with a decade of idolizing Hollywood lawyers like Rudy Baylor in *The Rainmaker* led him—and almost everybody else we knew—to imagine a star-studded life. But his conversations with clients deviated wildly from the kinds of closing statements he imagined delivering in civil disputes.

At a sturdy card table in the bowels of the county jail, Ryan learned quickly to lay down the law, literally, to the kinds of tough men he didn't know in real life—the one in which he followed recipes for apple-prune crisp with Irie, sorted baseball cards with Leo, and paced the house, humming contralto, baby Fern sacked on the wide bank of his shoulder. Ryan and I were prolific reproductively, but he was no rainmaker, quickly becoming comedic and ill-tempered instead, like Vincent Gambini from *My Cousin Vinny.*

"If you're going to get caught red-handed, at least steal shit I can justify," Ryan said to Derek Green the very first time they met. At that point, Green had been charged with misdemeanor theft of movable property from Open Pantry.

Much to our surprise, the Winnebago County Jail had relocated from the second story of the Oshkosh Police Department downtown to its own state-of-the-art facility, built larger and to accommodate future expansion, on a scenic plot of land adjacent to the tri-county dump. Older, more jaded defense attorneys in town entertained Ryan with stories about the old jail. "Do you honestly believe crime has increased that much since the sixties?" one grouchy old lawyer said. "Hell, no. They just started making more stuff illegal. They make a lot of money incarcerating the poor."

Green was a chronic shoplifter: seventy dollars in gasoline from Kwik Trip, a bottle of Gordon's vodka, Reese's king-size candy bars, batteries, hot and greasy tornado rolls. But on the day in question, months before *the* Walmart heist, with only three cents' worth of stamps on his electronic benefits card, Green should have considered a food pantry in lieu of Open Pantry.

The attendant at the gas station recognized Derek Green in his faux-leather jacket and ball cap, his mannerisms familiar and antsy as he circled the store, waiting for the right moment to pocket Slim Jim beef sticks and whatever other five-finger discounts might tide him over.

We truly wondered, if Green and his family were starving, why didn't he consider snitching applesauce or Chicken of the Sea? Of course, what difference would it make? Green was known by police to "intentionally take and carry away merchandise held for resale, without the consent of the merchant," and he was known to get caught. Whether his getaway vehicle was a kid's BMX bicycle or a Walmart shopping cart, Green tripped over his own feet and backed himself into corners.

On this evening in November, the attendant had called the police before Green even sailed past the register, looking baffled, as if pointing a finger at his own dumbfounded face. When officers arrived, Green ran anyway, perhaps for appearances, through the parking lot, across a busy street, and into an unsuspecting neighbor's backyard. The officer pursuing Green issued verbal commands for him to stop, and finally, Green calmly flattened himself on the ground like a little boy taste-testing dirt and dew. He tucked his hands behind his back, accustomed to the step-by-step procedures for arrest, and began his confession.

"I'm sorry," he said. "I didn't mean to do it." Green always apologized, an exemplary and well-mannered thief.

"Come on, man," Ryan said during their first meeting. "You've got a baby to take care of, and here you are stuffing beef jerky down your pants? It's not like you stole a canister of formula or something." Back then, Ryan could still mill around with jailbirds on "pod." It was a large cafeteria that didn't serve lunch. "How the hell am I going to cast you in a sympathetic light?"

One trait Ryan shared in common with movie lawyers was his gusto and his wide-eyed quest for justice, even though, as time ticked, his gusto would wane, replaced with a less optimistic attitude. Just months before Ryan rented his eighth-floor office suite in the old First National Bank, memorializing the start of Ulrich Law, 404 N. Main was used as one of many Wisconsin backdrops for filming the John Dillinger biopic *Public Enemies*. Hollywood crews descended on Oshkosh, temporarily restoring our downtown to its former 1930s glory, implementing tracks for a cable car, outfitting storefronts with dramatic awnings, and nailing up old-fashioned billboards for Haddon Hall cigars and Sparkle Desserts.

On set, when the actors emerged from the First National Bank Building on the corner of Washington and Main—our designated spot for watching the Oshkosh holiday parade—they were pretending to steer five hostages onto the running boards of their Ford Model A getaway car. After Johnny-Depp-as-Dillinger and friends sped down Main Street, tossing nails to slow the squads, the First National Bank Building remained, in our collective imagination, a Hollywood movie set.

The public defender's office, or as Ryan's clients call it, the "public pretender's office," is located on the second floor of the First National Bank Building, hidden behind a staircase, a speakeasy for indigent criminals who qualify with meager incomes and secret knocks. The fourth floor is haunted and empty, but others are populated by a mishmash of oddities—dental hygiene for the elderly, the carpenters' union, Kirby vacuum cleaner sales, and an acupuncturist specializing in care for veterans. Longhaired Tom cleans the building, his mop of twisted yarn sloshing murk across the floors.

In character, Ryan was the lawyer with the salt stains on the cuffs of his pants and the frayed corduroy jacket, patting clients on their backs; "that guy with baby geese on his tie," hand-selected by his children. It was difficult to determine if being a father was an advantage or a liability, as his instincts caused him to parent his clients, becoming the male figure so few of them knew intimately in their own lives. As he compared his clients' shortcomings to ours, he failed to see big differences between a guy like Derek Green and himself. Instead, Green reminded Ryan that our pockets were also empty.

In fact, we almost wondered in seriousness if Ryan, with his cut-the-crap lecture to Green early on at the jail, made himself an unintentional coconspirator in the Walmart heist. After all, Sony home theater notwithstanding, Shaffer had filled her cart exclusively with trappings any parent might justify, in the name of Destiny on her first Christmas. We weren't that different from Derek Green, even beyond the money struggles. Sometimes it seems like a miracle we didn't end up in more trouble as kids. Together, we egged a crotchety school board member's house; we trespassed on old abandoned houses; and we drank Malibu from the bottle, driving against traffic on one-way streets.

When Ryan was in eighth grade, he and his buddies would ride their bicycles one-handed, a cavalry, up over Highway 41, the sun puffed out like a dandelion gone to seed. Racing to Walmart, they would pitch their wheels against the superstore, and Ryan, designated thief, would venture inside alone. He was never antsy, ambling with what kids today call swagger. He walked straight to the aisle with the baseball cards and, without hesitation, pocketed dozens of Topps Stadium Club packs into his Nike zip-up. His paper route was not nearly enough to subsidize his pastime of acquiring and trading players. The guys tossed litter like paper airplanes across the parking lot as they waited for their own folk hero to emerge from Wally World and to reveal the faces of Major League Baseball from behind those cellophane seams.

At high-school parties, Ryan orchestrated our seating arrangements when we hunkered down to play poker in somebody's kitchen. He'd study his hand, fresh from the cut-and-shuffle, and pass his best cards to me. Under the table, we'd make the exchange—his winning cards for my rejects. As I won, oftentimes the only girl at the table, he'd laugh knowingly. We were cheaters of the purest kind. Ryan and I disappeared into tree forts and farm fields, when we should have been socializing platonically. Eventually, in the later years, our friends stopped searching for us, our romance implied by our constant cahoots. We look back now on our petty but criminal wrongdoings with nostalgia rather than with shame or regret, as if shoplifting, cheating, vandalism, trespassing, and underage drinking were rites of passage, as they arguably still are for many kids who will become well-adjusted adults.

When Ryan and I graduated from high school together and finally moved away for higher education, we vowed never to return to this godforsaken town. Caravanning beyond the Oshkosh city limits, we felt triumphant and rebellious, like escaped convicts, having traversed the barbed-wire fence surrounding our former lives. While we were becoming enlightened in places like Madison, Ann Arbor, and Madrid, we were actually more like fugitives, wanted back in Oshkosh by some godlike warden who governed our lives. When we left Oshkosh in 1996, we were our *parents' children*, but when we returned, permanently, in 2008, we had become the inverse of our former identities—we were now our *children's parents*.

When officers began questioning Green and Shaffer, in a parking lot on the frontage road hillside after their Walmart heist, their mouths formed contrails on the air, long vaporous chains of words. If the policemen were cold, Destiny was colder. I'd like to think Shaffer ripped the tags off one of the pilfered stocking caps, gifting it two weeks early over the bald crown of her baby's head. When one of the officers asked about the cart, Green responded with "permission from the manager." When he asked why the merchandise was not in bags, Shaffer said they "just didn't bother with that."

"Can I see a receipt for your purchases?" the officer asked.

Green and Shaffer patted down their pockets and scrounged in their wallets as Shaffer offered her best spontaneous explanation, vastly underestimating the sixty-three items in her cart and the value of products such as the Gerber crib set for $79.88 and the George baby blanket for $13.38. She told the officer she checked out in aisle 18 and paid exactly $500.00 in cash, receiving no change. Strangely, Shaffer had packed empty Walmart shopping bags for the caper, intending to masquerade as a paying customer, but for panic or apathy, she never used them. They remained wadded up in a corner of the cart.

"I've got it here," Green said, finally. He handed the policeman a receipt for orange juice, a jolt of vitamin C he had purchased earlier in the week with food stamps.

"Ma'am, it's below freezing out here," the backup officer said to Shaffer. "Why don't you sit in my squad car to warm your baby up?" I wonder, were Destiny's eyes sticky with pulp and did she cry from the cold wind, or was she still warm, a bun pulled not so many months before from Shaffer's oven? Our Fern still seemed to radiate four hundred degrees Fahrenheit from hot coils deep down inside her small belly. A receipt later created when a Walmart manager scanned in Green and Shaffer's loot proved nearly everything in the cart was for Destiny. Though she was only six months old, nearly $1,000 worth of goods had been stolen on her behalf.

Succumbing to the temptation to steal new baby accoutrements is easy to imagine. I've been drawn, without warning or reason, to new baby things in magazines and stores, much prettier than the secondhand vestments in which we usually dressed our children. The siren call of baby garb was surely composed in some mystic enclave, on some secret clef unknown even to musicians, thousands of years ago. The lure of something brand-new—the baby and her swaddling clothes—is irresistible. Babies are the blank slate, the second chance, the rewind button in life, as Allison Shaffer must have known. Babies—new life, new blood—are known to cancel out shitstorms and snowstorms and all manner of stress, at least temporarily.

For me, the natural hormones of pregnancy, childbirth, and breastfeeding proved the only effective antidote—the only reset toggle—for my long-term depression. Since my elementary years, sadness, trapped inside my body, had traveled to my heart, my lungs, my brain, even my limbs, like water in a blister that sloshed around but wouldn't drain. Motherhood siphoned the intense malaise from my body in ways I'd never fathomed, and I wonder, was it the same for Destiny's mother? Footie pajamas and itty-bitty socks, soft, delicate, and as yet unsullied, are really just the second coming of our babies; it's no wonder we are tugged unwittingly toward Baby & Toddler at Walmart.

But I was not there to lobby for Derek Green and Allison Shaffer, not that meditations on motherhood have any real place in a court of law, anyway. Police officers mandated that Green and Shaffer sign the Temporary Physical Custody Request paperwork for Destiny, to guarantee her a safe haven while they awaited court proceedings behind bars. No chance Destiny might wear those new fleece pants and that hollyhock LOVE bib on Christmas two weeks later, wherever Child Protective Services delivered her for the holiday. Even when certain stories were fun to tell, punch lines fell flat. For Ryan, this story was about a father trying to provide. For me, it was about a mother losing her baby into a tangled maze known as Child Protective Services. I grew light-headed imagining any small infraction leading to the loss of my own.

From the refuge of our home, I snuggled and read with my kids. One of our favorite picture books was *Good Night, Gorilla*, and I'd envision Ryan as the ape, knuckling the zookeeper's keys, liberating the animals, everyone from the elephant to the armadillo. In my version, they followed him from the courthouse to the iconic bank building and slept on the faux-leather hand-me-down sofas. I studied Green's mug shot and imagined him there, the gorilla's sidekick, towing the banana on a string. If Green was the keeper of Ryan's livelihood, meager though a single piece of fruit might be, who was the keeper of his?

Second only to our house on Hazel Street, our son Leo was our most expensive commodity. During my second pregnancy, we had guilelessly ignored red flags from our new health insurance company about delivering him at the Madison Birth Center. In a phone call we failed to document, a representative of our new provider of student-spouse health insurance, purchased through UW–Madison while Ryan was in law school, promised to match benefits available to us previously. Throughout my first trimester, in 2005, our provider covered my prenatal care at the birth center; and we assumed, based on vague reassurances, this coverage would continue in 2006. We were young, Ryan not yet a lawyer. We should have confirmed the company would match providers, not just benefits, but we didn't, and they ultimately refused to cover Leo's birth at the Madison Birth Center with the only midwife I'd ever known. We later learned, when the center went out of business, that insurance companies made a habit of not footing their bills, preferring instead to fund major hospitals.

Eventually our midwife sued us for $8,000, hiring a collection agency called Stark, as in stark reality, or if I were to buy another vowel, as in stork looming. We might have expected such a bird to deliver our children, delicately balanced inside the knotted hammock of a clean diaper. Instead this "Stork" Agency was the yawp of a ringtone, a carefully trained heartless voice. I worried irrationally that a phalanx of winged creatures would scoop up our baby and carry him into some unknown pattern of migration.

I worried that the universe, if not our midwife, would reclaim Leo, some version of "removable property" I could not safeguard with breast milk or love. Leo had emerged on Mother's Day. Mothers everywhere celebrated as I pushed him triumphantly into existence. Irie, kneeling at my bed, clamored to catch her brother, in the same room at the birth center where she was born. He was still attached to my insides, a fish on the line. Unable to pull his slippery limbs into her own, she cried.

No Mother's Day gift could compare to this naked boy serving knuckle sandwiches on my chest, but months and years later, when the Stork Agency came knocking, my memory of Leo's arrival became fraught with worry. In a small claims supplementary exam, under the supervision of a Winnebago County judge, one of Ryan's colleagues, another attorney, embarrassingly grilled us about our income, debts, and spending: used furniture, one television, two old cars, and a house with a modest mortgage on which we were upside down once the housing bubble burst a few months after we purchased it.

"What about monthly expenditures?" the birth center's attorney asked.

"Well, student loans between the two of us—that's about a thousand dollars a month. And we pay two hundred dollars per week, per child, for day care, so that's about twenty-four hundred a month." Just as addicts go broke on drugs, we were going bankrupt on children. Eventually we came to a settlement agreement and paid off the debt, but we learned, quite quickly, that being uninsured in America and being a deadbeat were synonymous. The plaintiff's attorney had treated us like crooks. We reminded ourselves that Ryan advocated for criminals but was not a criminal himself, even though, humiliated and deeply ashamed, we knew dividing lines were not so easily drawn.

While I was pregnant with Fern, two years later, I interviewed for and was offered a tenure-track position at my current institution in Oshkosh, which meant blessedly fewer classes per semester at a higher pay rate. At the Modern Language Association convention in Chicago, where the national search and interview took place, I ran into an old friend from graduate school. "You have a lot of guts coming to an academic interview pregnant," she said. Her sharp tongue cut both ways: compliment (for my courage) and warning (for my naïveté). When Fern was finally born, in a hospital, under our new insurance, she slid from me like a buttered noodle in under two hours. In my mind, governed by metaphor, her birth was cheaper because I had labored so much less.

High on Fern's recent birth, I plunged into my three-week literature class, five days postpartum. Fearful of making a bad impression on my colleagues (many of them childless or child-free) and in dire need of a paycheck, I taught through my recovery period. My mom, Fern, and I, three generations of women, set up an ad hoc nursery in an empty classroom. Whenever Fern awoke, I'd give students a break as I tucked Fern beneath a blanket to relieve my breasts. A College of Nursing student cohort expressed support for my tandem act—teaching and mothering—as did others, mostly women, one of whom thanked me months later. "I didn't know it was possible to have babies and work too, until I took your class," she said.

But the following academic year, a new director for the Office of Equity and Affirmative Action was outraged to hear, through the grapevine, about my breastfeeding in front of students. She asked the associate dean to reprimand me, even though no student had filed a complaint. She glared at me in the tiny cubicle where we met, after I requested further explanation. "On behalf of the chancellor, we feel you crossed a line." Although not formalizing the incident, she said I jeopardized my students' classroom safety and their right to learn. "Students in the Midwest are just too polite," she said. "If this were New York, they'd come right out and tell you, 'Professor, that's gross.'"

Shortly thereafter, a clerk at an educational resources store said, "So, you're not going to believe this, but I heard a professor breastfed her baby while she was teaching!" Holding a now one-year-old Fern on my hip, clamped there with paws like a koala's, I cleared my throat and said, "That was me. Guilty as charged."

After this incident, when the draft of a child-at-work policy for UW Oshkosh stipulated termination of employment for bringing children into classrooms, I knew, deep down, some ghostwriter was anonymously lashing out at me, somebody who'd been emboldened by our former chancellor, no doubt. When Fern was still a baby, he had hosted an orientation for new faculty in the union ballroom. As I stood, obviously not as inconspicuous as I believed, at the back wall, he pressed his lips against the microphone and said, for all to hear, "Not all of us are fortunate enough to have our children with us here today." He pointed to me and winked oh so cleverly. Years later, I'd feel vindicated—if just a little bit—when that same chancellor was sued by the UW System after being accused of illegally transferring $11 million to major real estate developments, a controversy that would taint his legacy.

A baby's fetal cells can remain inside a mother's body for as long as twenty-seven years after birth, free-floating biological units comingling inside us, overlapping, little Venn diagrams of our children's predispositions, nature before it is nurtured. Like most parents, I hoped to mitigate the worst and cultivate the best of their genetic makeup. I was quick to admit my flaws, in the interest of honesty, and I tried to set good examples, in hopes of nurturing conscientious children. If we found ourselves accidentally shoplifting baby wipes, left on the bottom rack of the shopping cart in the chaos of checkout, I returned them to customer service immediately, swiping our debit card for an apologetic second transaction. Sometimes, though, we didn't return the wipes. It was raining or snowing, or maybe one of our babies was screaming for milk, already buckled into a car seat.

Early on in Ryan's career, we took our children to see a local abridged version of *Les Misérables*, all of us becoming enamored of Jean Valjean's story, learning the lyrics of the songs by heart long before our children could truly pronounce the words. Oblivious to the Broadway musical's complex themes, they became fixated on one detail, repeatedly asking, "Would somebody really be sentenced to nineteen years in prison just for stealing bread?"

Answering our children's questions was never clear-cut. How might we explain to them, for example, the disproportionate number of poor people or people of color in the system, even here in Oshkosh? It's a majority white city, only 2 percent black, yet Ryan estimated, roughly, that one-third of his clients fit the latter category, no surprise given Wisconsin's highest incarceration rate for black men in the nation. How could we promote Badger pride? And how could we explain our own wrongdoings—accidentally swiping wipes, shirking car seat laws, and speeding well beyond the reasonable uptick—combined with our good fortune in circumventing any kind of prosecution?

"Jesus," Ryan would lament from the depths of his criminal-defense practice. "A lot of my clients are getting charged for doing the same types of shit we used to do." It was difficult for him to reconcile how the state felt compelled to incarcerate or "supervise" his clients while we were looked upon as examples of professionalism and good parenting. How many years in jail or prison might we get, or better yet, how many years didn't his clients deserve? At the same time, however, Ryan's clients turned him into the kind of overprotective parent I never imagined he'd become. He defended his clients but refused to let our children fraternize with theirs. He'd cite meth labs in basements and handguns in unlocked drawers.

We realized we'd be stuck in our house on Hazel Street until we could bail out of debt and afford a home in a safer neighborhood. Exposed every day to the underbelly of our community, he overreacted, and I underreacted. In many ways, we were revealed as products of our own parents' styles. "I'm surprised you're not living in a bubble!" I'd scream at my helicopter husband, who was raised by hypervigilant, arguably alarmist parents. "Really . . . really?" he'd retort. "Well, I'm surprised you're not dead, facedown in a ditch somewhere!" Our marriage and teamwork in child-rearing dangled precariously over some abyss.

In the flow of genetic information, long, long beforehand, I'd received instructions to be skeptical of marriage. My dad married three times, and my mom, upon divorce, made clear she'd never tie another knot. Before our wedding, my heart was as cold as my feet. Marriage would be nothing but taxing and painful, according to the stories on which I'd been reared, which my parents learned from observing their own mothers and fathers. My dad once intercepted a note from his father's mistress, and my mom was often charged with supervising children at her mother's child-care center, the Teddy Bear Nursery, while my grandmother, Jean, for whom I was named, excused herself for mysterious hours-long lunch dates. To believe in marriage was to be sweet and gullible, nothing more than a babe in the woods.

My partnership with Ryan begged the question: how do we adjudicate our family's patterns, not to mention those of other families? Criminal minds were frighteningly identifiable, and when crimes bewildered others, they secretly made sense to me. Although not yet one of Ryan's clients, Tina Last, a mother of one of Irelyn's classmates, fascinated me. With ear piercings, eyebrow piercings, nose piercings, lip piercings, and chin piercings, she was like a voodoo doll, pins protruding from her burlap skin, invoking evil. She was beyond eye contact, hypnotized by the flurry of parents and teachers, high on marijuana. She was how I imagined myself if I'd gone wayward longer.

In early elementary school, a teacher said I was mean. I received D grades in citizenship. My mom repeated this word— *mean*—maybe to remind me I was the opposite of what we valued, which was, of course, kindness. Around the same time, other teachers said, "There she is with a smile on her face!" Was I smiling? I hadn't even realized my outward expression, but somehow the repetition of these mixed messages confused me. When I felt sad, why did I smile? And when I felt happy, in what ways was I mean? Did I feel threatened or jealous, as my psychoanalytically inclined parents told me, and if so, by whom or of what?

Even if I looked pretty on occasion, I'd imagine these sharp protrusions inside me, like the barbed triangle teeth glinting from wolves' mouths in fairy tales. My outsides were soft, but my insides were metallic and hard. People with good eyesight—teachers, coaches, friends' parents—could see them the way X-rays detected metal plates used to reconstruct bones. Maybe this was the depression talking. It's hard to know, but certainly, when I laid eyes on Tina Last, I identified her as me, turned inside out. Even our children had been linked. Irie, my daughter, and Xavier, her son, were the naughty kids of Miss D's kindergarten room—babies we'd produced separately but then combined five years postpartum.

Ryan and I were not yet willing to concede, in those early years, that the good judgment required of responsible parents contained, inevitably, a degree of *judging others*. Parents of modest means who didn't steal bread to keep their children nourished gave up entirely instead, and Tina Last was one of them. I wavered between identifying with her and worrying about keeping my children safe from the likes of her. As for Ryan, the further he submerged himself into the lives of his clients, the more desperately he wanted to provide better lives for our children, which meant, in true American fashion, earning more money.

On Saturday nights, when we'd hear police sirens, the first thing I'd do was a head count. So long as everybody in my family was safe, I could laugh and say, "Thank God for job security." Truthfully, just as many crimes happened on weekdays, after school, when children—including our very own—returned home, sweaty, hungry, excited, and exhausted, and the witching hour commenced. They dumped their backpacks, ransacked cupboards, and foamed at the mouth with repressed speech, metamorphosing into beasts, testing our love and patience. Some of us rose to the occasion, just barely, and others, like Tina Last, would break under the pressure.

Derek Green, the first parent Ryan represented in his criminal-defense career, was not a father so much as a child himself. Two weeks into his eighteen-month term of probation, after being released from jail for the Walmart heist, he returned to the same Walmart on a June day, mounted a shiny new bicycle for sale in the Sporting Goods section, and tooled up and down the toy aisles. Maybe he popped a wheelie or squeezed his horn like a performer in a parade.

It's almost impossible to believe, but true: when nobody was looking, he fired up his nerve and pedaled right past the Walmart greeters into the parking lot, up the frontage road, and back to the halfway house where he now lived, tired of begging bus tokens off his parole officer. Nobody chased him. Nobody even noticed him. If the sight of a gleaming new bicycle had not waved itself like a red flag, proud and patriotic among the secondhand wheels his housemates owned, he might have pulled off this heist, olly olly oxen free.

If he were not a repeat offender, and if he did not appear again years later for forgery charges in another county, I might argue, before the assistant district attorney or the judge, that Derek Green was an innocent man deluded simply by the fantasy of never growing up, Peter Pan in a world of hard knocks. It's actually really difficult to make enough money to support a child—"never mind three and counting," Ryan would say.

How many times had Ryan yearned for the days of his own youth, nostalgic for endless bike rides and hours of trading baseball cards, when money was neither suspicious nor dirty but exciting and hot, burning a perfectly patchable hole in his jeans pocket? What wouldn't any father give to relive the indiscretions of his adolescence, long since left behind in the backwind of parenthood? I knew Ryan well enough to know he would not turn around, but I didn't know yet how much further, how many babies more, I could push him forward, running along behind, having wrenched free and ditched the safeguard of our training wheels.

CHAPTER 2

Brown-Sugar Skies

Just as I was realizing how addicted I'd become to pregnancy and childbirth, Ryan was beginning to realize that drugs were the epicenter of his clients' crimes. Rob McNally described himself as the quintessential junkie. When McNally was a little boy, his old lady, owned by Hells Angels, would ferry him to the nearest amusement park once a year, but no roller coaster compared to McNally's first joyride when his mom "gave him wings." She spiked his arm, and McNally, just fourteen years old, rose up, leaving their nest for brown-sugar skies. What did she say, as she pushed the plunger, heroin filling his veins? "Baby, it feels good" was a mantra she repeated daily. "Blood-red, skull-white" was a lullaby she sang.

When McNally was five, at the pediatrician's office she finagled a prescription for Ritalin to personally abuse. When McNally was ten, she revealed a secret: What he assumed were Pixy Stix were actually straws drained of sugar and replenished with cocaine. He swallowed the granules and played video games, all jacked up. When he was thirteen, she mentored him in cooking up the family recipe for motor-oil meth. They manufactured it together, mother as master craftsman, son as apprentice, in the bathroom where gangsters pissed in the sink, and together they indulged.

But their mother-son bond was not all highs and hoopla. One time, McNally recalled, sadness like phlegm in his throat, he found his mother at the Hells Angels clubhouse strapped with jump ropes to a kitchen chair, beat up like an old shoe box, begging to die. Thank God for a needle chamber filled with sweet dreams, which might just as easily as death alleviate Mama McNally's problems and her son's too. As every parent knows, pleasure is the opposite of pain.

"What's the latest on McNally?" I asked Ryan. I'd met Rob McNally, and he'd told me his story, appearing grateful when I listened.

"Fuck, I don't know," he said. "The guy's probably dead." Ryan had developed a habit of cursing at home, all manner of four-letter words, including D-E-A-D. One of our small children was attempting to smuggle chocolate chips from the pantry and piped in, "Who's probably dead?"

"Mind your own business," Ryan snapped.

Since he had begun his criminal-defense practice, it always seemed clients were dying—a fatal car accident, complications from alcohol and obesity, a couple of drug overdoses. Winnebago County had become a labyrinth of drugs. Wisconsin law enforcement blamed major thoroughfares between Chicago, the central hub for heroin in the Midwest, and northeast Wisconsin. Smack traveled one way from Chi-Town to the Fox Valley in three hours. In Winnebago County alone, dozens of heroin overdoses per year resulted in death, and statewide, users were dying from drug overdoses by the hundreds. Paramedics drained dosage units of Narcan, the antidote to heroin overdose, by the thousands. Arrests for heroin-related offenses spiked more than 50 percent between 2010 and 2012, and an abundance of those users became Ryan's clients. His job was to allay charges against his habitués while maintaining face with district attorneys, which meant, from time to time, convincing people like Rob McNally and another woman named Darlene Eaves to become confidential informants, or CIs, in an effort to keep them in their self-described normal lives as Wisconsin citizens.

Unlike McNally, Darlene Eaves, also facing felony charges for possession with intent to deliver heroin, appeared on the road to recovery. She would admit, "I shot heroin," always in the past tense, whereas McNally described the ritual as ongoing. Eaves's safest option, for the sanctity of her health, was to help build a conspiracy against three known drug kingpins by recreating a paper trail of purchases and submitting it to Lake Winnebago Area Metropolitan Enforcement Group (MEG) officers. Eaves worked with drug agents from within the refuge of Ryan's office. Rob McNally, however, would need to complete so-called fieldwork. Facing six years in prison for three counts of delivery of cocaine and two counts of delivery of heroin, McNally was assigned to hit the streets, seedy back-alley apartments, and bars like Tony's Deluxe where haggard patrons stood smoking over their graves.

"We could drop him into any social circle in the valley, and he would produce a dealer immediately," a MEG officers told Ryan. "I just don't know if we can control him."

McNally was tattooed from earlobes to knuckles. The inky scar tissue in the folds of his arms could be mistaken for old chicken pox, the same bumps all pre-vaccine kids scratched into permanence. When he balled his fists, they read B-O-R-N R-E-A-L. Drugs were emblems on his skin—marijuana leaves and pill-shaped outlines labeled XANAX, OXYCONTIN, and ADEROL [sic]. His face remained untouched by sun. He spent most of his adult life behind bars, according to the calendars above his pectoral muscles, etched like ancient scrolls.

My only markings are moles, a scar where I carved a boy's initials onto my thigh with a razor blade, and stretch marks from pregnancy. I've always hated tattoos; ink on skin—from a marker, pen, ink pad, or needle—unnerves me, turns me queasy. Everybody is a puritan about something. McNally's torso was labeled like an illustration in a textbook of anatomy: CARNEY, ANARCHIST, 100% FELON. In fine print the Bible passage: FOR THE WAGES OF SIN IS DEATH, BUT THE GIFT OF GOD IS ETERNAL LIFE. Smack-dab in the middle, where paramedics would perform CPR compressions if necessary, was a tattoo of Eeyore from *Winnie-the-Pooh*, whimsical yet despondent, fallen under the weight of his woes.

"My mom used to call me Eeyore because my eyes were always red. I was always like *boo*," McNally told me, voice languid and faintly Southern. With nothing but an army bag full of clothes to his name, McNally flexed his forearm, lamented the serious matters. "I seen a lot of dirty stuff," he said, but he refused to boo-hoo himself. "We're all dealt a hand," he continued, "and this is mine."

McNally opted out of a GED in juvy but was proud of his street smarts. He gave me a detailed lesson in the alchemy of prison tattoos: "You take an electric shaver, the spring from an ink pen, and the pen itself. You cut the heel off the state-issued boots, catch the black soot in a bag, scrape it out and combine it with an ounce of water and a half ounce of alcohol. Ink is powder before it becomes a liquid form. It's redefined soot."

"You sound like you could mix up anything," I told him. "You sound like a magician."

While earning his law degree, Ryan received his lowest grade in criminal procedure because he idealized civil litigation, *not* a life defending addicts: his clients and eventually his wife, whose addiction to babies would become the most shocking but pleasant surprise of her life. Just as the state charged Rob McNally and Darlene Eaves with drug offenses, feminist colleagues accused me of delivering babies to sell women down the river, treating me as if pursuing maternity—to an excessive and environmentally dangerous degree—and a professional identity were a crime, a sign of witchcraft, or both. Plenty of women in academia chose not to become mothers at all.

"You're a baby factory," a friend told me, bitters on her tongue. In earlier decades, people seemed to gawk less in public at families of ten or twelve, and therefore I was slow on the uptake about how to handle myself socially when claiming three, and later four, children. People today expected me to be self-deprecating and humorously apologetic. "Oh, you know, I'm the old lady who lives in a shoe," I learned to say.

While friends and family joked about our proliferation, oftentimes with sports references—"You'll have your own basketball team" or "Now, you just need a goalie"—I'd always recall a colleague who pontificated about adoption when I was seven months pregnant with Fern, swollen as a planet. "I can't imagine why someone would give birth when so many children need to be adopted," she said. "It's so wasteful to keep bringing babies into the world." As Fern skinny-dipped through my waters, I nodded and tried not to appear like an extraterrestrial having descended on academic culture bearing the unsightly gift of Jupiter.

My closest students continued to confide that English majors and professors talked about me behind my back. "She's no feminist," they'd whisper. "She has babies and wears dresses." I'd begin my courses in women's studies with discussions on the misconceptions of feminism just to clear away the clutter before teaching about what I really loved—language and stories. The assumption also, of course, was that Ryan and I probably had lots of crazy sex, throwing caution to the wind.

Everyone, not the least of all Ryan, troubled over the rapid-fire pacing of our children. By 2009, a year after Fern's birth, I'd begun to actively campaign for baby number four, hopeful I could deliver him on or around Fern's second birthday. A MEG officer might argue, if babies were converted into bindles of dope, I'd delivered twelve kilos or forty-five thousand dosage units in little more than half a decade, serious drug trafficking, more heroin than Rob McNally could jack up in a lifetime without dying. I'd need to either cluck my habit or get more cunning about my grind. I was just as addicted to the birdie powder as McNally was, and Ryan was burned out, wasted, totally cashed. But facing neither prison nor execution, I was fighting my own demons. To make meaning of life, people I knew turned to religion or drugs, opposite ends of a continuum for solving the existential crisis, and I'd landed in some bizarre hybrid of both, feeling spiritually devoted and chemically addicted, simultaneously, to my body as vessel.

I wasn't just imagining or willing it into existence. Babies had rewired the pleasure center of my brain. Like my aunt who was addicted to eating and QVC, my brother to drugs, my stepbrother and a half brother to booze, all I could fixate on was landing more pleasure. I reminded myself of those cautionary tales about Wisconsin sports enthusiasts. They'd drink to stay warm while deer hunting or ice fishing but then end up so numb, they'd fail to notice the frostbite as their toes turned to bones of ice.

How much of my baby complex was physical, and how much was psychological? As medical researchers discovered that synthetic oxytocin was a potentially viable treatment for opioid addicts, I began to wonder how I'd fare when and if my own organic supply began to taper. Would I need to inject, imbibe, or inhale the man-made variety just to avoid withdrawal symptoms?

It's no surprise that sex was my gateway drug. During our high school years, when Ryan and I began officially dating, just seventeen-year-old kids, we'd make love wherever we could: a parking lot between Oshkosh and Madison on a summer day; beneath the foothills on campus at the University of Colorado; eight times one weekend to the soundtrack of a televised Cardinals–Braves playoff series at an Estes Park hotel, paid for with a buy-one-night-get-one-night-free coupon from the back of a Boulder phone book; in my Wisconsin Avenue apartment with a view of the state capitol; in Madrid, where daytime and nighttime were transposed; at Niagara Falls to the onslaught of hydro power; and in Prague, in the communist-style dormitory, where we copulated passionately and quietly behind heavy iron curtains. We didn't know yet that by the time we'd accumulate more than our replacement value in children, we'd need to pay babysitters just to make love, clandestinely, in his office, on the eighth floor of the old bank building.

When Ryan was appointed by the state to defend Eaves, she and Ryan met there with MEG agents, who were plotting a strategy to bring down the head of the largest-ever heroin-delivery drug ring in Winnebago County: eighteen thousand dosage units of crack cocaine and ninety thousand dosage units of heroin, a multimillion-dollar venture worth more than fifty arrests. MEG guys, working undercover, craggy and weathered as real users, layered Ryan's desk with mug shots of suspects. They matched numbers to faces, dates to purchases, and dirty deals to previous criminal records. Jabbing her fingers like darts popping balloons, Eaves burst one after another until the MEG agents decided her statement was substantial enough to win the grand prize—a conspiracy case against Lazarus Jackson, the big shot. If Eaves agreed to testify, consistent with her statement, in the slim chance of trial, the state agreed to amend her charges to possession of drug paraphernalia.

This is what I'd think about when we'd retreat to Ryan's office late at night, after a few drinks and a good meal, the babysitter's clock ticking. I felt a little exhilarated and a little filthy about lovemaking there. And much like the purity of a drug supply, sex, for us, was always changing. When we were twenty-five and stopped using birth control, we expected many more months of uninhibited sex. We drank sidecars and made love, tucked inside the red walls of our third-story pretty-penny apartment in Madison. It was like mating inside Georgia O'Keeffe's red canna lily. But within three weeks our first baby was conceived and growing fast.

Pregnancy nausea astounded me. I slept odd hours, alone in bed, exhausted from teaching and desperate to deaden my insatiable hunger pangs. My first job after graduate school was teaching at EAGLE School near Madison, earning a handsome salary of $26,000 per year, no benefits. I'd drop Ryan off on the UW campus, our source for student-spouse health insurance, and then journey to my four-in-one position: Spanish teacher, English teacher, student council advisor, and drama director. I took only one sick day that year, the second Monday of the first semester, as I curled into a ball and wept, wondering how I'd grow a child while mothering nearly fifty adolescents for seven hours a day all year long.

Halfway through the pregnancy, when my sickness retreated, I felt robust, but my conversion from Ryan's nighttime lover to round-the-clock mother figure was imminent. Upon Irie's arrival, I discovered something more pleasurable than sex—the self-indulgent and gluttonous ritual of maternity. I latched her mouth to my breast, incubating her nakedness on mine. Sexual pleasure paled in comparison to this high. Thanks to oxytocin, Mother Nature's liquid bliss, not to mention the divine event of nurturing my daughter. Irie, also known as Oxytocin Girl in my world of everyday superheroes, had rescued me.

I would later discover in the course of my research all over the internet that journalists compared babies to drugs, based on neuroscience. As it turns out, my brain had been commandeered by motherhood; I'd never get it back, and this exhilarated me.

Although I could not yet articulate the needs of my limbic system at that time, intuitively, I didn't just want a fourth baby. I needed one.

"How would you describe the feeling you get from shooting heroin?" I asked McNally.

"I'm free," he said. "Take a nap for five minutes, wake up to no worries. It's a buzz I would want to keep forever." Better than pot, better than meth, better than oxy. OxyContin was a popular choice for McNally and other addicts between 1995, when the FDA approved it, and 2010, when Purdue Pharma LP reformulated the opiate so it could no longer be crushed to powder and snorted. Efforts to recodify OxyContin as abuse-resistant were so successful that the majority of abusers picked up a heroin habit instead. It was suddenly cheaper, more available, and more efficient to use.

Oxy from Greek means sharp, pointed, acidic, intense. Perhaps, by way of an *oxymoron*, it might also mean smooth, because oxytocin furbished the edge off my depression, a feat traditional antidepressants—Prozac, Zoloft, Celexa, Wellbutrin—had failed to accomplish. In heroin overdoses, opiates cause bodies to relax so profoundly, they forget to breathe. In the same way, I'd feel laced and placid upon breastfeeding, the glorious "pleasure hormone" released in generous but modulated shots by my pituitary gland, as it had been during orgasm and childbirth, *only stronger*. At my breasts, my babies—fuzzy, eyes dilated like pain-relief tablets, fingers clenched into little heartbeats—sucked hard enough to pull euphoria from the dark chasm inside me and force me to notice it. Breastfeeding was my version of self-medication.

Mental illness was a household catchphrase when I was growing up, on the highest point, topographically, of Winnebago County, where my childhood house sprawled like a fat, stoned cat. Everything there seemed to die. We dug shallow graves for birds that choked on paint fumes, hamsters that perished from neglect, a cat my mom flattened beneath the tires of our car, and a pet rabbit that blindly convulsed under the willow tree. My mom's favorite album was Don McLean's *American Pie*. "Vincent," a tribute to Van Gogh's suicide, was the soundtrack we listened to while washing floors. My mom was a former psychiatric patient of my dad's; he had wooed her after signing her discharge papers and divorcing his first wife.

In summertime, an archaeologist would dig in nearby fields for arrowheads left by Winnebago Indians, our county's namesake, otherwise known as the Ho-Chunk people. Did relics of loss and grief stretch downward through centuries of soil? Did the Native Americans for whom our land was named imbibe peyote, commune with holy spirits, and if so, were they healed? As I was coming of age and into a disconcerting awareness of my troubled mental health, I wondered how I compared to the grown-ups in my parents' offices. I resented the assumption that children were happy and blamed my dispiritedness on genetics and landscape in equal parts. Beyond our rural plot of land, parachutes from Skydive Adventure along Highway 21 mushroomed against the sky, hallucinations, fleeting dots of beauty we'd remember later, some of us hopped up on drugs, others desperately seeking other forms of pleasure. I never suspected that my body contained the means for both sadness and elation.

When McNally was not in jail or prison, he was a gamer with Tip Top Rides & Attractions in Wisconsin and Florida, migrating between North and South along some invisible groove. There is no lifestyle in America more transient, more unstable, or more unsightly than that of a carnival game operator. Step right up to the Ferris wheel, bumper cars, the Sizzler, corn dogs, fried heartburn on a stick. The guy with the smooth clothes and nice shoes, sweet-talking customers at the balloon-and-dart game, is

McNally. The rules: shoot a needle at the vein and watch it pop.

"We'll set you right up here! Come on now, don't be a cheap date. Go for the big prizes," he called out, demonstrating for me inside Ryan's office, voice fast and clipped like an auctioneer's. "The faster you talk, the more money you make. I could play them till they were broke and I was taking the chains off from around their necks." Most important: the gig kept drugs in his pockets.

Ryan, straightlaced and sober, hated amusement parks and carnivals and any of their sundry associations—fireworks, bubbles, balloons, chewing gum, lollipops, roller coasters, streamers, and Disney World. If it cost money and combusted, he despised it. "You might as well light a hundred-dollar bill on fire," he'd say. He loathed miniature toys, otherwise known as choking hazards—marbles, bouncy balls, and plastic beads. Worse yet: Slinkys, jump ropes, or any novelty that might be awarded as a prize and strangle a child. "Who invented this shit?" he'd shout to anybody in earshot.

Nor did he understand the merits of bargain-basement diversions or my instincts to maintain domestic harmony with food. One afternoon, I was checking out at the Oshkosh Pick 'n Save in front of an old friend from youth orchestra. She'd judged me back then, certainly, for skipping entire measures of music.

"Excuse me," the clerk said. "This check won't clear." She printed a receipt embossed with two simple words: INSUFFICIENT FUNDS. I was genuinely surprised, as this was the first time I'd been caught with a bad check. The technology of linking check numbers to bank account balances had finally caught me. The clerk generously directed me to customer service. What did the violist think of me now, as I brokered a deal for customer service to keep my food cold while I scrounged up the cash?

When I called Ryan in a panic, he growled, "I thought you were only buying a couple of things to get us through the next twenty-four hours." As was my reckless habit, I'd overspent by thirty dollars or so. Ryan said he'd swing by and pay for the amount we could afford. When he brought the groceries home, the kids and I hid in the sunroom as he plunked the plastic bags on the countertops with shaming force.

Ryan even hated the Dollar Tree—his clients shopped there; and money was money. Yet he also wanted me, year-round, to entertain our small children on the cheap. We'd make homemade play dough, chalk the sidewalks, crumble crackers into the ant-hills, collect pinecones and sticks, but at some point, a mother had to spend a nickel or dime. Prices at the tiny amusement station at Menominee Park across the street crept higher between our first and third babies, but in the early days, a ticket for the little red train and caboose cost a dollar. Small children with tattooed parents were little versions of McNally, getting started early on their carney careers.

Inside my own pockets were candy wrappers and pennies for the moon water, our wishing well in Oshkosh, where I'd pat the fire in my belly and imagine more children, an endless supply of my own vice, each baby a talisman for happiness, new human life the remedy to a family history of mental illness—unless, of course, I ended up passing on my depression like a burning hot potato, mental anguish paid forward into perpetuity. What great virtue distinguished me from Ryan's clients, users and addicts who became informants on the witness stand to sell out Lazarus Jackson? Though they were younger than me by traditional calculations, their faces were taut as old rope. A processional of informants filed to the witness stand. They were clean now, so help them God. Each testified to buying forty-dollar bindles of heroin, three times per week.

Darlene Eaves would end up testifying three times, in spite of MEG agents' predictions that chances of trials were slim. Each time she was subpoenaed over the course of three years, she'd call Ryan, wringing her voice like a rag over the kitchen sink. "This is getting ridiculous," she'd say. "I feel like the state owns me. When will it stop?" With blue eye shadow and dusty-rose lipstick applied thick, as if she'd emerged from the 1980s, Eaves was otherwise an innocuous woman, a smoker and a drinker, a truck-stop waitress type, but not a serious addict. She appeared to have gotten her life together *enough*, calling Ryan for advice on mundane legal issues such as landlord-tenant disputes and personal injury casework. But she also worried about testifying in front of an audience. The deal was not worth dying for.

In childhood, I'd often dream of death. I'd wake from nightmares, traverse the empty hallway to my parents' room, where I'd wake my dad. We'd walk together in the dark toward the kitchen cupboard, from which my dad would produce Children's Triaminic Syrup—the "orange medicine." Twisting open the childproof cap, he'd pour a generous dose into a cereal spoon perfectly sized for my mouth, opened wide like a baby bird's beak. The sticky goodness of antihistamines would lull me drowsy enough to sleep in my own bed, where I'd crash hard and dream I could fly.

I would never raise lonely or anxious children, or so I believed, but I worried I was raising instead a generation of addicts. Every time I got my oxy fix, my babies did too. Nursing on demand, they'd go slack in my arms. Inhale: their eyes opened. Exhale: their irises rolled back under the steady pump of their eyelashes. Other mothers said, "My baby just quit one day, cold turkey." Mine pleaded for milk. They'd unhook zippers and buttons, break sewing thread, unknot scarves like magicians, pulling my nipple from my clothing like a coin from behind the ear. Weaning was never easy for us.

I could blame only myself. I'd soothed every child's fuss with a shot of milk. We co-slept and co-bathed, starting with Irie, my nipple in her mouth like a stent or an IV needle, a second umbilical cord that kept us connected. She was perfectly Gerber Baby–plump. But into her late elementary and tween years, she remained so, eating voraciously, third and fourth helpings, tranquilized only by the ability to suckle and nosh. A bowl of sherbet or a smoothie doused in whipped cream melted in her mouth like the *hush-hush* cadence of our breastfeeding. Perhaps Mama McNally and I passed on to our children the same intolerance for discomfort and pain.

From early on, mixed messages cross-wired inside my brain. My midwife encouraged on-demand feeding, but family members said I overindulged. "Crying is good for babies," or so they'd say, but mine preferred the pistil of my skin to a pacifier or lungs full of air. Spare the NUK, spoil the child. Worse yet: lay a foundation for lifelong cravings. My babies rarely cried longer than ten seconds—the time it took me to produce my breast. I wondered what kinds of formidable pleasure-seekers I'd created. Leo and Fern were fiends for chocolate, and one summer at Bay Beach Amusement Park, when Irie spilled ice cream, she sobbed until her ears blushed, as if she needed the fix. We soothed her with the promise of an extra ticket for the Zippin Pippin. "I just love to eat, Mom," she'd say. "I can't help it."

One of Ryan's newest clients at this time was a mother with no previous criminal record, charged with smuggling marijuana to her son in prison. I could relate. I probably would do anything to make my daughter happy, at the risk of overindulgence. "All these moms are enablers," Ryan would chide, and I wondered, sometimes, if he meant me too, mothers being the trees from which any bad apple falls.

I recall fondly my own father's medicine closet, which housed free trials, boxed up and shipped to their private practice, Mental Health Consultants, thanks to the marketing efforts of pharmaceutical companies. My dad stockpiled medicine against the nuclear threat of depression and despair. I sought solace by opening the medicine closet and sniffing the nest egg of tonics and cures. It smelled of licorice, aspirin powder, and spirit tinctures. The room was cool and dry, and I liked to hide there, basking in the pleasure of aromatic content. I never took any.

Depression at our house was governed by a godlike force. Although we shared genetics, my full brother, Christopher, became more truly and wholly possessed by what the poet Jane Kenyon calls the "unholy ghost." In high school, the counselor pulled me from Spanish class and drove me home because of rumors my brother was plotting a carbon monoxide suicide. Maybe she believed we could save him. Shortly thereafter he overdosed on a cocktail of prescription meds and ended up in the psychiatric ward at St. Elizabeth Hospital. Doctors healed him temporarily.

Just as I entered graduate school, my third in a line of therapists diagnosed my mental illness—what I perceived to be general purposelessness—as bipolar II disorder. At my lowest, I'd be ravaged by night terrors. From the time we married in 2001 until my first pregnancy, starting in 2003, I'd wake to the sensation of tarantulas crawling up my neck or bats catching in my hair— dozens of dreams about nocturnal creatures. I'd claw and scream for upward of sixty seconds, once even breaking my pajama straps like some pathetic version of the Incredible Hulk.

After two troubled years in my fine arts program, bored of my mood stabilizer, depression workbook assignments, and weekly visits to a phlebotomist to test my valproic acid levels, I healed myself by getting pregnant instead. With children, sleep became a dream. I floated downstream on a human-size leaf. But if I couldn't endlessly gestate, then what was plan B? I was fairly certain I could sway Ryan's vote toward four; once, long before we understood what having children *really* entailed, we'd talked of sets—two older, two younger, for a grand total of four. But why four? The four chambers of the heart, the four elements, the four Gospels? It was an even number, and I was superstitious; Wisconsin sports greats Paul Molitor and Brett Favre were number fours too. Maybe it sounded impressive to us, not just an everyday "hobby" family, but also not reality TV–worthy.

But no act of superstition or faith could save McNally now. He was adamant he'd never recover. After all, he could easily turn to Lifepoint, part of the North American Syringe Exchange Network, whose goal is to eliminate the epidemic transmission of diseases such as HIV and hepatitis C. He could walk out of the needle exchange, grocery bag filled with all the amenities for pleasure: a hundred needles, cookers, powder to break down crack cocaine, and enough Narcan in case he "falls out." As an experiment, he tried the antidote once. He shot up more heroin than he could handle, and as soon as his lips turned purple and tingly dots clouded his eyes, he injected the Narcan the way a paramedic would. "I came right out of it," he said. "I got real sick—the shakes, diarrhea, you know, but I survived." Ryan numbed himself against the real possibility of McNally dying.

In January 2010, a distressed Anna Weaver, a potential new client, called Ryan with pressing legal questions, and they agreed to meet, but Weaver never materialized. Ryan thought nothing of it, no-shows fairly routine, but three months later, he awoke to grisly details in the newspaper of Anna Weaver having been bludgeoned to death on Main Street, up the road from Ulrich Law Office. Investigators would determine that Weaver and her murderer, Collin Smith, had carpooled to Milwaukee to score oxy, all the while Smith intent on some bizarre drug-world vigilante justice. Who buys, who uses, and is it fair? Ball-peen hammers are traditionally used to harden metal fabric, but back home in Oshkosh, high as a bat, Smith beat Weaver's existence into a soft, bloody pulp, and then he stabbed her arm with a needle because "that's what the junkie deserves." The murderer's fiancée and seven-month-old son looked on. A baby, like Mercer Mayer's little mice, would always be found in some square inch of these snapshots. I could never wrap my brain around these ghastly scenes of family togetherness—or wrap my arms around my own children tightly enough. Was there anything Ryan might have advised Anna Weaver to prevent her gruesome death?

Certainly my dad, when wearing his Dr. Ralph K. Baker hat, had played a role in familiarizing me with violent crimes in childhood. As a psychiatrist, he testified in court about whether regional atrocities were attributable to mental illness. He submitted reports in high-profile criminal cases ranging from the mutilation and murder of Carla Lenz by John Ray Weber in backwoods Wisconsin to Eagle Scout Gary Hirte's quest to "get away with" the murder of loner Glenn Kopitske. He talked unabashedly about his work life. Now that I was a parent, protective instincts were plaited into my existence, and I'd think longer and harder about drugs, violence, and the short circuit between them.

No single case in Ryan's criminal-defense career was ever a duplicate. Each case was resolved in its own way, depending on t he client's record and overall attitude, the assistant DA working up the case, the judge at the helm, and, generally, everybody's moods just as much as the state's laws. This time around, Ryan finally managed to strike a deal with the DA, in exchange for McNally's hand-to-hand purchases for the MEG unit, taking down the group of dealers that emerged after Lazarus Jackson was locked up. He shot heroin between setups, and Ryan kept expecting a call from agents to report an OD. "They don't care if you shoot dope on a setup," McNally told me. "All they care about is getting convictions."

When Ryan arranged McNally's deal, he said to the DA, "I thought Darlene Eaves and the other CIs already brought down the big dealers."

The DA laughed, sarcasm a tone he struck only after hours. "What do you mean? Putting people in jail doesn't solve the drug problem?" After a long pause, he continued, "Prices just double for a little while until new dealers take their place."

Before reporting to jail, to serve six months instead of six years, McNally, cranked up on heroin, stopped by to see Ryan. A buddy who came along with McNally—in fact a future client—picked up Ryan's old guitar from the corner of his office. McNally was a walking cadaver, so gaunt in the face the outline of his teeth protruded through his sallow cheeks. His eye sockets were like a fun-house novelty. As McNally's pal picked an elegant rendition of "Nutshell" by Alice in Chains, McNally nodded out, and back in, rhythmically, eyes rolling around, possessed.

He'd been using smack with his latest in a string of girlfriends, and according to McNally, she had a nine-year-old daughter. Ryan imagined the girl locked in a bathroom or hanging out at the library, Burger King, a coffee shop—wherever children hide from parents who are users. "I'm an addict. She's an addict," McNally said. "This is no place for a kid." As Ryan meditated in the wake of their departure, sober and depleted, he looked around his office and then picked up his phone, placing an anonymous tip to Child Protective Services, even though he waffled briefly between his loyalty to McNally and his paternal instincts. In any event, his call proved moot. McNally's girlfriend overdosed on heroin a few days later and ended up hospitalized.

Lazarus Jackson wept to the judge before his sentencing, "The allegations against me are just crazy. I can barely sleep at night thinking about this." Winnebago County had suffered the seventh highest rate of heroin-related arrests out of seventy-two counties in Wisconsin that year. Wisconsin was hard at work on producing alarming statistics. We witnessed more accidental deaths from opioid overdoses than from car crashes; we landed runner-up status in pharmacy robberies—committed by desperados hell-bent on obtaining heroin's pharmaceutical alternatives; and we redeemed heroin from Mexico as pure as 80 percent. Nowhere in America was the crisis deeper than in the Midwest. The Wisconsin attorney general called it the greatest challenge in his twenty-five years of law enforcement.

It's no wonder the judge sentenced Jackson to nineteen years in prison. Eaves testified, as promised, against the third and final dealer charged in the conspiracy, but without hand-to-hand buys as evidence, the jury was deadlocked and Jackson's accomplice was set free. When Ryan heard this news, he called the DA to ask about Eaves's testimony, to ensure she had followed through on her promises and was absolved of her troubled past.

"Yeah, she testified consistent with her statement, but you know what?" the DA said. "I heard she ODed this weekend." Ryan's lungs imploded. He had noticed Eaves's cell number in the backlog of messages on his voice mail that morning, and the memory compelled him to hang up quickly with the DA and listen, when usually he let the messages accumulate to the point of inertia.

"Hello, Ryan, sir. This is Darlene Eaves's boyfriend. I'm afraid I have some bad news. Darlene is deceased, at the moment." Ryan played the recording a dozen times. Her boyfriend seemed to believe Eaves would rise from her gurney, but heroin had been nicknamed "dead on arrival" for a reason, and Eaves would remain deceased now and for an everlasting fermata of moments.

At times like these, Ryan felt more bewildered than sad. He drifted through work, seeing double—versions of Eaves, living and dead—as if the effects of drug use were contagious. He'd drafted McNally's obituary in his mind a dozen times and was therefore stunned when Darlene Eaves was the first to require a eulogy. What pushed her to use again? She was certainly a judicial system pawn; to some extent, everybody involved was a user. To memorialize her death, Ryan thought maybe he could play a preventive role in other clients' lives. He mustered up what little energy remained for the workweek, before compassion fatigue settled back in, to lay out options for his other heroin addicts, first and foremost McNally: inpatient treatment at Nova Counseling Services, serious detox, a good dose of willpower. Ryan made personal visits to McNally, now in jail, to ensure he had a plan for sobriety when he was released, and when he was, Ryan was the first person he visited.

"I want to help you, man," Ryan said, reaching over the surface of his desk toward McNally on the other side. "I'll make it my mission."

"The craving won't ever go away," McNally said. "I'll be a sixty-year-old man, and I'll crave the smack."

Ryan tried to imagine this junkie older and wiser, he'd tell me in recounting the conversation.

"You looked like dog shit the last time I saw you," Ryan said. "Glad to see you fattened up in there." In four months, he'd gained about thirty pounds, McNally more efficient at bulking up than I was during any of my pregnancies.

Before going to jail, McNally had told Ryan and me about the time he found himself outside a Kwik Trip, crushing and shooting up five Ritalin, and he couldn't even get high. "I looked down at my bloody arms, and I realized I didn't have nobody, I didn't have nothing, except you," McNally said to Ryan, choking up, some unseen force willing him to speak. He and I were on opposite corners of Ryan's desk, facing each other, and I leaned hard into the sharp edge, attempting to close the distance between us.

"If you could change anything about your life, what would it be?" I asked McNally, yearning to possess something hard and real from his private war against addiction. He made a fist as if coaxing out a vein, and I stood up to hug him, his body rigid and unaccustomed to affection. "I wish I had different parents," he said, and then he began to weep.

Ryan was never sure when McNally departed if he'd ever see the guy again, but I'd see illusions of his mother, Mama McNally, everywhere and often, in the phlebotomist at the hospital, the plunger of the syringe cocked; or on the back of a Harley along Highway 41 between Milwaukee and Oshkosh, laughter caught up in the full-throttle rumble of a Sunday joyride. Sometimes I even saw Mama McNally in my very own bathroom mirror, and I'd ask myself, *Well, what kind of mother will you be today? And tomorrow, and a year from tomorrow?*

CHAPTER 3

The Bandwagon for Animals

The first time Ryan's casework made the news, I was shaking hands and kissing babies: I'd won the campaign for our fourth child. Ryan muttered in private, cracked jokes in public. No sooner had I matured into a globe on a spindle than I happened upon a geologist from campus who was genuinely shocked by my girth. "Is this number three, now?"

"Number four," I told him.

"Imagine that," he said. "That's a lot of carbon footprints."

This pregnancy marked a shift in Ryan's casework from behind-the-scenes to public-eye advocacy. He couldn't always advocate quietly for his clients anymore, especially when the news media caught wind of whom he defended and for what. Although family came first, Ryan's sense of duty to provide for his clients, to provide for us, had ratcheted up, causing him to double down with twice the anxiety. As defendants looked at him with the eyes of needy children, he slept less, often on our sofa, without blankets or pillows, sports commentators crooning him to sleep. He wheezed on the brink of an asthma attack, sighed constantly, and bit off our heads for breakfast. "God, what's he crabby about?" people asked me. They had no idea he was like one of these guys discovered, impossibly, to be supporting two families at once, on opposite ends of the map.

Irie and Leo couldn't believe their dad was on TV. We listened to him feed the reporter standard defense attorney lines, clutching his poker hand tight against his breast pocket, in his first high-profile case, *State of Wisconsin v. Joseph A. Michalik*, in which an Iraq War veteran was charged with killing his ex-girlfriend's cats, facing two counts of felony mistreatment of animals resulting in death.

"A lot of evidence wasn't heard today," Ryan said. "My client is innocent until proven guilty, and that is how we are proceeding should we go to trial."

In Oshkosh, where Memorial and Independence Day parades yield larger turnouts than elections, where Veterans of Foreign Wars *and* Humane Society dogs make parade-goers weep, the needles on spectators' moral compasses spun in endlessly confused circles, Joseph Michalik greeted simultaneously by salutes and damnation. This fusion of love and hate also characterized Michalik's short-term relationship with the cats' owner, Cali Ziegler, a young woman sympathetically bulging, pregnant with Michalik's son. The evidence against Michalik—necropsy reports and feline remains—symbolized the end of their romance, though nobody knew yet what to make of Ziegler's baby and the umbilical cord connecting these estranged lovers as much as it yoked mother to child.

Their June due date was only days before our fourth child— our second son, Francis—was predicted to arrive, two boys muscling up in separate wombs on the same side of town. Ziegler and I were under care of the same midwives at the same medical center. The boys' fathers were leading news, more scandalous locally than the war itself ever was, animal rights activists landing a brighter spotlight. Ryan expected picketers around every corner, their acronyms a jumble of nerve-racking letters: ASPCA, PETA, HSUS. They printed T-shirts, pinned orange ribbons to their lapels, and staged protests at Michalik's preliminary hearing, arraignment, and pretrial conferences.

Ryan reviewed the evidence meticulously and arranged plot points in his head. As every lawyer knows, and as every *Law & Order* enthusiast believes, trials are theater, even though what makes for riveting TV does not always make for justice. Joseph Michalik was a name we learned to say at home, enjoying its onomatopoetic quality, cathartic as the *f*-word. Linked in consonance with *click* and *lock*, *Michalik* sounded like a prison cell door, lights out, a fate Ryan guarded against for the first time, as prior to Michalik, his clients had only faced time in jail. In some ways, Michalik reminded us of Derek Green because he was utterly sympathetic, but our allegiance to him was further accentuated by the fact that he'd never committed a crime before returning from Iraq.

As Ryan grated out public defender appointments, it was easy to take his clients' wrongdoing for granted, but his job also entailed looking at crimes from a levelheaded perspective. Transgressions were not always as egregious as prosecutors argued. He met every DA at the line of scrimmage and tried to prevent overwhelming defeat, using pure and simple common sense: a voluntary program instead of probation, probation instead of jail time, or a short-term stay in the clink instead of a longer stint in Wisconsin's prison system.

The state's case against Michalik began a week before Christmas, stockings hung by Cali Ziegler's stovetop with care. Michalik crashed at her upstairs apartment in Oshkosh, where they'd briefly coexisted, allowing their possessions to commingle. He stayed this night with Ziegler's permission, while she worked hospice care. I've always wondered, whose spiritual needs did Ziegler tend to on the night in question? Did she crush ice chips or massage the lifeline on an old woman's palm?

Of course, nobody recorded details of Ziegler's nightshift or of her journey home at sunrise. Instead investigators focused on the scene of the crime. Aside from one thud in the night, downstairs neighbors neither heard nor saw anything suspicious, but in the morning, Michalik texted Ziegler to report bad news. Her orange-and-white cat, Wilson, had escaped, and Michalik could not find him. Michalik laid Ziegler's house keys on her kitchen table, pulled the door closed, tightened his backpack, and bicycled twenty miles to his mother's house beneath weeping, sleeting skies. When Ziegler arrived home from work, not many hours later, she called out for her furry companions, but she could find neither Wilson nor her black kitten, Molly.

"Molly, come here, girl," she said, but she did not hear the clack of claws.

Perhaps because I was raised with indoor-outdoor cats, in the country, a missing feline never signaled foul play. When Fluffy, Tiger, Smokey, or Puff—all uninspired names, I realized too late—disappeared, we assumed they were hunting mice in the woodpile, chasing chipmunks in the field, or taking a vacation in the Doemels' barn. Our faith in their return was always rewarded hours or days later, and this experience made Ziegler's instinct to call Oshkosh police seem strange, but she called them twice.

The first time police responded to Ziegler's phone call, they searched her backyard as if trawling a frozen river, searching both sides of the fence alongside the duplex, beneath the ice-dipped shrubs, whistling and cooing, "Here, kitty, kitty, kitty." Ziegler traipsed down the wooden fire escape, joining officers, packing snow into a semisweet glaze. Near the driveway, she bent to peek beneath a snowmobile trailer, and because she had committed Wilson's markings to heart, she spotted him immediately, even though he was camouflaged, his white-and-orange patches identical to the rust-colored cottonwood leaves strewn across the snow. His fangs were clamped against his furry lip, body gone stiff, dead from blunt-force trauma to the head.

"Oh my God, oh my God, oh my God," Ziegler likely wept. "Joseph must have shot him with his air rifle." On hands and knees, officers scraped Wilson from the ice, taking his congealed body into their arms for evidence. His grimace looked ferocious like a cougar's despite his domesticated size. Ziegler disappeared upstairs and returned quickly, still in some muted version of hysterics. "The air rifle is gone," she cried, referring to one of many items he'd left behind after their breakup. "He must have taken it with him." After they left, police contacted Joseph Michalik, but he denied taking the weapon or harming the cat.

Nearly two full days passed before Ziegler called the police again. They had not searched her garbage for evidence, Ziegler insisted, and Molly, the kitten, had not materialized. An officer drove his squad car to Ziegler's apartment, and upon his arrival, Ziegler stood eagerly waiting. Nobody wants to dig through days-old rancid trash and come upon devastating evidence alone. Ziegler handed the deputy a bag of trash as she searched another, both of them pushing aside food scraps and used tissues like human scavengers. That's when Ziegler unearthed a wad of black mesh and gasped, "This looks like it's from a boxspring."

Back inside her apartment, with Ziegler's guidance, the officer matched the mesh to the undercarriage of Ziegler's sofa, fitting it against the ripped-out portion. Just like Wilson, Molly was camouflaged inside—black fur blending into the black cavern of the hollow furniture. The officer spied her tufted ears and pulled her through the opening, like a magician pulling a limp rabbit from a hat. Molly's matted and wet fur was curled into the shapes of metal sofa springs, and like Wilson, Molly was dead.

Ziegler glowered at the wet cat, each millisecond of disbelief fueling her frenzy. She ricocheted from room to room, hypothesizing and efficiently stockpiling evidence against Michalik. She found a plastic storage bin with kitty scratch marks on the inside, a wet towel coated with cat fur, and last but not least, the most damning evidence of all: an army uniform name tape labeled MICHALIK peeping from the bathtub drain, over which, one might imagine, Michalik had hovered as he filled Molly's plastic death chamber from the cold tap. Joseph Michalik was the only person in Ziegler's apartment when the cats went missing. Dozens of text messages between Michalik and Ziegler proved he was the last person to see the cats alive.

As Ryan prepared for trial, he worried the jury instructions read like a worksheet for a literature course titled Contemporary Courtroom Drama, and "army name tape" was the answer for a fill-in-the-blank question regarding the mistreatment of animals according to Wisconsin statutes. When Ryan appeared on TV a second time for the same case, he furrowed his brow, discussing Michalik's life before the war, a criminally unblemished record, not even a speeding ticket. The pompadour thickness of Joseph Michalik's wavy dark hair looked wet, his forehead equally pleated in surprise at the events of his own life, and his face twitched as he turned toward Ryan the way boys turn toward big brothers. Brain damage from his encounter with an IED in Iraq manifested as symptoms of Tourette's. He was twenty-nine years old, but his mother had chauffeured him to the arraignment, on fumes of gasoline, from the Veterans Affairs hospital where he was voluntarily seeking treatment for his post-traumatic stress disorder.

For Michalik, the dividing line between lawfulness and crime was once clear, but this distinction had been erased during his tour of duty in the Middle East. When my grandfather Frank, a journalist for whom Francis was named, suffered his first stroke, his vocabulary talents powdered into the sides of his brain, and he'd stare at me ashamed when I brandished his transistor radio and all he could say was "phone book." Michalik had suffered the stroke of combat. He spun the Rolodex of names for the campaign for which he had fought, but he wound up baffled, speechless, in a courtroom with bright lights. Was it the Iraq War or the War on Iraq or Operation Iraqi Freedom or the Second US-Iraq War or Gulf War II?

Ryan was bigger than Michalik but softer, a prizefighter in only one school-bus skirmish, decades earlier, but he was not afraid to sit beside this sniper educated in the school of firing hot bullets into the temples of insurgents' heads, because Michalik, unlike the Malik Turners of the world, was afraid of himself. When police picked him up shortly after his return from Iraq for disorderly conduct—his first offense—he bellowed on a long exhale of booze, "You have no idea what it's like to stare down the barrel of a gun and watch somebody's head explode."

When the IED exploded and knocked Michalik from his wits, killing a handful of his troops and the commander of his platoon, blunt force was written like code into this soldier's head. His body would remember without any conscious effort the true impact of violence. Poor Wilson. Was he the most plausible victim when Michalik awoke, in the bruised hours of a winter night, in his ex-girlfriend's bed? Did Wilson yawn and stretch, also awakened, on the same set of sheets where Michalik had tried to replace lives he'd ended in Iraq with desire, sex, and a new baby boy? A flashback to combat would explain the thud heard that night; terracotta flowerpots smashed to bits on Ziegler's apartment floor; curtains pulled from rods, wrestled to the floor like ghosts; the large, wet bin, sticky with black cat hair where Molly lay lifeless before her burial inside the living room couch, not returned to the earth properly as cats should be.

Michalik's crime nagged at Ryan from some kind of fathomless place inside him, not because of the violence but because the defendant and his alleged crime were intuitively incongruent. As spring thawed, Ryan planted the seeds of his strategy, hoping to use Michalik's PTSD as a defense when up against the assistant district attorney prosecuting *State of Wisconsin v. Joseph A. Michalik*. A former army ranger, perhaps remembering his own service, this DA, although tough as pumice on crime, showed signs of empathy toward Michalik. When I met him grocery shopping one day, he pumped a gallon of milk in each fist and looked more like I'd imagined Michalik should—the face of America's armed forces, fit, brawny, gritting his square jaw. But he also seemed to feel some sense of loyalty toward Michalik, perhaps the glint of fidelity we all feel for soldiers.

"Look," he said to Ryan. "About the PTSD, we'd be satisfied with NGI. If you get Michalik a good doctor to evaluate his mental health, we won't contest the doc's opinion." Not guilty by reason of insanity, otherwise known as NGI, seemed like a fair and proper resolution to Michalik's case, given the catalog of evidence against him. Though Ziegler would want some greater sense of justice for cruelty to her cats, Joseph Michalik *was* the father of her unborn child, and Ryan hoped NGI would provide a satisfying settlement all around. For a moment we thought we heard a bugler playing "Taps" in the background, not for a soldier having died but for his resurrection.

An orange-and-black stray cat began living in our garage around the time Ryan arranged for Michalik's psychiatric evaluation. I remembered Ryan—at ages eleven, twelve, thirteen—attending parties at my house. In self-imposed exile on our porch, he rubbed his swollen eyes and rasped, misery to which he subjected himself for six more years before I'd euthanize an ailing Fluffy. His allergies were so serious, sometimes an eye would swell shut and we'd be forced to try home remedies like Preparation H. Between dating and marriage, we broke up once, and I immediately adopted a cat, as Ryan was the only reason I wasn't already raising one. When he and I reconciled fully within a couple of months, I reluctantly gave Mr. Bay to a neighbor—inadequate, even pathetic consolation for a late miscarriage she'd suffered.

The kids and I never named the stray in our garage because we lacked consensus, Irie, Leo, and Fern jostling over favorite candy names: Reese's, Skittles, and Milky Way. Not to mention Ryan's adamant opposition to the stray. "We're not keeping that mangy varmint," he'd mutter, as we ignored his wishes, feeding her cold cuts and milk, filling an old toaster box with hearty plaid and inviting her to roam the house. Irie had learned to whistle and would crouch on our driveway, fish-mouthed, until the cat slinked into view, an ethereal rebuke of Ryan's good intentions to exonerate Michalik. A week later, however, much to our children's disappointment but Ryan's relief, we entrusted her to the Humane Society, where she was christened Tess and adopted immediately. The children felt sad, but I taught them as my parents taught me: cats, dogs, rabbits, and other pets were worthy of love and affection, but relinquishing a pet to a shelter or to euthanasia was just another practice test for "real pain."

At times, Ryan was an irritable husband, and I was a mean wife. He'd overreact to spilled milk, and I'd call him a "baby," an ironic and harsh epithet Irie once shared at circle time in pre-kindergarten, as in, "My mom says my dad is a big baby." When exercise and diet management seemed impossible, Ryan procured a prescription for Valium; he was supposed to pop one if he felt an anxiety attack coming on as he rushed between courtrooms in the train-wrecked schedule of preliminary hearings. Even when he swallowed only half a dose, he'd wind up cashed on his office sofa, without even flipping the OPEN sign to CLOSED, his body paralyzed in the deep afternoon light. When I married Ryan, he was easy-go-peasy and patient with my volatile moods, but by now we had swapped roles. Weary of his bad temper, I could be hard on Ryan, but I was surprisingly blithe with the children in ways he couldn't pretend to be. When something thudded, he'd wince and clench his fists, as if he himself suffered the PTSD of combat. Since I'd become pregnant with Irie, I'd passed my disquietude on to him.

Ryan was especially nervous about the Michalik case. Based on his litigation experience, jurors in small Midwestern cities respond not to evidence, as judges must, but rather to personally tailored versions of how the world ought to be. What then, he wondered, would this mean for Joseph Michalik, our Iraq War veteran, whose wartime experience was more complicated than anybody at home could fully imagine? Would it hit a nerve to suggest that punishing Joseph Michalik was like punishing our own zealous support of a foreign war?

If it were not for Cali Ziegler's second phone call to Oshkosh police, Ryan would have added Joseph Michalik to his long list of sorry scofflaws. In the evenings, when our children slept, Joseph Michalik and uterine magic were what remained in our clouded minds. Ryan pasted his palm between my legs, Francis's kicks strongest where my body opened, life tied perpetually to intimacy. Though Michalik would never feel his baby's limbs inside Ziegler's body, I imagined his boy marching like a soldier inside her womb.

Ryan had become increasingly suspicious of Ziegler. The evidence against Michalik appeared more like choreography than like discovery. Wasn't it awfully suspicious that Ziegler managed to gather clues so quickly once that police officer arrived at her apartment? Ryan speculated that forty-eight hours between investigations was certainly sufficient time for Ziegler to have manipulated evidence and staged her apartment. Ziegler, not the Oshkosh

Police Department, suggested rummaging through her garbage for additional proof; and Ziegler, not the officer, unearthed the sofa mesh *and* Michalik's name tape, pulled from the bathtub drain like sleight of hand.

Ryan began to poke holes in Ziegler's version of events, slowly and methodically, as if plugging brightly colored pegs into the dots on a Lite-Brite. If Ziegler found the name tape in the officer's presence, this meant Ziegler had not bathed in forty-eight hours. And if Michalik's name tape had been used to plug the drain, this meant one of two possibilities: Michalik had dressed in his uniform to kill Molly, and the five-pound kitten had yanked the name tape from his uniform with her tiny claws; or Michalik himself had sliced it from his clothes to plug the drain, as if no other stopper would work. Ryan said to me, repeatedly in those days of reckoning, "Even a mediocre soldier would know better than to lose his name tape in the bathtub, for Christ's sake."

This one piece of evidence—a rectangle of fabric meant to withstand modern warfare, meant to outlive the soldier himself—was what Ryan dwelled upon, the alleged murder scene turning increasingly ridiculous. Why was Molly still wet, if Michalik had drowned her forty-eight (or more) hours earlier? And how was Ziegler so swift to patch together a report, a plausible play-by-play, if the evidence she discovered, in the presence of the police officer, was as surprising as it should have been?

While initial evidence against Michalik was damning, Ryan scrutinized the theatrics with which Ziegler produced additional proof, seeing more and more clearly that Ziegler's clues were too perfect to believe. If Ryan were to focus exclusively on refuting seemingly uncompromised evidence against Michalik in Wilson's death, jurors might believe he killed Molly too, but if Ryan were to raise suspicion in Molly's death, jurors might believe all the evidence was planted. But if Michalik had not killed the cats, Ziegler was the only other possibility, and the image of this pregnant mother wrestling her whiskered creature beneath the water, black legs thwacking the plastic tub, was less conceivable than a soldier reenacting violence against animals. Dressing in his army uniform to drown a kitten as if laundering dirty shorts, his face reflected in the water above Molly's writhing claws: this sounded like the kind of formulaic and predictable tale jurors would believe.

Nevertheless, Ryan became increasingly convinced that Michalik was innocent, at least in Molly's death. As spring thickened and he taught our children, in order of birth, to ride a bike, to memorize the Milwaukee Brewers lineup, and to speak in clear and complete sentences, I spent time thinking of women like Andrea Yates and Susan Smith. Both had drowned their human babies, debunking myths about motherhood we once accepted. Was Cali Ziegler willing to sacrifice her cats if it meant locking up the baby's father, denying him access to their child? If Michalik were behind bars, Ziegler would be free to raise their son entirely on her own terms.

Was Ziegler a professional victim, and attention-seeking a symptom? Was violence its manifestation, and if so, against what other living things, her own child included, might this violence be used? One does wonder if flashbacks are contagious, memories of explosion and death stamped like DNA onto the egg at the moment of conception, then incubating there. Perhaps Michalik and Ziegler suffered from strains of the same delirium. Maybe Michalik killed only one cat, but in an effort to draw the community's attention, Ziegler drowned the second, before settling in to bathe her own weary body, filled mysteriously with life. Joseph Michalik and the mother of his unborn son might lean over the same bridge between stability and madness, right where I too hovered. Was the inheritance of heartache passed genetically through the devious games of science?

Around the time Irie was born, we learned, through ancestry research, that one of my maternal great-great grandmothers, Wilhelmina Krohn, lost eight of her twelve children to infant death. On the cusp of the twentieth century, infant mortality plagued families. Before widespread post–Industrial Revolution improvements in things like public health, clinical medicine, and sanitation, between 15 and 30 percent of babies in America, depending on city and region, died before turning one. It's no wonder mothers are still superstitious about naming their children. Is it possible that Wilhelmina's period of mourning, a century later, has yet to expire? While mothers then were conditioned not to attach too quickly to their babies, the physical experience of pregnancy has remained unchanged. To birth babies that readily die, one after another, must fray the psyche.

When my counselors diagnosed my inherited strain of depression, perhaps they meant this to include a predisposition for feeling Wilhelmina's pain, siphoned from her genomes to mine, homage to babies who wasted away or died suddenly from the same germs traveling different pathways—bad water, unpasteurized milk, a sick crib-mate whose lips shone humid with microbacteria.

Wilhelmina Krohn was my Grandpa Hilbert's grandmother, and my Grandpa Hilbert, known as Hilly to his friends, suffered severe depression. In the 1950s, he was a patient of electroshock treatment—particularly brutal for him, as his body would not fall under the hypnotic spell of anesthesia—and in later decades before his death in 1979, the recipient of many experimental drugs. He rarely worked, instead collecting disability insurance from the Department of Veterans Affairs.

Soldiers today board planes for the wasteland of war in the Middle East and return frazzled, images of dead bodies burned into their brains. Women who conceive babies travel back in time through the sacred ritual of childbearing, one of the only ways in which we can know our grandmothers, and along that journey, we come upon babies in shrouds.

The egg from which I hatched was inside my own mother's body, which in turn, was inside my grandmother's body when she conceived my mother. Every one of us springs from some container within a container, family sets of Russian nesting dolls. If we count our lives as starting two generations back, how many losses might we add to our emotional resumes? Perhaps this explains why clinical psychologist Martha Manning describes depression as a "legacy"—"a complex weaving of genes and expectations, biochemistry and family myths, and the configuration of our family's strengths, as well as its vulnerabilities."

We are not so far removed from women of a century ago who lived shorter lives, mothers who gave birth and died, met death head-on after babies were born. In our case, though, fatherhood was the silent killer. I wanted to continue as a container for life while Ryan shuddered at the threshold of exhaustion. He had gained eighty pounds since his first year in law school when the stress of starting and supporting a family happened to coincide, a lawyer-father double whammy. To call our brood complete was to resuscitate him, even if it marked the return of depression in me and a slow plodding toward death.

Cali Ziegler's outline, on television, as she raised her pink-manicured right hand, was blurred to protect her anonymity. She enunciated her side of the story with an unambiguous Wisconsin accent, vowels hard and cylindrical as ziti before it is boiled. Perhaps Ziegler endured months without food as I did in pregnancy, eating only the unholy wafer of pregnant women everywhere, saltine crackers, and sipping lemonade. How exactly does malnourishment of first and second trimesters affect the mother's lucidity? Police officers had come to know Ziegler on a first-name basis long before she met Michalik. In a statement to police about a domestic dispute with a previous boyfriend, she claimed to be pregnant but was later discovered not to be. Now Ziegler really was flowering on the inside.

Nor did the case of the dead cats earmark Ziegler's first time in court. Before Wilson and Molly were killed, before Michalik and Ziegler broke up, before Ziegler knew she was pregnant, she alleged Michalik threw a cell phone at her during an argument, and he was charged with battery. The morning of Michalik's plea and sentencing, Ziegler called Ryan and offered him help in the form of an ultimatum. If Michalik was willing to sign over to Ziegler the title to his Jeep, she would give a statement to the judge in Michalik's favor, but if Michalik was not willing to bequeath his vehicle, she would state that he was more monster than former lover. When Ryan called her bluff, she stormed out of the court-room, forged Michalik's signature on the title, and peeled from the courtroom parking lot in his Jeep anyway. One full year later, she would be charged with two felony counts of forgery.

The true turning point in this ever-changing story ultimately arrived in the mail as an unsolicited letter from Ziegler's brother, Brent Ziegler, to the Oshkosh Police Department. In the four-page memo, he addressed Ziegler's history of lies and manipulation, in fact revealing that he had discovered the Crosman American Classic 1377 air pistol, the weapon used to kill Wilson, in Ziegler's dresser drawer. He wrote, "I strongly believe that Cali is wasting the city and county resources and paints a picture that is not true to gain the benefit and the attention of others. If Joseph Michalik did actually kill her cats, he probably was driven to do so by Cali's ability to play mind games. However, I believe that Cali might have done this herself to gain the desired attention she was not receiving."

When the deputy DA stood before Ryan and Joseph Michalik, six months after the alleged crimes, the judge asked, "Are you dismissing the charges against Joseph A. Michalik for burden of proof issues?"

"No, Your Honor. We could easily prove Michalik guilty as charged, but I have reason to believe the evidence is not genuine."

Brent Ziegler wrote in his letter, "Cali alluded that her decision to become pregnant with Joseph Michalik's baby was intentional. During the conversation Cali stated that she stopped using birth control." He went on to detail Ziegler's drinking vodka and chain-smoking cigarettes throughout the pregnancy. "While I understand that Cali has the right to make these decisions for herself, I feel that she is endangering the child she is carrying." As a fellow mother, I wondered, at this point, whom we should worry about: Wilson and Molly, long gone, or Ziegler's baby boy, my son's comrade, born safely on the tail of one war but potentially into the jaws of another.

When I was in labor with Francis, at the end of June, Ryan asked our midwife if a mother named Cali had recently delivered a boy. "We have a Cali in labor right now," she said, and briefly, though she turned out to be somebody else, I wondered if Ziegler and I would birth our boys in sync, and if I might orchestrate an accidental meeting in the hallway or at the nurses' station. New mothers do not share rooms anymore, at least not here, but I felt connected to Ziegler briefly, and in a way, Joseph Michalik lived on in my baby boy. That year, 2010, was the Year of the Tiger for babies who promised to be courageous, hotheaded, and rash—warriors of various kinds. In the whirlwind of Francis's summer birth, I failed to add his name, officially, to our health insurance plan. Our second son, like our first, was an uninsured baby until the university Human Resources Department helped me sort the mess.

We'd been deliberately careful about everything else, even Francis's name, perhaps because of Michalik. Our son's nickname, Frank, pays homage to my grandfather; his other nom de guerre, Franco, is a halfhearted, perhaps ironic tribute to my Spanish major and studies in Madrid. Our little boy, like all babies, was a miniature Francisco Franco, a dictator, demanding Mama's milk and skin-to-skin contact. But his given name, Francis, was a superstitious effort to counterbalance the everyday discord of Ryan's life defending criminals.

As a young girl, I adored the youngest boy, Francis, in Disney's *Swiss Family Robinson*. While his older brothers, Fritz and Ernst, appeared somber and harrowed, taking responsibility for their survival after being shipwrecked, Francis was exuberant, inventive, and playfully optimistic about his family's future. He investigated wildlife, tamed ostriches and zebras, and amassed his own menagerie of loyal animals. The actor who played Francis, Kevin Corcoran, also played Arliss in *Old Yeller*, a wide-eyed, animal-loving boy with an unmatched zest for the well-being of all living things. And if Francis Robinson were not auspicious enough, I believed Saint Francis of Assisi bore good fortune, a namesake protection against some kind of unpredictable violence, a prophet sent to us in peace, flag of surrender undulating, like a whitecap in the wind.

At which Madrid museum did I see my first-ever original painting of Saint Francis—the Reina Sofía or El Prado—and was the artist Maestro Nicolás Francés, El Greco, or Francisco Goya? I studied his countenance, as our professor lectured on the patron saint of animals, who preached to his sisters, the birds. According to legend, Saint Francis put an end to the chronic threats of a wolf against nearby townsfolk. He tamed the wild beast, blessed him, and ensured that in exchange for human safety and security, the citizens, collectively, would fill and replenish a porringer of fresh meats, fish, and berries—all the sustenance required for the pacified creature to endure the brutality of winter.

Ryan often forced me to admit that pregnancy was not the perfect cure. It did not alleviate my depression without side effects, such as nausea, hunger, and delirium. My first pregnancy with Irie completely altered my perspective on "morning sickness." Nausea was no longer a joke but rather a serious malady, my insides tightening like shoestrings into a triple knot just beneath my rib cage, releasing an aftertaste of rotten chemical eggs. My stomach actually hurt, especially in the evenings, and looking at little alien-ghost babies in the early weeks of development, from *The Pregnant Body Book*, convinced me I had eaten something rancid—my own baby.

I dreamed I was swallowing jellyfish and eating teacups to kill them, like the old lady who swallowed a spider to catch the fly. I learned pica was a mental disorder, more common among pregnant women and children than the general population, in which those afflicted crave nonnutritive substances such as clay and sand. I diagnosed myself as suffering from pica, as most smells and tastes caused me to gag, and in my dreams I began eating scraps of paper too.

Sometimes I'd cry out in agony just thinking about the recommended spinach diet for loading up on folic acid. Candy tasted good, especially when I chain-sucked Jolly Ranchers, the sourness an effective antidote against acid reflux or vomiting, but real food did not. I was skinny and malnourished, losing, on average, fifteen pounds during each of my first trimesters. For the first twenty weeks, each baby grew inside me like an infection. When I was pregnant with Leo, my midwife prescribed Zofran, an anti-nausea medicine prescribed to cancer patients, and in addition to regular checkups, I scheduled weekly appointments to be pumped full of IV fluids because I could not bring myself to drink. Writhing in bed, feeling ravenous but also queasy, I inexplicably begged my mom to buy me a cheeseburger at Hardee's. I picked at the sesame seeds while sobbing. Somehow, throughout every pregnancy, I continued to teach. I'd sway, lurch, lean against students' desks, and try not to vomit up my lectures.

When I was pregnant with Fern, I thought I'd discovered the answer in microwave popcorn. After eating a whole bag at work, I loaded Irie and Leo into the bucket seats of a city bus. When we disembarked, after a twisting drive home, I threw up on my neighbors' lawn, the hulls from the popped corn flickering in the afternoon sun. The neighborhood dog licked them up. By the time I was pregnant with Francis, I had learned to hypnotize myself into drinking soda, the bubbles massaging my nausea into brief submission. I was weak, dizzy, and trapped deep inside my personal tunnel of survival.

"I can't understand how anybody suffers chronic pain," I told a good friend.

"Just think of it as a prison sentence," she said, laughing. "You're up for parole in a couple of weeks." And of course, the second half of the pregnancy always compensated for the first. I was more like the Very Hungry Caterpillar, fattening up for some noble transformation, and when my uterus worked hard to squeeze out babies, the pain was barefaced and intense, not covert and mysterious like morning sickness. Getting pregnant was a secret, but giving birth felt like a public event. In the early stages of pregnancy, I whispered, but in labor, I screamed with joy. Madness came in many colors, and I preferred the rapturous lunatic I became while pregnant to the somber woman I was otherwise.

"You look happy," a colleague once said, surprised, as I was front-heavy, enormous with the tumor of pregnancy, ready to fall forward on my face. "I'm growing a human inside me," I said, dotty and moonstruck, not of my right mind, smiling into the distance. Cali Ziegler was capable of anything, and so was I, along with all the other uberous women who'd been walking the earth for thousands of years.

Less than a year after Ryan resolved Joseph Michalik's mistreatment of animals case, police responded to an anonymous tip that would lead Ryan down a familiar path. An emaciated pit bull was frozen to the sidewalk a block from our house on Hazel Street. Necropsy reports showed the puppy died from systemic multi-organ failure, secondary to severe malnutrition. Rocco looked more like a premature fawn or an aborted fetus than a puppy, his rib cage accentuated by his thin fur coat. He was all bones, no meat. One of his back digits dangled from a sinewy thread, bloody and raw, and his haunches were mottled with the markings of his own feces.

Through the anonymous tip, police were able to trace Rocco to his owner, Brandon Fredrickson, and Brandon's girlfriend, Alyssa Brandt, who were living in complete squalor: dirty dishes growing mold, feces-stained sheets, McDonald's drive-thru bags and crushed soda cups, soiled clothes, and an empty box for a First Response pregnancy test—by all accounts, Brandt's urine having conjured up two pink lines. In a cloudy green fish tank, police discerned the webbed feet of a pet turtle, and in addition to an empty dog crate, too small for Rocco, police discovered another pup named Princess, not nearly as emaciated as Rocco but edging in that direction. The day after Fredrickson's case appeared in the *Northwestern*, Ryan called me at work and said, "Well, I'm defending the dog killer's girlfriend."

"Another animal cruelty case?"

"Yup. Another one."

I imagined myself connected to any defendant who was also a mother or mother-to-be, as Ryan did with guys like Derek Green and Joseph Michalik. Although both Fredrickson and Brandt were only nineteen years old, they were pretending to be married, Brandt having adopted Fredrickson's last name for Facebook appearances. They were playing house. Brandt would have been in the early stages of pregnancy the night Fredrickson removed Rocco from his cage and carried him like a baby—"he was too weak to walk"—to Oak Street, where he laid him down to die, the March air frigid, even though spring had officially arrived. Fredrickson was Brandt's first boyfriend, a good-looking guy with a limited IQ, living exclusively off his $680-per-month social security stipend, which he received for his cognitive disabilities. Perhaps these dogs were practice tests for real parenthood, which Brandt and Fredrickson obviously and egregiously failed.

Animal rights activists returned to Oshkosh with a vengeance, raging protests against Alyssa Brandt, even though her dog, Princess, was rehabilitated at the Humane Society and quickly adopted to a loving and more capable owner. Charged with being party to the crime of mistreatment of animals resulting in death and intentionally mistreating animals, Brandt faced twenty-seven months in prison. The judge received hundreds of letters with local, national, and international postmarks, advocating a tough sentence.

Brandt was a young woman with no criminal record, on track to attend the technical college in the fall. Inquiring minds wanted to know: what was her excuse? She had adopted Princess to save her, the runt of the litter, from being killed—an obvious gesture of compassion, the same as Fern's benevolent act in *Charlotte's Web*. Irie and I were so touched by the 2006 cinematic adaptation of the novel that we decided halfway through our first viewing to name our next girl Fern, in honor of E. B. White's animal liberator, and of course, we did. Now here was Alyssa Brandt, who had shopped at Walmart for formula, a full-fledged mother who had bottle-fed Princess hourly, humming sweet lullabies into the puppy's ear.

Nothing seemed to explain why she slowly began limiting Princess's food and water after Fredrickson bought Rocco via Craigslist, and nothing explained why she never stepped in to prevent Rocco's gruesome death. The tipster working with police described Brandt and her "husband" watching movies, talking, and laughing while Rocco wasted away in his crate. This friend—this spy—developed a ritual of biting her chicken nuggets in half and pushing the fried McDonald's morsels between the slats, Rocco snapping them up and swallowing them whole. One explanation in this case is that Rocco was hostile; he would bite Fredrickson's hands and attack Brandt when she opened his cage. But at what point do neglect and hunger begin to manifest as a vicious dog?

More than preoccupied by Brandt's behavior, though, I was worried about my own lack of moral outrage, desensitized to animal cruelty after only two high-profile cases. As the wife of a criminal-defense attorney, I wondered, was I becoming numb as a matter of self-preservation, and would I continue to make a decent mother?

Admittedly I found myself baffled by friends who compared their cats and dogs to children. Colleagues would discuss dropping their Labradors off at doggie day cares as if feeling the same separation anxiety that mothers of breastfeeding babies experienced. I politely smiled, knowing we were comparing the equivalent of apples and some exotic fruit like the African horned cucumber. Other professors stormed through the department, "overwhelmed" by their students' requests, mounting stacks of papers, never-ending to-do lists, but I knew, secretly, work was a vacation from child-rearing. Pet ownership was not the same rigorous boot camp parenthood was, even if a couple of my fellow professors were busy managers of their cats' Facebook pages. Sometimes, when I'd tell people I wanted another baby, they'd say, "Get a dog instead." Not only did this preclude my active role in conception, pregnancy, and birth—animal mothers got to conceive, grow, and nurse those puppies and kittens—but plainly, bluntly, I did not believe animals equaled people on the continuum of living things.

Our dog, Mr. Owen, was an impulse buy when I was pregnant with Leo, but we loved him as most families love their pets, because he was jolly and dopey. We gave him outrageous haircuts like Mohawks or buzz cuts with leftover leg warmers, and Irie dressed him in T-shirts. Mr. Owen participated in every imaginary game she wished, though he also liked to be naughty, bolting off in parking lots and jumping into strangers' vehicles, a regular Houdini dog. Ryan once received a phone call from the YMCA parking lot, where Mr. Owen had leapt into a stranger's car. The good Samaritan who had found Ryan's phone number on Mr. Owen's tag said, "I think I've got your dog here," but after a moment's delay, he followed up with, "Wait, he just ran off and jumped into some lady's van." Ryan hung up and called me, flabbergasted to realize I hadn't even noticed Mr. Owen leave and return. Our magician pooch resembled the dog who swallowed the canary, and this goofy half golden retriever, half poodle made us laugh out loud.

In spite of our affection for Mr. Owen, back when I'd begun lobbying Ryan for a fourth baby, I had eagerly exploited our lovable pooch for leverage. "You're right. The only way I can see having a fourth baby is if we give up Mr. Owen," Ryan had told me. "We just won't have the time or space to be good pet owners." I hesitated very little. Comparing children to dogs did not require a balance scale. We quickly relinquished him to my stepmom Nancy's sister, Anna, with the unusual perk of keeping him, marginally, in our lives.

After several happy months with his new owner, Mr. Owen was diagnosed as having a stomach tumor. Thanks to Anna's devotion, he received surgery and post-op veterinary care, but on a June morning shortly thereafter, the exact day Francis was born,

Anna found Mr. Owen dead. Nancy withheld the bad news for a few weeks, as we settled into life with another newborn, eventually calling me one evening. "There's something I need to tell you," she said. Intuitively I guessed that Mr. Owen was gone, and though bummed, none of us dwelled on his departure. We stared up into doggie heaven, smiled, and then walked our little humans endlessly around the block instead.

At Alyssa Brandt's sentencing, Ryan debated whether he'd speak his piece, knowing PETA and ASPCA members waited, to do what, he was unsure: spit in his face, force-feed him gruesome photographs, fall to their knees and cry on his leather shoes? But as Princess's new owner made a statement, the "victim" in this case, lobbying for Alyssa Brandt to be sentenced to the fullest extent of the law, Ryan could no longer resist the urge to proclaim his position.

"There just isn't any comparison when it comes to a pet and a child," he said. "This is coming from somebody who lost his four-year-old dog the day his son was born. I can tell you the joy of bringing home my son completely overshadowed the loss of my dog." He paced and gestured, realizing how unpopular he'd become. "People can compare animals to children, but they are just not the same," Ryan continued.

"Yesterday I learned of a case in Outagamie County where a woman is accused of starving her child. Late last night I looked into how many letters had been received in support of this infant that had been almost starved to death. There wasn't a single letter of concern, a single letter of support, a single letter arguing this mother should be punished to the full extent of the law. There is something about animal cases where it really tends to cloud people's perspective."

When he finally rested his case, he expected punishing remarks from the judge, but, much to his surprise, he had unwittingly opened the door for the judge to provide a long-building meditation on human beings versus animals, as she addressed the court. She could not reconcile why she never saw "a groundswell of community support for those children as victims" of abuse, neglect, sexual assault, or homicide; and she could not, for the life of her, understand "why people jumped on the bandwagon for animals," for although pets were members of the community, their lives could not be equated with human existence. "Certainly animals are helpless and can't speak for themselves, but neither can infants, and we don't see people getting up in arms over infants being neglected and abused," she said.

Instead of imposing the maximum sentence, the judge sentenced Alyssa Brandt to four months in jail and two years of probation, holding out the possibility of the expungement of felony charges, should she adhere to the stipulations of supervision. While Brandt never showed remorse for neglecting Rocco and Princess, what struck everybody involved—Ryan, the DA, the judge, police officers, and other investigators—was that she did, in fact, cry. She wept from her chest, wet and sticky with phlegm, whole-body moisture, the kind of grief that surges from some internal hot spot. Brandt cried not because Rocco had died, not because Princess went hungry, but because, between twelve and sixteen weeks' gestation, she had miscarried her little boy, whom she would neither birth nor breastfeed, nuzzle nor neglect.

As our little Saint Francis grew hair, we noticed that his eyelashes—black wisps like the feathers of a magpie—compensated for his unimpressive coiffure. Unlike Irie, Leo, and Fern with their "serious hair" flowing from their scalps in corkscrew curls and horsehair rivulets, Francis's hair grew straw-straight, but fortunately his eye hair curved thicker and longer than any of the others'. His favorite kiss was the flit of our lashes together, the butterfly. When I looked into his brown eyes, some days, all of the earth's winged creatures fluttered there, infinitely alive, and we wondered, naively, if pets—an ark full if necessary—might be the answer to what maternal yearnings remained even after Francis was born.

We adopted the first of our two rabbits, Mr. Edward Nibbles, saved by his first owner from a meat farm—"Ever heard of rabbit stew?" he asked. When that Flemish giant didn't satisfy my unmet needs, we adopted yet another bunny from the Winnebago County Fair, Mrs. Eleanor Nibbles, but in my heart, two pets did not equal a baby. I barely felt surprised, much less sad or grief-stricken, when she died on a hot summer day. Reaching into her cage with our red kids' snow shovel, I scooped up her corpse and laid her in the garden, whereupon Ryan returned home in his suit, dug a small hole, and dropped her inside. Although Leo and Fern cried a bit, we clapped our hands together, like erasers filled with chalk, and as soon as the dust settled, we all went inside to eat lunch.

Life was full of inconsistencies. Pets could never assuage my longing for children, yet I felt wildly animalistic, instincts cued to procreate, an entire litter at a time, if possible, as if this were my life's purpose. Neither Ryan's stress nor all the violence in the world suppressed my desires. Even my rich intellectual life at the university, hard won by feminists before me, felt meaningless if not attached, like some blood-hungry parasite, to my procreative function. The creativity of my mind and of my body had become inextricably linked; when my womb was empty, my brain felt vacant too. With each pregnancy, hormones had revitalized the circuitry of my brain, consolidating gray matter, clearing space for more highly energized and expectant thinking. Being pregnant was like feeling smart and falling in love at the same time, and nothing made me more productive than the ever-enchanting oxy rush of baby amour.

CHAPTER 4

Bedside Manner

When the family of Aloysius Jungwirth retained Ryan for charges their son faced for sexual assault, I hoped, prayed, and temporarily believed the boy's crimes were examples of innocent games gone awry. Our own sex life had already mutated into an obstacle course I worried we'd never complete against my biological clock. Four small children and work-related stress had nearly killed Ryan, and now we were inundated with the details of disturbing sexual crimes that deadened our libidos too.

Long before Ryan, my own brother once tied me with jump ropes to a boy named Timmy and forced us to kiss in the corner of our basement. Christopher and Timmy's older sisters had married us, at five and six years old respectively, with all the accoutrements of modern-day weddings, including white mosquito netting over my face, before holding us hostage on our honeymoon. If this was love, and obviously it was, I have often wondered, how did we go about labeling other dalliances into the strange world of adult intimacy, such as the stripteases we young girls performed at our cottage, emerging from behind pleated closet doors that opened like spellbinding accordions?

Aloysius and his sisters also played imaginative and purportedly innocent games in which they experimented with physical closeness, one of which they called Ozone. Aloysius would toss a nubby green blanket up over their heads and wait patiently to devour the sister unlucky enough to be caught in the boggy fabric as it descended to the ground in an artichoke cloud. Sometimes his sisters called him Ali—the younger of two boys in a blended family of four, quiet and demure. Other times, they called him Wes, though it sounded more like *Wish*, as in *I wish we had put an end to all this madness sooner*.

I myself had referred Wes's family to Ulrich Law Office, as I often did when friends or acquaintances got into trouble. I had known his mother, Annie, since childhood, when we attended church together. In spite of its robust population—sixty-six thousand—Oshkosh remained a small town. At stoplights, turning to stare at other drivers and passengers is customary. The likelihood is we know each other, or recognize a familiarity. I respond to every mention of a first name with "What is his (her) last name?" and therein begin to map the connections, at most three degrees of separation. We're one big family tree, a reality every Oshkosh small business owner must acknowledge and overlook in order to remain viable.

Annie was melancholic but charming, softening tragic experiences into childlike and mildly unsettling whimsies like illustrations in a Maurice Sendak book. Dark-featured and somber with a port-wine birthmark on the bridge of her nose, Annie spoke in a sweet fairytale whisper, as if she possessed some spell to convert evil into gingerbread.

Having met Wes through Annie before knowing him in these criminal circumstances, I found him a bit odd but only in the way that acne-dotted, chubby boys with buzz cuts are all, for the most part, bumbling. He avoided eye contact with adults, slouched sitting or standing, a true master of social awkwardness, which would have explained his inept attempt to engage in romance when he put the moves on his sister's friend during a sleepover—this being Annie's version of events, based on which I asked Ryan to take the case *State of Wisconsin v. Aloysius Jungwirth*. Just as Annie knew how to candy-coat her own life story, a spoonful of sugar helped *this* medicine go down. According to their mom, Wes and Sabrina had been flirtatious for months, evidenced by exchanges on Facebook. When a weekend slumber party turned to drinking, Wes found himself emboldened to act on his attraction. Sneaking into his older sister's bedroom once the girls were asleep, he sought out Sabrina, eager to test the waters of their coquetry, inept by daylight but hoping to possess a small dose of confidence by darkness. Standing by her bedside, he took a deep breath, and then he burrowed his hand underneath the covers, running his clumsy palm up her thigh and into the notch between her legs. What boy waits until a girl is asleep to practice his overtures? How on earth could she consent if she was not conscious? Wes considered neither of these questions, motivated only by his desires.

Waking from a sound sleep, Sabrina blinked into reality and instantly hissed at Wes, "What are you doing? Stop it."

Like a cat burglar in a cartoon who fears his own shadow, not as confident as he would have liked, Wes ducked to the floor, crawled under the bed, and emerged on the other side. He escaped to his own bedroom and fell asleep, but by morning time, Sabrina had decided to tell her parents about Wes's maneuver, and her parents quickly called the police. Within a few days, the DA's office had charged Wes, on the brink of nineteen years old, with second- and third-degree sexual assault of a child. Sabrina was fifteen years old.

By now, Ryan had been practicing criminal law for almost four years, and he was feeling discouraged by all of the cases in which the supposedly secret world of teen romance had become a breeding ground for the ever-expanding Sex Offender Registry in Wisconsin. Several clients facing sexual assault charges were high-school boys risking consensual sex with their high-school girlfriends. Ryan and I might have qualified for such persecution ourselves, Ryan nearly three months older than me, born in a separate calendar year, but we never thought twice about our young sex lives. Losing our virginity was a rite of passage, a task we checked off our list, like most boys and girls we knew, before earning diplomas. Before reading the criminal complaint against Wes Jungwirth, Ryan believed defending him would require little to no sacrifice of his own professional integrity, as most likely, we guessed, this was a one-and-done transgression, a failure of couth and grace. Sabrina had every right to be outraged, and we applauded her courage in reporting the assault, but we also imagined Aloysius's offense would be added to Ryan's list of second-string crimes.

Regardless of where Ryan's give-a-shit meter was pointing that spring, most of us who knew Wes's mother, Annie, had filled her bucket with genuine sympathy. After divorcing Wes's father when Wes was a little boy, Annie, not unlike her son, set out blindly in search of an intimate connection. Unfortunately, her gauge pointed twice in the direction of dangerous men, the first of whom lured her overseas, on business in Japan; the second of whom enticed her back to Seaside, Oregon, still thousands of miles from her roots in Wisconsin. Both physically abused Annie to the point at which her eyes would always resemble bruises. Wes traveled everywhere with Annie, her only faithful companion in the murky waters of courtship.

After my own parents divorced, as I embarked on the sixth grade, my mom actually began writing letters to inmates on death row with the Cook County Department of Corrections. Their return letters arrived, cockeyed print engraved on the envelopes like braille. One of the men, named Johnny, sent his photograph, which my mom kept tucked inside her wide oak credenza, such that dangerous men seemed the obvious byproduct of the dissolution of marriage. I felt torn. I wanted the death penalty abolished, but I also wanted these men to die, putting an end to their efforts at wooing my now-single mother.

Unfortunately, the dangerous men Annie attracted were not behind bars. In the second of her rebound matrimonies, Annie became not just a victim of abuse but also a victim of poor health, exacerbated by stress and hardship. Annie's doctor diagnosed breast cancer. Weak, depressed, and depleted as she underwent treatment, Annie was not strong enough to parent Wes on a daily basis, and therefore she placed Wes in the care of another troubled family whose matriarch, though mentally ill, was physically well.

When Clayton, a ten-year-old boy in Wes's surrogate family, invited him into his closet, the purpose was none other than to molest Wes and further to suggest that the abuse remain a secret. Only seven years old, Wes followed the older boy's instructions—to enter his dark bedroom vault, to remove his pants, and to show Clayton, in the privacy of the closet, his private parts. What began as show-and-tell quickly evolved into Clayton's suggestion—request, demand—that Wes open his mouth and inhale Clayton's manhood, biting him there, gently, playfully. Having watched three of my own boys in bathtubs, plucking their penises, little ornaments of dough dangling between their legs, how can I not be tempted to soften this story by referring to Clayton's penis as his "boyhood"? All small boys are amazed, and rightfully so, by these delicate appendages. They tug and twist, marveling at their elasticity, as we mothers, perched on toilets and the sides of bathtubs, behold the innocence of their self-discovery.

Despite Annie's illness and the ubiquity of abuse, Wes chose against returning to Wisconsin to live with his father, Zane, when presented with the option, worried for his mother's welfare, sure that murder or suicide would snuff her in the end. One day, Wes watched Annie's husband strangle her; perhaps he intervened, coming to her rescue, though reports remain unclear. In any event, the next day, when he came upon his mother's body, half-conscious in the bathtub after a suicide attempt, he wondered which kind of loss would truly be worse.

Although we conceive of mothers as absolute, immortal, even godlike, I'd long known motherhood to be a precarious station in life. My own mom met my dad, her psychiatrist, after a suicide attempt, and mothers, at least in my life, were either martyrs or sacrificial lambs. I was an elementary-school girl when my soon-to-be best friend's mom, Laura Chapman, suffered doom at the hands of her baby's father. Laura had arrived at his parents' home, the Franz residence, to pick up baby Travis after a long day at a new job. As she unzipped her coat, having entered through the side door, a voice called out from the depths of the basement, "Laura, down here." Her eyes adjusted, and she discerned Harold Franz's shape, hunkered against the bottom step, something like a bayonet protruding from his armpit. Before she could turn toward the kitchen, she felt something hot and deep like a cigarette stubbed out on her heart. He'd fatally shot her.

As Mandy's soul sister, when she showed up in my classroom the year of the murder, I too treaded the dark waters of bafflement and grief, grappling to make sense of how and why fathers killed mothers. Could anybody have prevented the irrevocable course of events? According to testimony Ryan collected, Aloysius Jungwirth was actually believed to have prevented his own mother's death, child as bodyguard, even if she failed to protect him. Several family members and friends, eager to paint a saintly picture of Wes when he faced sexual assault charges, would testify that Wes saved his mother by remaining in Seaside until she was strong enough physically and emotionally to return home. Eventually Annie used the legal system to file restraining orders against her third husband, and finally, in the end, to divorce him before being beaten to death.

Aloysius Jungwirth's long backstory was important to all of us, the only defense strategy at Ryan's disposal. When this boy, the youngest of adults, was detained by police and asked questions about touching Sabrina without consent, he confessed to far more than his mother or I imagined possible. Annie maintained some hope that he could enlist in the US Army, perhaps leave town, as vanishing was her go-to solution for heartache and trouble. If he were able to pursue his life in the army, perhaps Wes might later return home, truly a man, labeled a kind of hero. In her heart, he deserved all kinds of medals, but as she imagined Wes in camouflage, what she did not yet know, or perhaps what she could not yet admit, was that Sabrina was not Wes's first and only victim. His first two victims were actually those girls squatting beneath the descending fog of the green blanket, waiting for the depleted "ozone layer" to murder them by pollution.

Despite my coaxing Ryan into taking the Jungwirth case, he tried to maintain a policy of not representing sexual deviants. When he first received a request from the public defender's office to represent Randy Foote, who was charged with theft of movable property from the new YMCA, it seemed a no-brainer. What could possibly have been stolen from our community Y—weights, kickboards, soccer balls, hockey sticks? He thought fondly of Derek Green and laughed, but strangely, only ten minutes after Ryan accepted the case, Randy Foote called him, insisting on a meeting, a curiously urgent response to charges of theft. Foote was so persistent that he and his wife materialized in Ryan's office within seconds after Ryan acquired the file and sat down to read it.

Foote was a young guy, short and slightly hefty, apparently bland. His wife appeared old enough, by a fair margin, to be his mother. Ryan shook both their hands. "So tell me what happened, in your own words," Ryan said, trying to stall for more time. As Foote began an unwieldy account of his charges, Ryan skimmed the criminal complaint. He had reached a point in his career of speed-reading case files, quickly and judiciously, scanning for key words, to gauge what kind of evidence he was up against, and in the case of *State of Wisconsin v. Randy Foote*, he felt instinctively unsure about taking on Foote's case. This guy was no regular thief. He was no Derek Green, stuffing beef jerky into his coat pockets or stealing baby clothes from Walmart. This guy was a pervert and a pig, and a panty sniffer. Randy Foote was not stealing exercise equipment or other sundries from our YMCA. He was sneaking into girls' lockers and pilfering their panties for his own personal collection.

Up until this point, as our children multiplied, the easiest place for me to let down my guard was the YMCA. When we swam there, the weight of the water slackened our movements, and our frenzied life clicked into slow motion, all of us free from the pressures we otherwise felt when cooped up at home. The swimming instructors at the Y were free-spirited twentysome-things with dreadlocks, mermaid tattoos, and endless supplies of optimism and candy. After swimming, washing off in the communal showers at the nearly defunct downtown Y, Fern and Francis would strip and run through the mist, using the tile floor, rife with foot fungus, as a Slip 'N Slide. The showers served as a walkway between the locker room and pool deck, but I never worried about strangers' eyes on my children's nude bodies, as if lulled into a false sense of security by the Y's Christian mission.

Swimming at the YMCA was so fundamental to our lives that Irie quickly advanced through the skills levels and joined the Oshkosh YMCA Swim Team at age six. Strangers or acquaintances might refer to Irie as "big-boned," but I would describe her as exceptionally prone to gravity. When she was in kindergarten, she complained for weeks of pain in the arches of her feet. A doctor's appointment revealed she was just a heavy walker. Everything about Irie was voluminous. Her head, large and bright as a disco ball, seemed to flicker constantly with noise and flashing lights. Granted solos at concerts and in musicals, she'd nearly break the microphones with her lung capacity. Her body was just as solid. We once played a game of trying to knock Irie off her feet, and in spite of our combined efforts, her siblings and I failed, the threads of her leg muscles rooted into the floorboards of our house.

Nevertheless, the magic of pool water transformed Irie into a lithe and dexterous sea creature. Very little gave me more aesthetic pleasure than watching her swim laps, freestyle or the butterfly, her arms, torso, and legs streamlined in a way that was impossible for Irie in tennis shoes. She seemed to inhabit two separate bodies—a bovine body on land and a goddess-like body in water. Perhaps this blessing was just another reason I felt safe about dropping Irie off at both Oshkosh YMCAs, including the new state-of-the-art facility on the west side of town—until Ryan met Randy Foote, and I learned that neither Y facility was immune from real-world perversions of the kind that Ryan encountered every day at work.

It was too late for Ryan to jettison Aloysius Jungwirth, as our paths crossed often with his family's. Our Oshkosh upbringing put Ryan in the tough position of preserving family allegiances and using his JD to maintain relationships, but maybe this was the perfectly timed moment for telling a guy like Randy Foote to hit the road. Although Ryan always remembered that law, not morality, governs society, and he could uphold a judicial stance even if it meant sacrificing personal beliefs, he could not imagine advocating for Randy Foote, an adult who'd infringed on our daughter's world; so Ryan ushered the guy from his office under the guise of "needing time to more closely read the complaint."

Back at his desk, listening to the quiet buzz of street traffic below, he began to study evidence against Randy Foote, looking for a justifiable reason not to accept the case. That was when he discovered the escape hatch, a detail he was able to discern based on parents' names. One of the girls referred to as a victim was one of Irie's friends, another eight-year-old girl whose safe haven was the YMCA. He felt sick but ethically absolved of the burden to guarantee Randy Foote's constitutional rights. For the first time ever, Ryan returned a file to the public defender's office, and most likely, at the end of the day, he drove our daughter to the YMCA where she would swim, none the wiser, single file between her teammates, fingertips to fins.

When Wes returned with Annie from Seaside and began spending weekends with his father, Zane, he also began seeking intimacy in all the wrong places—first and foremost, in his sisters' hampers and drawers. Like Annie, Zane had tried his hand at marriage again, though his second attempt also failed. Nevertheless, when Wes returned to Oshkosh, the boy had gained two half sisters and one stepbrother. All of them were suitcase kids, traveling between their mother's and father's houses, and surely all of them were grappling for some sense of affection and security.

What began with swiping his sisters' panties evolved quickly into an obsession with their bodies. He lured one of the girls out behind the garage, and somehow—*somehow*—coaxed her to pull down her shorts and push a metal coat hanger up inside her vagina, as if playing some dangerous version of Doctor, or more specifically Obstetrics. Was he helping her to abort a pretend baby? What the hell kind of a game was that? She might have lacerated her own delicate contents, blighting her body with infection. In his confession with the investigator for the Oshkosh Police Department, Wes conceded, "I don't know what I said to make her do it, but I must have said something."

From that moment on, Wes admitted, he began to exert even greater persuasive skills on the next sister in line, tricking her into the unfinished basement and forcing her to lie naked on top of him so he could penetrate her. If they were not in the basement, they were in closets. One sister was assigned as the lookout in case a suspecting adult was headed in the general direction of the abuse. As it turned out, Ozone was not the imaginative child's game parents believed it was. Rather, under cover of the green blanket, Wes would force his hand into the girls' panties and clench their most special parts.

He gave up early on forcing the girls to give him blow jobs, developing a modus operandi much more devious. Once the girls fell into fitful sleep, Wes would skulk to their bedsides and kneel beside them, a sinister doctor making a house call. He ran his hands up their legs and into the warm spots between their thighs. According to Wes, his sisters often remained sleeping while he used his fingers to get his fix, but I can only imagine they merely pretended to sleep in denial or as self-defense. Wes told the investigator he "never hurt them," except for the time he punched his sister in the panties and another time when he forced his fingers inside her. Wes's testimony reminds me that we owe our children, at the very least, the gift of vocabulary. What good does it do to teach them only a singular definition of such a complicated word as *hurt*?

A friend that Annie and I shared in common wanted to know, if Wes was such a flabby guy—such a passive kid—"why didn't those girls just punch him already?"

"I get the sense they did punch him," I said. "But it didn't make a difference." Besides, shouldn't we be asking the opposite: why couldn't he just leave his sisters alone? In a case like this, Ryan's job was rarely to explain or even justify his clients' wrongdoing but rather to make sure that his clients were not overly punished. But how many years in prison were too many, when sexual abuse was such disquieting territory? We knew we'd be devastated if this happened in our own family.

We admittedly spend endless energy teaching our children the value of family loyalty. We expect them to defend each other. Therefore it's hard to imagine that our girls—even Irie the Almighty—would want our family to implode upon the revelation of such circumstances, even though, of course, we also advocate openness and truth-telling. And what role does gender play in a family like ours, in which the girls are more physically forceful than the boys? In the same calendar year, both Irie and Fern would be reprimanded at school for grabbing friends, Fern for seizing a classmate's wrist in a fit of jealousy, and Irie, similarly upset about a rival being awarded a music solo, for clawing at a girl's shoulder.

Irie and her best friend, Layla, from our neighborhood school, once hatched a game called Punishments in which an authority figure (principal, teacher, parent, or police officer) penalized a disobedient subordinate (a rowdy, wayward child). Layla was always in charge. She loved to devise outlandish retributions for Irie. She would lock Irie in the bedroom closet or force her under the bunk beds. As when we played Cops and Robbers as kids, the bandit—or in this case, the "bad kid"—was permitted only bread and water for sustenance.

At first the game seemed creative, even comical. They weren't just rotting their brains on iPods or TV. But as weeks turned to months, we noticed they began to adopt the rules of their charade at school. Layla set up Irie for legitimate repercussions, and Irie, headstrong and mischievous, relished her post beside the secretary outside the principal's office. Their self-fulfilling prophecies unnerved us, and when the girls began to reckon with each other, without our suggesting it, we watched their friendship dissolve with sadness but relief. Even the dynamics of playful intentions could turn dangerous.

At home, Fern was forever weaseling her way into Francis's bed at night, greedy for his comfort and warmth. We've tried to create gender equality in our household, but perhaps in doing so, we've allowed the girls too much power over the boys. Ryan jokes that I tricked him into conceiving Leo and Fern, if not Francis too, but it's funny only because husbands are assumed to enjoy sex with their wives. During the time period Ryan was defending Aloysius Jungwirth, we rarely felt in the mood. Sexual desire was tainted with every incriminating detail Ryan was forced to read, and this worried me, just another offshoot of Ryan's work in criminal defense, invasive and ugly.

In "A Father's Story" by Andre Dubus, the short story I've perhaps taught most often, Luke Ripley covers up his daughter's hit-and-run accident, not because he believes it's the right thing to do but because he loves his daughter more than he loves God. I can't count how many times I've uttered, upon kissing my children's foreheads, "I would do anything for you." I'm not sure exactly what I mean, but I instinctively whisper these words when the ferocity of love overtakes me. I'd sacrifice myself with a lone bullet to my heart if it meant, in exchange, my children remained safe.

I could identify with Annie Jungwirth and her sweet gingerbread-scented denial. Raising children is gloriously but also frighteningly uncertain. Although we make choices every day to protect and to teach our children right from wrong, parenting is like rolling dice, and I'm not sure which digits add up to a more disastrous loss—child as perpetrator or child as victim. Until Ryan took on this case, I had forgotten to allocate a percentage of maternal worry toward these kinds of dark thoughts: What if my child commits a heinous crime? How would I manage to console a child who was locked up, far away from home?

Ryan's only argument for why Wes should be sentenced to probation without serving any prison time was to blame his parents for their son's volatile childhood. After all, according to many witnesses, Zane knew of his son's misdeeds but was passive about enforcing a remedy. All the abuse transpired under Zane's roof, and at one point Zane was even described as stumbling upon Wes in bed with his sister but doing nothing.

"I thought it was about cigarettes, or drugs, or alcohol. If I'd known it was sexual abuse, I would have done something."

Ryan would argue Annie was responsible for having dragged Wes on her journey of transience and abuse throughout his childhood, even though Ryan was not, by nature or profession, accusatory. How else could he explain the vile crimes his client had committed? Ultimately, Ryan's sentencing argument would hinge upon that turning point in Seaside, Oregon. "When I went in that closet with Clayton, I didn't know any better," Wes told investigators. "I just did whatever people told me to do."

While Wes had committed certain crimes as an adult, he began committing those crimes, including the most heinous of them, as a boy. Ryan argued that ten-year-old Aloysius would not have been sent to prison, and therefore eighteen-year-old Aloysius should not be either. Wes was never allowed to develop a true appreciation of his deviance, and his parents failed to guide him in meaningful ways. It was obvious to Ryan, though, that eventually Wes began doing whatever *he* wanted, using his sisters' bodies for foreplay and then masturbating in private and public bathrooms, unusually preoccupied with his own sexual gratification.

Over the course of familiarizing himself with Wes's story, Ryan had developed a kinship with the boy's maternal grandparents, not only because they paid him for his services and treated him with respect but also because they reminded him of his own extended family. He repeatedly referred to Wes's grandfather as the patriarch, trustworthy, and altogether lovable. Sometimes it seemed impossible to understand how inherently good people raised deviant kids.

In a final effort to build a case, Ryan enlisted the help of a well-respected Oshkosh psychologist, Dr. Hammond, hopeful that Wes's history of trauma, combined with his young age upon first committing abuse, would result in an appropriate diagnosis. A personality disorder or PTSD would prove useful legally in mitigating his sentence. Ryan wavered constantly between feeling a professional, and slightly personal, obligation to help Wes's family, and bottoming out with a sense of disgust. "It's all a bunch of sick shit," he'd say. More than anything, Ryan wanted to ensure that Wes would get help so as not to re-offend in his adult life. Defense attorneys, like everybody else, worried over recidivism. We sat back—or perhaps forward, on the edges of our seats—and waited for the psychologist's official evaluation. Even Wes's siblings became advocates for allowing Wes to remain part of their family and the community. Neither of the girls wanted Wes locked up.

Our own boys take turns suffering from what I call little-boy big-boy syndrome. In the throes of weaning, a process I approached passively, the boys would alternately brandish swords, playing pirates like big boys, and then crawl into my lap for "milky" like little boys. Even as Leo matured, he would reject hand-holding in public but crawl into my lap in private, clutching my wrist like a chew toy and blowing warm peppered air into my palm. One step forward, one step back was a dance we memorized. Leo would take enormous risks, like throwing fastballs across city streets or intentionally belly-flopping into deep water, but if he hurt himself, often bleeding from the nose, he'd come running, calling, "Mama, help me," his voice nostalgic and infantile, a baby wailing to be held.

When mothers exchange pleasantries, we say, "They grow up so fast" or "Enjoy these years while they last." There is no way to forestall their growth and maturity, even if we document their rites of passage, fastidiously marking our children's coming-of-age. Whereas breeching, an occasion in which mothers first dressed their little boys in britches, was once momentous in a son's life, what now, I wonder, has replaced this ceremonious event? And for girls, what has replaced such old-fashioned coming-of-age rituals as shortcoating or donning a bodice? Perhaps for all children today, those first rites of passage entail learning to walk, talk, read, and ride a bike, or the first pierced ear, the first Swiss Army knife, the first sleepover, the first house key, the first cell phone. But it was not so long ago that girls celebrated their "coming out to society" by wearing their hair off their necks—elaborate updos—at public parties or balls.

Among contemporary generations of children, certainly we'd include the first kiss, the first drink, the first cigarette, the first joint, not to dismiss the most taboo of all the coming-of-age rituals, losing our virginity. But how do the rules of such ceremonies change when our first encounters with intimacy, aside from our parents' love, present themselves by force? Having been sheltered by his mother from more traditional influences such as popular culture and friend groups, Wes was younger emotionally than physically, by a long shot. Mathematically, would it be fair to say that when twelve-year-old Wes hid away in his bedroom watching porn instead of Disney Channel, he gazed at the screen with the eyes of a nine-year-old?

My own parents taught me about sex when I was only six years old. Since I had seen my brother's and other neighbor boys' penises, my only source of confusion was the male erection. "If it's so wiggly, how does the man get it inside?" I asked. When I was fifteen years old, I would learn the difference between hard and soft, coming of age with my eighteen-year-old boyfriend, one of a few partners before Ryan and I officially became a couple. By legal standards, my first lover was an adult. Did I become an adult too, when we closed the gap between our bodies on the floor in my TV room? In a world where sexual intimacy is considered a secret passageway to adulthood, what kinds of lines, if any, might be drawn, even if they remain invisible, blurry, or shape-shifting?

Parents, mothers in particular, experience a kind of hallowed proximity to our children as they metamorphose. Newborn diapers become training pants, and later, for our daughters, underwear becomes the drop cloth for menstruation. I launder my children's undergarments, carefully, in hot water with lavender-scented Downy. These V-shaped cotton intimates will cover, and protect, one hopes, their most delicate parts, all of which, I can't help but remember, are the anatomy one day required for reproduction. It's no wonder jokes abound about the "family jewels."

Purposefulness was what I loved so much about making babies—intercourse removed from all the mixed messages we are bound to encounter in a lifetime about self-gratification and pleasure. Trying actively to conceive a baby was arguably the opposite of being victimized. My goal was to reproduce, and sex was a means to that end.

After Wes touched Sabrina, his third victim, in the middle of the night, she was admitted to the hospital for symptoms of PTSD, namely paralysis. Sometimes, it seems, each baby I birthed, or perhaps each umbilical cord, was my own version of an awareness ribbon, purple and fleshy, looped inside me like perennial hopefulness. Now that Ryan had probed his way into the darkest realms of criminal defense, I worried about sex in new ways. Neuroscience reveals that we nourish our bodies and procreate because reward centers in our brains urge us to repeat what's pleasurable. But what happens to our circuitry when our brains get misappropriated by sickening stories of sexual deviance?

When Harold Franz murdered my best friend's mother, Laura Chapman, I was taught by my father to forgive transgressors their mental illness. The *Oshkosh Northwestern* revealed that after extensive evaluation, "a psychiatric report, prepared by Dr. Ralph Baker, Oshkosh, determined that Franz is not competent to aid in his own defense." Most of my dad's mental status examination focused on Franz's low self-esteem: difficulty graduating from high school, an inability to perform basic arithmetic, and suicidal thoughts. The diagnostic impression was atypical psychosis, mixed organic brain syndrome, and features of a dissociative disorder as well as a major depressive disorder, all connected to his underlying multiple sclerosis.

Franz made courtroom appearances for first-degree murder, propped in a wheelchair. He murdered Chapman in February, and by June the *Oshkosh Northwestern* reported, OSHKOSH MAN FOUND GUILTY AND INNOCENT. The district attorney specifically stated Harold Franz posed no danger to society at large, and he was sentenced to Winnebago Mental Health Institute instead of prison. By my own father's recommendation, the man who murdered Mandy's mother was found not guilty by reason of mental disease or defect, or NGI.

In spite of Franz's diminished muscle tone and cloudy vision predicting a low likelihood of perfect aim, a lone bullet burst the bubble of Chapman's heart, and she died almost instantly. But according to my dad, we could not justifiably hold Harold Franz, plagued by paranoia, dissociation, and mental anguish, accountable for the pain he'd caused. Did this NGI verdict make us more or less afraid of the world, more or less merciful?

Nearly three decades later, with my husband instead of my father holding the reins, Aloysius Jungwirth was not to be evaluated as leniently, even though Ryan worked just as diligently for Wes as possible. When Dr. Hammond called Ulrich Law Office, Ryan was relieved to finally hear something, as cases were always tied up and postponed. Resolving any set of charges provided a reprieve, some small deliverance from the anxiety of his career. But when his cases took surprising turns, he'd be injected with adrenaline and regret.

"What do you have for me?"

"Well, I'm not sure you're going to want me to write a report."

Dr. Hammond's formal evaluation and letter of explanation were more damning than his innuendo. Just as Ryan and I had observed ourselves, Aloysius demonstrated little guilt, shame, or embarrassment, and therefore no psychological evidence could help his cause.

As opposed to psychopaths, whose mental illness is inborn, sociopaths are shaped by their environment, especially during their formative years, and sociopaths, unlike psychopaths, can form connections with others. But, in this case, impaired social function is precisely what thwarted Ryan's case. Was Aloysius Jungwirth a sociopath, perhaps the first or only one Ryan had defended, or was he one of many? Even a client like Alyssa Brandt, criticized publicly by the judge for her lack of remorse, had demonstrated some degree of sadness, if not for her dogs, Princess and Rocco, then certainly for her own miscarried baby.

After Wes's diagnosis, I would think often of his tumultuous childhood, but even more about his intense—almost fatalistic—bond with Annie. She sheltered but neglected him. She kept him safe from exposure to violent movies and music but exposed him to her own destructive instability. Annie leaned on him as a life partner when he was not yet potty-trained and still sucked his thumb. No "how to" manual can right these inconsistencies. We vaccinate our children to protect them against measles, mumps, and rubella, but there is no vaccine for inoculating against devious behavior, children's worst impulses, which not unlike savvy viruses, evolve in order to constantly outsmart our best intentions.

Prior to sentencing, Ryan dedicated himself to working tirelessly with the assistant district attorney, hoping that, given the high-profile nature of this case, he could figuratively enter the courtroom hand in hand with the prosecutor. As Wes had offered a full confession, Ryan's primary task was to provide his young client with a fairly definitive notion of how the judge would sentence him. Judges were less likely, in Ryan's experience, to supersede a joint recommendation. When defense and prosecuting attorneys came to a compromise, judges tended to reward these middle-ground covenants, and in this case, probation would also entail counseling. Ryan accomplished this joint recommendation without as much as a paragraph from Dr. Hammond.

Annie often wondered why the psychological evaluation had not yielded more favorable results, but Ryan could not bring himself to tell her. There was no generous way to say, "Well, it turns out your son is probably a sociopath." Of course, Annie would have gone on loving him anyway. And maybe the judge used her intuition to reach the same conclusion as Dr. Hammond, possessing neither a mother's love nor a mother's blindness.

Much to everybody's surprise, the judge in the case of Aloysius Jungwirth offered a long meditation on Wes's unyielding pattern of abuse and then "dropped the hammer," as they say, sentencing him to far more than the jointly recommended probation. She sentenced Wes to thirteen years in Wisconsin's prison system and a lifetime on the Sex Offender Registry. By the time his mother would see him again, a free man, he'd potentially be in his thirties. Annie would not be able to see, hug, kiss, console, or nurture Wes on a daily basis. She would now be forced to envision her son in prison stripes instead of camouflage, serving time instead of serving his country.

Throughout the remainder of the calendar year, Annie's voice grew more saccharine than ever. At one point, she appeared to be entirely coated in candy. A longtime receptionist at a veterinary clinic, she began to adopt cats from the Humane Society, two at a time, until she reached a dozen, desperate to fill the void Aloysius left behind. She rented an old farmhouse and rejected a marriage proposal, determined to wait for her baby to come home, like a wife whose husband is off at war.

The Jungwirth case soured Ryan on baby-making and baby-rearing. Irie, Leo, and Fern, speaking on Frank's behalf too, often asked, "How many more babies will we have, Mama?" I would smile sweetly, but Ryan, with dregs of exhaustion in his eyes like he too was using junk, would say, "Our days of making babies are over."

With Aloysius Jungwirth away at prison, guys like Rob McNally returned to the forefront of our minds. We both knew I was the real addict, not fearful enough of motherhood, but what, if not Wes's distressing sexual abuse case and his mother's anguish, would stymie my urge to keep birthing babies? The olfactory joy of a newborn baby's scalp, eau de uterine parfum, makes fiends of women like me, but the makers of Narcan can't reverse the lifelong responsibility of raising our children once they're born, which explains why Ryan was completely "done." Time was up. He'd set his pencil down, having completed an arduous task, but I associated finality with the end of a golden era and the onset of middle age. I resisted climbing up and over the hill, even if in Ryan's mind bringing our baby-making to a close was the fastest route to a second youth.

To make his point, Ryan began sorting and piling my over-the-belly leggings and tunics alongside size 0–3 month footie pajamas at the bottom of the basement steps one afternoon. When we bought the house, we almost didn't make an offer because of that dreaded staircase, constructed nearly upright as a ladder more than a century earlier, in 1888. I could jog up and down it now, nine months pregnant if necessary, holding a toddler and a load of laundry.

Ryan had come to a standstill upon unearthing a fuzzy pumpkin suit, a gift from my friend Shelley, worn by all four children for their first Halloweens. "Hey, honey," he called to me. "Can we give this away?" His moment of pause provoked in me a deep, angry sadness, and without warning I charged down the stairs and began boxing at Ryan's face. He dodged and ducked beneath the pipes suspended in a copper maze above his head.

"I can't stand you," I hissed. "Go away. Go upstairs." Ryan had become, in that moment, a man no longer useful in making babies. When he had climbed up and away onto the first floor, where our four children were making the music of death metal—fighting, dumping marbles, crushing Goldfish into the upholstery—I stood deliriously over the mounds of clothes. Finally calmed down, I told Ryan I'd finish sorting, but nearly everything I owned had been laundered in sentimental value.

My "keep" pile grew tall and tipped over as I added a favorite black maternity dress, shapeless as an old fitted sheet; my green XL baby doll shirt; and a button-up white cardigan patterned with baby geese and miraculously not stained. I told Ryan I kept a few items, but secretly still hoping for a fifth pregnancy, I kept most of them, giving up only the soiled clothing; I easily cached as many clothes as Allison Shaffer attempted to steal in her Walmart shopping cart years before. That evening, once the kids were in bed, I sobbed on the couch. Ryan and I faced each other. We were holding each other's feet in our laps, whispering hoarsely, domestic messiness to remain unattended to till morning.

"Having babies is the only thing that has ever made me happy," I said. I'd experienced other forms of joy—(temporary) accomplishment, (temporary) satisfaction, (temporary) relief, and (fleeting) euphoria—but nothing would ever provide me with sustained human contentedness like back-to-back pregnancies and childbirth. I envied fruit-bearing trees their abundance, their succulence, their purposefulness, and honestly imagined, after birth, I'd shrivel back into the earth.

Ryan had scheduled an appointment for a vasectomy consultation, the receptionist encouraging my attendance. A vasectomy was, in many cases, a "joint decision," she said. We actually knew a guy who sabotaged his marriage by getting snipped without his wife's consent. Virility, it turned out, was just as important to the laws of attraction as strong hands or thick hair.

Further complicating Ryan's commitment to the consultation was his own squeamishness. Much as women enjoyed sharing birth stories, sterile men loved to regale us with tales from outpatient surgery. Mere mention of a slit scrotum sent Ryan to the nearest bathroom, where he never vomited but thought he might. He'd even lose his appetite over predictable jokes my dad cracked about sporting a jockstrap post-op. Neither of us was motivated enough, so he canceled the consultation, and we never seriously visited this as a birth control option again.

A baby, I reasoned, remained a possibility. Psychology was the only roadblock to biology. I possessed the resolute and single-minded desire for a fifth baby, and I was intent to deliver another little bindle-bundle into our lives, come hell or madness. But how tricky was I willing to be? The women in my life—mother figures, friends, and mentors—perhaps worried for my big-picture mental health, urged me *not* to add another baby to the mix. "Slow down," one of them said. "You're already running yourself ragged." Another told me, "You have perfect symmetry. Why ruin that?" They stopped short of telling me I was a junkie or a fiend.

Four children no longer seemed like the right number. As a child and teenager, it was true, I'd envied perfect proportions. I'd scowl at my crooked nose in the mirror, only to exaggerate my disproportionate face, believing bilateral symmetry equaled beauty, and even—not odd—numbers predicted good fortune. Before language colonized all the space in my brain, I was gifted in math, and when the answer to a calculus problem was even, not odd, I'd celebrate with relief. Nevertheless, as I grew older, turning to art more than to science, my expectations and tastes changed, odd numbers, asymmetry, and chaos appealing more to me spiritually. Pregnancy and child-rearing also worked at flipping that switch, such that I no longer enjoyed the predictability of patterns, and I believed, perhaps too boldly, in the risk and possibility of breaking them.

When Ryan visited Wes at the county jail as he awaited processing, Wes looked Ryan in the eyes for the first time in their acquaintanceship. Quite thoughtfully he said, "I've been doing a lot of thinking, and I'm going to tell the other inmates I'm in for burglary." While he had demonstrated no remorse or shame in the psychologist's office, his self-preservation instincts had been restored.

In all its gruesome and troubling detail, defending Wes for charges of sexual assault was its own rite of passage—unfortunately, the first in a string of cases in which victims were children. If Ryan was going to make a living in criminal defense, he was learning, he'd have to be less choosy. He'd have to set aside his moral hangups. And he'd have to hug our children more protectively when he returned home at night. When the public defender's office called him nearly three years after Wes was sent to prison, Ryan considered taking a new case, a defendant charged with capturing images of nudity without consent, but by now he had learned to review the charges of sexual misconduct before making a decision. When he opened the file, on the doorstep of the public defender's office, the name Randy Foote flashed familiar in his brain, but the face of the old panty sniffer did not come fully to mind until he began reading this latest complaint.

Foote had invited a father and his children to swim in his pool and then secretly videotaped them changing in his bathroom. The children's father found the camera and submitted it to police, at which point investigators also found child pornography on Foote's memory card. For Ryan, the complaint invoked images of our own children, Irie especially. Our favorite way to imagine our eldest child was in her bathing suit, droplets of pool water like sequins on her skin, thick hair hiding under her latex cap.

Ryan turned to one of the secretaries in the public defender's office and reported, "I'm going to pass on this one." As he headed back to the elevator and pushed the button, waiting for his shuttle toward higher ground, he realized the pressure to protect our children was just as strong as the pressure to provide for them. As the inevitability of a debate over more children crystallized, he noted Randy Foote and other creeps like him as evidence for his side. With one more baby, how could we possibly keep them all safe?

CHAPTER 5

Hell's Lovers

Furthermore, I wondered, could we protect our children from the likes of ourselves? As Ryan's filing cabinets grew glutted, choking on evidence against his clients, many of them parents incapable of managing their misfortunes and distress, I measured their fuses against ours. Patience was essential, but how much was there to go around? Ryan, the overreactor, and I, the underreactor, had both developed bad disciplinary habits: I mollycoddled the children, unfazed by their antics, while Ryan launched extravagant, empty threats into their faces, his thunderous voice a missile unto itself.

"I'll throw all your toys in the garbage!" "I'll give you something to cry about, so help me God!" "If you touch your brother one more time . . ." he'd threaten before a fill-in-the-blank kind of silence. His favorite Midwestern curse sounded worse than the f-word on his tongue, fully adulterated. What was he even screaming? "Gal blasted" or "God bless it"? None of us knew. Wasted food infuriated Ryan most. "We're not going to be those parents who cut crusts off the kids' sandwiches," he said, but without meaning to be, we were. When one of our children didn't finish an egg sandwich or touch the baked ziti, Ryan would seize the plate, grab a utensil, and scrape the meal into the garbage, swearing until the plate was clean.

Corrections officer is just one of many ways to describe a parent's duty. Once when we discovered "somebody" had purposely shredded pages from a hardcover library book and nobody confessed, Ryan held a trial in the living room for "criminal damage to property," calling each of our three eldest children to the witness stand. When Fern ignored our subpoena, offering up household chores instead ("I'm just washing windows over here," she cooed nonchalantly), we knew we'd found our culprit. Another time as Irie and Leo boiled up bedlam in the back seat of our van, Ryan drove toward the Winnebago County Jail, swerved into the parking lot, and threatened to drag them inside. "I have plenty of connections," he growled. He was melodramatic, over-the-top, and outright laughable, but other parents he met through criminal defense launched grenades, plumb-full of explosives, not blanks.

When a woman named Liberty Cabot suspected her seventeen-year-old son, Jared, of stealing from her purse, for example, she made the mistake of calling her husband, Wayne Pomeno, down at his biker establishment to complain. An associate of Hell's Lovers Motorcycle Club, Pomeno was the quintessential tough guy, and he admitted his reaction to Cabot's phone call wasn't pretty. "I went ballistic," he told police. By his own reckoning, Pomeno was an automatic weapon with a chamber full of ammo, and his stepson was the spoiled punk tripping his trigger.

Somebody had burglarized Pomeno's private residence weeks earlier, and now, more than ever, Pomeno was convinced that his wife's kid was the offender. This biker knew how belligerent he could get, especially when provoked, and he claimed he begged Cabot to keep Jared as far away from the bike shop as possible. If the kid showed his face, Pomeno warned, he'd have a hard time practicing restraint. He was splenetic, pacing and kicking tools around the garage.

According to Jared, however, Cabot did just the opposite. She woke her son from a late-afternoon nap on the sofa. How many moments in mothers' lives are spent mastering the art of the wake-up call? We rouse our babies for birth, orchestrating flashes of light with our furious labor, and they emerge as if baptized, awash in luminescence. And so begins the painstaking litany of years, waking our children from literal and proverbial sleep. Sometimes we've got to knock sense into their heads.

"You need to work things out," Cabot said to Jared. "Make things square." She gave him specific instructions to meet Pomeno downtown. Maybe, she urged, Jared could help with bike repairs in his free time to pay his stepdad back. Was she an idealist, truly believing in the possibility of reconciliation between her son and husband, or was she actually an accomplice, uttering beneath her breath, "Spare the rod and spoil the child"? Either way, Jared's grandfather was seemingly also either optimistic or duped. He personally chauffeured Jared down to the bike shop while Cabot ran a few quick errands. She would be there soon, she said, to see how it all turned out.

The faint trail of leather, ink, and hot rubber led bikers and friends of Hell's Lovers to the repair shop and clubhouse. Motor oil burned like incense when Jared walked in that day. Jared's grandfather attempted to chaperone him through the repair shop and into Pomeno's office, but the boss stopped him at the door. "It's OK, old man," he said. "Go on and wait outside." Jared was a black belt, after all, the kind of boy who would "kung fu up" to protect himself, if necessary. Jared could handle himself, and Pomeno wanted this done man-to-man, one-on-one. But when Jared entered his stepdad's office, an entourage of Pomeno's friends was waiting for him behind the door, which they quickly locked. Pomeno grabbed Jared by a chain around his neck, as if he were a disobedient dog, then he yanked him flush against his tight chest, close enough to steam the kid's face with his hot breath.

"If you weren't your mother's kid, I'd kill you," he said.

Somebody embraced Jared in a bear hug from behind and restrained him, with the help of another unidentified lackey whose strong arms pushed him, hunched over, onto a rolling swivel chair. That's when Pomeno pulled out a baseball bat from behind his desk, perfected his stance, kicked around the dirt at home plate, and began thwacking the butt end of his Louisville Slugger against Jared's chin. Within seconds, pockets of blood bulged from the boy's bone like cysts.

"You don't want to fuck with Hell's Lovers," Pomeno cursed.

When he finished his portion of the assault, he signaled his cronies to take turns drubbing Jared with bamboo rods on his back, his arms, and his legs. Who needed the justice system to corroborate Jared's alleged burglary when Pomeno could take matters into his own hands, vigilantism in its most gruesome form? Which old-fashioned method of corporal punishment for disobedience did the beating most resemble—flogging, birching, caning, or something else altogether? When the muscled fists of Pomeno's henchmen finally released Jared, his whole body tingled with pain, as if his funny bones had ruptured.

"That'll learn you," Pomeno said and signaled for his buddies to open the office door. Lacerated, bloody, and swollen, Jared cowered his way out of his stepdad's office. He never looked up or sideways when leaving, instead shuffling slowly to his grandfather's car in the parking lot, where he resumed his spot at shotgun.

"Jesus Christ," his grandfather said. "Mother of fucking Mary." Then they both gulped when they recognized the sound of Cabot's car. She pulled into a parking stall beside them and emerged from her driver's side door, catching her son's punished face through the window glass. Maybe at first she thought his gnarled face was just an optical illusion, but when Jared rolled down his window, she wept instantaneously. When Cabot cried, seventeen-year-old Jared cried too.

"This was not supposed to happen," she said. Her sobs were like hiccups. She took Jared's face delicately in her hands, as if he were covered in thistles, prodding his injuries, tapping his wounded skin. This was Jared's version of the incident in the criminal complaint, but even as different renditions would emerge in the coming days, nobody disputed the fact that Cabot had insisted Jared show up at the clubhouse. Her son's poor face had been tenderized, nothing to Pomeno but raw meat. If Cabot had coordinated the effort, what kind of mother was she, after all these years?

Irie was our only child who needed barbaric reminders to behave. She stirred the beast inside me. Perhaps we overindulged her moods and whims, ready, when she was born, to be parents but not yet disciplinarians. Both of us were pushovers the first baby-go-round, blessed with a girl who seemed not the product of Ryan and me but rather offspring to an opera singer and gladiator—fierce, unreasonable, and gifted at hooking adults into her highly emotional paradigm of the world. Who was to blame—us or her, nature or nurture?

One time, Irie refused an antibiotic by biting her tongue until blood streamed from her lips. Another time, she lopped off a chunk of hair at a sleepover, enough strands to fully stuff a business-size envelope, which was how the friend's mother sent the locks home. The list of parents, teachers, coaches, principals, and supervisors she would drive to madness in her early childhood and elementary years was long and unforgiving. Whenever an adult approached me head-on, I'd stop breathing, bringing on self-induced dizziness, preparing to endure the next installment of ongoing bad reports.

In kindergarten at our neighborhood school, Irie's teacher compared her to Tina Last's son, the wild and unruly boy with an underbite and the voice of a cartoon monster. Later to be diagnosed with EBD, emotional behavior disorder, and relocated to a school that could accommodate his needs, Irie's counterpart lived under the supervision of the voodoo doll mother. Neither tattooed nor pierced, except in my earlobes, a von Trapp girl in satin sashes, I'd stare at her spiked face as if looking in a mirror, fully aware we shared something in common, our children evil twins of the monogrammed ABCs reading carpet.

Tina Last appeared in constant need of exorcism, and I wondered, what did I look like to her? She slicked her hair to the scalp, tied it in a blood knot at the nape of her neck. Every week, she sewed a new metal hook or grapple to the sleeves of her army coat, a garment that surely also served as a torture device. Most of us wear our negative emotions, be they umbrage or grief, beneath our flesh, alongside our guts, hidden away, opting instead for polka dots and paisley, living, literally, under wraps. Tina Last would not conform to such norms. She walked about in public inside out. Each buckle, hook, sharp pin, and clasp represented pain, and I'd wince just looking at her.

She hovered in my peripheral vision, in school hallways and on sidewalks around our neighborhood, a reminder of my own depression history. Sometimes I wondered if I'd conjured up this alter ego. When I was first pregnant with Irelyn, a friend warned us of her nickname: "*Irie* sounds like *ire* as in anger, just one letter's difference." Pregnant and still teaching seventh and eighth graders at EAGLE School, I surprised myself once by screaming, truly at the top of my lungs, unendingly, to quiet the classroom. Although I was mostly too relaxed a mother, once our children began to arrive in quick succession, Ryan teased me about my quarterly meltdowns. Four times a year, I'd scream so fiercely our kids scattered like bugs, to hide from me beneath their beds. In small doses, I scared the bejesus out of them, as Tina Last did me.

Whenever we'd brainstorm options and investigate loopholes for sending our children to different schools, I'd think of Tina Last. Her son's EBD diagnosis had afforded them the opportunity to receive an education elsewhere in the district. We'd later learn that Irie was not disturbed, just anxious, therefore naughty—nature and nurture. Her eldest-sibling status mixed up inside her a carbonated concoction of love, protectionism, and resentment. Anxiety brewed within our daughter as depression had percolated in me. Once when my stepmom asked Irie how she felt about Francis's birth, she said, "Just one more kid to worry about."

Even before siblings, Irie's intensity burned hot. When she was only two years old, we were stuck awaiting Leo's arrival in an Extended Stay America hotel room. We were no longer renting in Madison, but Leo's due date and Ryan's final exams coincided. We needed to be geographically proximate to the Madison Birth Center and the UW Law School, which were fifteen minutes from each other but nearly two hours from Oshkosh. A long weekend became two weeks, the three of us packed into a small room off the Beltline. Irie had arrived ten days early, so at four centimeters dilated and mostly effaced, my cervix seemed poised but unwilling to release Leo. Larger than I'd grow with any other pregnancy, not to mention continuing to indulge Irie with breast milk, as nursing was known to stimulate labor, I was baffled by Leo's delay. Meanwhile, biting and twisting my nipples as a toddler bites instead of sucks on a straw in a milkshake, Irelyn was refusing naps, and I was desperate for daytime rest.

Surely she felt as trapped as Ryan and I did, if not more, plucked from routine. She refused to hold my hand on busy streets and would veer off into traffic with a smirk. In the hotel room, she jumped on the bed, opened and slammed doors, and then propped her eyelids open to protest naps. She'd sing, bellowing from her cavernous rib cage—the opera singer, the Broadway star—her fervor contagious, entering the bloodstream like an airborne virus, and it's hard sometimes, still today, not to feel jimmied up when she is around.

One afternoon while Ryan was on campus taking an exam, and I was ravenous for sleep, she escaped into the hotel hallway. After her fourth or fifth attempt, I lunged and grabbed her shoulders, digging my nails into her thick skin. Although I was delirious and swollen, the moment felt eerily rehearsed as I flipped Irelyn over and pinned her against the mattress, holding my daughter, white-knuckled, against her will. I was filled with love and also mysteriously with hatred.

A violent film reel unraveled in my head, featuring all the ways a mother loses her composure, strong and big enough to smother a child. The physiological urge to release anger in some unfettered gesture was like the fantasy of releasing doves turned vultures from a cage. I imagined gouging out Irelyn's face with my own claws. Later I'd revise the movie in my head, borrowing savage punishments from cautionary tales for children, as far back as the German and French writers our ancestors likely read—the Brothers Grimm, Heinrich Hoffmann, Hilaire Belloc. Little Suck-a-Thumb's hands were mutilated by the maniacal tailor while the mischievous Max and Moritz were ground to bits in a feedbag at the farmer's mill for their impish pranks.

In this literary spirit, my own father used cautionary tales as his number-one parenting strategy. According to him, mole people, mutant humanoid beasts, lived in our basement. Our "mole room" was a dark subterranean compartment where, pre-divorce, my parents stored Christmas presents and other keepsakes they wanted to protect from our dirty, pilfering hands. Similar to but distinct from the science fiction slaves in the 1956 horror film *The*

Mole People, ours oozed black slime. My dad warned me about these murderous rodents, cloaked like humans but whiskered like rats. My father knew how to wield power over us. With such playfully terrifying ruses, who needed rules? In our adult lives, when *mole people* entered the vernacular as the label for homeless citizens living inside New York City subway tunnels, the indigent subterranean dwellers seemed conjured by my father's imagination. My dad was unusual, born during the Great Depression, much older than my friends' parents. Cultural mores have largely changed by now to match our increasingly sentimentalized version of childhood. Instead of scaring or punishing naughty children, Pete the Cat sings them a groovy song.

But the physiological experience of raising children has likely not changed much over time, nor has the dire need for catharsis. In pre-Disney versions of "Snow White," the princess's biological mother—not her stepmother, in fact—demands her daughter be killed, and further yet, she requests Snow White's lungs and liver served on a platter at dinnertime. Sometimes, even when consumed by the purest love, I'd imagine eating Irie up. God, we love our children, but God help us, even the most sacred relationships are not immune to flashes of violence.

Mothers are taught to take deep breaths, to walk away, to lock themselves in bathrooms. Maternal love is what teaches us the art of restraint. That day in the Extended Stay America marked the beginning of many years spent "holding" Irie. She gazed back at me, perhaps watching that same horror film in reverse, each act of violence being undone, ending with a little girl fully intact, not yet corpus delicti. Sedate, merciful, and ready to sing me a song, Irie seemed always to emerge unscathed, resilient, rising from the ashes I had created with my fire.

Immobilization proved to be exactly what we both needed. I'd hold her at bedtime, and at playdates, and on days she threatened to blow our house down. Sometimes I'd clutch her more savagely than usual, and as if practicing a strange kind of acupuncture, it remedied our pain. As Irelyn and I developed our holding ritual, I came to recall my own father immobilizing me during childhood tantrums. He would become my straitjacket, straps stitched from his long arms and legs. Just as babies are swaddled, older children collect composure in the warm embrace of strong limbs, except when restraint makes them an easy target for abuse.

One day when my friend Jill and her children visited from a wealthy suburb of Milwaukee, I could not vacuum, dust, or hide enough clutter to prepare for their arrival. I gritted my teeth for hours before she arrived. After she'd weathered the long drive, and we'd sent the kids to play, she checked in to find them using Fern's doctor kit, including a bulb syringe for sucking up baby snot. She grabbed it from her son's fist as if he'd been caught with a heroin needle, and she replaced it with a sanitized toy from his diaper bag. Later, when we searched for costumes in the basement, she tried not to gasp out loud when she saw "the laundry project." At the park, when Irie misbehaved and I cornered my own daughter against the fence, holding her there, syncing our breath, I could see that my life on the wrong side of the tracks had stunned Jill. When she left Oshkosh, she appeared frantic but relieved, like she'd just missed colliding with a freight train.

The transition from one to two children would prove the largest upheaval in our ever-growing family, as we switched from providing undivided attention to multitasking, and I was already exhausted, but also eager for my hormonal fix. The rush of childbirth would carry me through the summer, I reasoned, if I could just force Leo to arrive. Ryan and I tried sex, when Irelyn was sleeping late at night. We were lovers trapped in hell.

At my midwife's recommendation, I was taking a supplement from Community Pharmacy, evening primrose oil, or some such medicinal wonder. We dined on spicy Indonesian food and then drove to a custard shop, where I dumped castor oil into my root beer float and slugged it back like an enormous shot of brandy. I was a living, breathing science experiment. Sadly, nothing transpired, not even a stomachache. Ryan and I were fighting over his allergies. "I'm walking around with a baby's head grinding against my pelvic bone," I said. "I'm sure you'll survive your stupid sniffles, you big baby." And of course, the big bambino was all we could think about.

Finally on Mother's Day—"a good day for birth," our midwife said—we ate a large brunch, including smoked salmon and pastries, before checking out of our hotel and driving to the Madison Birth Center. With a tool like a plastic crochet hook, our midwife punctured my amniotic balloon. It was a clean break, and the fluid poured from inside me like warm water from a jug.

After the bike shop beating, Jared Cabot's grandfather initially tried taking matters into his own hands by calling Pomeno to set the guy straight, but Pomeno told him in the most cavalier of ways, "What did you expect bringing the kid down to the clubhouse? I do shit like that all the time," pointing out he had recently pounded the piss out of his fourteen-year-old nephew, just to teach him a lesson.

Corporal punishment is still legal in all fifty states, after all, so long as paddling your kid's bottom with a wooden spoon doesn't become batting practice with your kid's head. If you slap your son or daughter to teach respect, you're operating under a special parent privilege in the law, but if you slap a stranger on the street, you've committed battery. Such are the intricacies of the criminal justice system. Two days after Pomeno thwacked his stepson, Jared, still bruised from the beating, reported the matter to the police, and an investigation was opened, which resulted in

Pomeno and two of his buddies being charged with felony child abuse.

When the public defender's office called Ryan to see if he could help, he was gratefully not assigned to represent Pomeno but rather asked to take on one of Pomeno's accomplices. A fellow named Carl Schunk was charged with being party to the crime of physical abuse of a child for allegedly having been one of the men who restrained Jared while Pomeno and his other associates whaled on the kid.

"Schunk was a really nice guy, totally normal," Ryan said. Schunk, like Pomeno, was a Vietnam veteran and a biker. He was also a husband and a father. A bit grizzled, with a ZZ Top beard and tattooed arms, Schunk smiled virtuously, cheeks round and merry, as if he were wearing rouge. Probably a bit of an anarchist, he was nothing to fear, and Ryan felt Schunk had been unfairly charged. There existed little, if any, evidence to indicate his role in the beating. In fact, in his statement to police, he asserted he actually broke up the fight between Wayne Pomeno and Jared Cabot.

Carl Schunk belonged to a growing number of Ryan's baby boomer clients, men and women whose formative influences—such events as the Cuban Missile Crisis, the JFK assassination, and the Vietnam War—made them largely suspicious of the government and, arguably, of all people and institutions of authority. Living on the fringes of society, they were usually quiet about their radical ideas, not planning to declare mutiny or anything. But every so often, this clientele would give in to their renegade instincts. Schunk was one such client. Crazy old Doug Nelson was another.

Just like Pomeno, Nelson married into fatherhood. When his unemployed forty-year-old stepson began living in his house, Nelson's wife promised "the kid" would be out on his own by springtime. "He should have a job by then," she said. But when tulips pried through the dirt, Nelson's stepson was still unemployed, probably because he spent every day lounging on his stepdad's couch, stuffing his face with potato chips, and not even glancing at the want ads. Nelson told him on multiple occasions to get busy looking; his vacation was about to end.

"Too bad, Pops," Nelson's stepson said. "I'm not going anywhere." That's when Nelson, all 110 pounds of him, produced his loaded handgun and aimed it point-blank between his stepson's eyes.

"You either leave on your own, or you're leaving here in a body bag."

Nelson's wife, fearing for her son's life and probably fed up with old Doug Nelson, helped her middle-aged son gather himself, and they left together, calling police almost immediately, proving, at the very least, that maternal instinct remains well-oiled for the full extent of its lifetime warranty, even when our children fail to reach their dreams or never dream at all.

Before long, the SWAT team had surrounded Nelson's house, assault weapons drawn. When they called through their megaphone for the suspect to exit his home with his hands in the air, Nelson meandered outside in his polyester robe and his corduroy slippers, stooped like the feeble old man in Shel Silverstein's *The Giving Tree*, slightly propped upright only with the help of his cane. What was all the fuss about—can't a father call his stepson to action?

At trial, Nelson put forth an affirmative defense called "defense of property," essentially arguing to the jury that, "Yes, I pointed a gun at my stepson's forehead," but much as in an instance of corporal punishment, he believed he possessed the privilege to act this way. Just as parents are protected with built-in rights in allegations of child abuse, property owners are likewise protected with built-ins, and therefore Ryan argued that Nelson was not guilty of intentionally pointing a firearm at a person, a misdemeanor, because, per the statute, he reasonably "believed in an unlawful interference with his property."

The state argued that Nelson's threat with a handgun exceeded his defense of property privilege because more peaceful means existed. For example, Nelson could have filed a formal eviction action to remove his stepson from squatting on his living room couch. Ultimately the jury was not convinced that the defense of property privilege applied to old Doug Nelson, and he became a convicted criminal for the first time at the age of sixty. Nelson's wife sided with her son, and together they continued living in Doug Nelson's house while Nelson, the rightful owner, was exiled to a trailer on the outskirts of town and Ryan handled his subsequent divorce.

Fathers like Doug Nelson and Wayne Pomeno would likely lament modern disciplinary practices. They'd say we coddle our children with time-outs and ineffective little sermons. Back in the 1950s, if a smart aleck mouthed off to his parents or, worse yet, pilfered from their money jars, he'd get a whooping, and if your no-good deadbeat mooch of a stepson wouldn't move out and get a job, he might have a change of heart after a short discussion with your Smith & Wesson.

Parents today are expected to show more restraint and better judgment, even when our emotions rise to the same levels that would have driven parents of previous generations to violence. Parents claiming not to have been pushed to a life-altering breaking point must be lying or, alternatively, not spending enough time with their children. I recall vividly the day that a neighborhood schoolteacher stopped to chat with me in my driveway. "I was afraid if I stayed in the house any longer, I'd wind up in prison for murder," she said, laughing but serious about her teenage daughter.

After Carl Schunk and Doug Nelson, Ryan and I had come to accept that his chemistry with Irie was grease on water. In every benign dispute, she used emotion, and he used logic, neither of them much willing to switch-hit. He often treated our domestic life with a lawyerly approach. When he wasn't swearing, grumbling, or bellowing, Ryan was deliberate in his speech patterns, even though, underneath it all, he carried the stress of working with criminals like a chronic illness. When Ryan would calmly lecture Irie—about being sloppy with piano practice or being cruel to a sibling—she would respond, hysterically and predictably, with, "Stop yelling." When he explained that he was not yelling, she'd raise the ante: "Stop being so mean." Her style was always to bait him into a fight, the opera singer yearning for the libretto of family drama. Ryan and Irie would work their way, crescendo-style, to yelling about Irie alleging Ryan yelled, irony at its finest.

One time, their fight escalated more quickly than ever before, and Irie trapped him into her emotional corner. As her level of disrespect and accusations mounted, the rest of us in the family receded to the outskirts of the living room. Ryan lunged toward Irie and grabbed her face with the vise of his strong hands. He began to squeeze and to push her backward. She seemed to waver above the floor like a human hovercraft.

"You make me feel like I want to kill you," he growled.

All of us were caught in the treacherousness of the moment. We felt dead ourselves, preserved with formaldehyde, momentarily beyond our bodies, until I finally intervened and screamed, "Ryan, stop it, you're going to hurt her!" When he let go of our daughter's face, the room was strangely quiet, even though Leo and Fern were crying. Frank, as usual, was nonchalant, oblivious, a fourth child in his own quiet world. Ryan snatched his car keys and left for a long drive along the lake, swaddling himself in the lullaby of the warm engine.

We'd recently received another foreclosure notice for our house on Hazel Street, this one from Aurora Loan Services, our mortgage company, which had swooped in to pay our back property taxes in 2008 but was now forcing us to escrow our taxes each year in addition to paying them back. Our mortgage had risen from $600 to $1,400 per month, and we were already three months behind again. I tried to tabulate Ryan's short fuse against the ledger of our debt. I worked hard on forgiveness. Without my daily dose of oxytocin, maybe I'd be just as much a menace.

Ryan had been considering a second job, added to his fifty-plus-hour workweek as a lawyer. Maybe he'd be a cook or wait tables. That was how we'd afforded graduate school in Ann Arbor. Or maybe he'd leave the profession altogether.

"I could be a pipe fitter," he said. He reminded me of his summer at Glatfelter, the paper factory where he fitted a never-ending network of lines that transported water to the pulp vats. "It was hot and miserable, but at least the paycheck was steady."

How much professional regret does one man's life contain? When I'd catch Ryan in action, singing or dancing, I'd swoon and assert, "You could have been an actor." Daddy's Dance Parties were our favorite home events. Ryan would crank up the iPod and blast everything from Beastie Boys to Paul Simon, lifting and twirling the children while headbanging and rocking his hips. He could have been an artist too. One evening he sketched a full-body portrait of my father, sitting cross-legged at the dining room table, depicting him more accurately than any photograph. But none of those forfeited talents would have brought us the stability we needed. Even our years of being educated at prestigious public universities seemed like a waste.

I too felt I'd missed my calling—midwife, pediatrician, childcare provider—any profession that might boost my oxytocin levels as part of my daily grind. I imagined sometimes all the surrogate children I'd nurture and how, according to science, children I'd not even birthed could wrench the throttle on my neurotransmitters. All those student loans, straight As, the flush résumé—what was it all for, if we couldn't afford to make a family or, worse yet, if we screamed at and threatened the family we'd made?

When Liberty Cabot pulled into the parking lot of Pomeno's bike shop, there's no doubt Jared's bruised and battered face transported her, at high speed in reverse, to a much earlier tragedy. Jared was not Cabot's only son. First came Jared, then five years later, Vaughn was born, the biological son of Liberty Cabot and Wayne Pomeno. It is quite possible—in fact highly probable—that Pomeno favored Vaughn over his stepson, Jared, from the day of Vaughn's conception.

When Jared was ten years old and Vaughn was five, Cabot was known to indulge ritualistically in smoking marijuana at bedtime. It was January in Wisconsin, dark before 5:00 PM, a month for hibernation. Surely Vaughn was already asleep when she toked up, but like all young children, he would wake up early the next morning. Where was Cabot headed at dawn, when she allowed him to sit shotgun without a belt or car seat, and how high was she after sleeping off the joints she smoked? Was Vaughn babbling and blowing warm air into the bubble of his clasped hands? Maybe he was not sitting on his pockets, but rather on his knees, high on the privilege of sitting in the front, as my children would be. I imagine his passenger's side window was frosted with ice, etched with fingernail train tracks, as our winter windows are, and that's why Cabot did not see the truck that blindsided them. She rolled the stop sign, right into the truck's forward trajectory. The judge would accuse her of still being numb from the THC.

Vaughn hit the windshield headfirst and suffered head injuries so severe that he died at Children's Hospital two days later.

The state of Wisconsin charged and convicted Liberty Cabot of negligent homicide and sentenced her to eighteen months' incarceration with five years of extended supervision. When Liberty Cabot and Wayne Pomeno lost their son, her guilt and his resentment likely made recalibrating their hearts impossible, and I'd guess Jared, their remaining child—not Pomeno's by birth—bore the brunt of their grief. Of course judges tend not to be interested in these kinds of hypotheses, though from the hands-off nature of neglect to Pomeno's hands-on abuse, Jared endured a range of disciplinary philosophies, and his mother suffered at both ends.

It is difficult to resist our children's requests—"Can I sit in the front seat, Mama?" Who does not want a companion at shotgun, a chance to talk, against the barren flat-scape of winter? By the time our fourth child, Francis, had arrived, I was laissez-faire about car seats. Our toddlers sat in booster seats meant for older children, and on the long extracurricular circuit about town (hockey, figure skating, swimming, softball, baseball, piano lessons, and theater) I allowed my children to roam the van or build forts. "You may freely walk about the cabin," Irelyn and I would often joke, although she worried.

"Mom, it's illegal," she'd insist. "You're going to get pulled over. It's not safe." But in this modern age, the pushback from bossy two-year-olds who won't sit in their pediatrician-recommended five-point restraints seems just as grueling as an imagined film reel of a deadly accident, and far more immediate. As they played house in our mobile home, I would stare deep into the rearview mirror, monitoring for headlights, wondering if those orbs of light were really closer than they appeared. Fern misunderstood our reference to the "oh shit handle" and would scream, "Grab on to the ocean handle!"

My parents always allowed us to roam our full-size van too, as we careened up mountain roads in Wyoming on vacation. We played hide-and-seek, curling into little kitten balls under removable cushions. Did my mom ever panic, even momentarily, when an oncoming driver laid on the horn? I often pulled in front of oncoming vehicles at interstate speed, blunted not by drugs but rather by exhaustion and daydreams. Liberty Cabot fell into line, somewhere between Mama McNally and Annie Jungwirth, as just another mother much more enigmatically human than the labels she earned in the database for Wisconsin court records might suggest.

For every praiseworthy act we committed as parents, we neglected another. A friend with two children once joked her kids turned feral, like mangy cats, while she ignored them for a day to paint the living room. With only two hands, I could rarely accommodate four at once on long home days. While I helped Irie with piano theory homework, Leo played too many games of *Madden NFL*, and while I baked with Francis, Fern ran off with the chocolate chips, devouring all sixteen ounces for lunch. One of my most neglectful offenses was the breastfeeding. As a working mother, all I ever needed to wake well rested and prepared to teach was to roll over in the night and pop my nipple into the warm opening of my babies' mouths, but as a result, my children's front teeth rotted. When Irie and Francis both needed dental surgery, doctors and nurses embarrassed us with long lectures on dental care. When Francis woke from his series of extractions in his hospital bed, a little crustacean beneath his hospital robe, I recognized my negligence in his whimpers.

Another doctor at Children's Hospital, where Leo was once treated for a urinary tract infection during his first year of life, looked at me as she pulled back his foreskin for the catheter, and said, "Wouldn't this be a lot easier, Mom, if he were circumcised?" I was mortified. "He would be more handsome too, if you know what I mean," she added, smiling wide, oblivious to the grave tyranny of her words.

Long before marriage, Ryan had decided against circumcision for our boys. In 1997, while in college, he happened upon "The True Story of John/Joan," an article in *Rolling Stone* by John Colapinto about David Peter Reimer's sex-reassignment surgery following the botched circumcision that burned his penis beyond surgical repair. The tumultuous life that ensued, in which he was lied to by his parents, bullied by classmates, and experimented on by medical professionals, ended tragically, thirty-eight years later, with his suicide. Ryan was horrified by the story of Reimer's life. In his extensive research thereafter, he was able to debunk typical Midwestern assumptions about circumcision, such as medical necessity and cleanliness. Leaving our boys intact was our gift to them.

I was quick to agree with Ryan's decision, as I tried to conjure up the heartbreaking, even nauseating image of my boys bound to molded plastic boards, mouths rooting for the comfort of my nipple as a surgeon slit open their foreskin. Just as a paring knife cleaves a peach, right? I've been told these babies, fully restrained and screaming bloody murder, are offered a ration of sugar water, as if to placate their first experience with pain, but what purpose does this hazing ritual serve, other than some test of pain threshold? Even Dr. Spock, who once favored circumcision, based on myths that persisted for decades, advised against it, in the end, before he died. The nurse at Children's Hospital of Milwaukee didn't care about any of that. In her mind, my baby's UTI was the result of my neglecting to have him circumcised. She and her fellow nurses chided me until we were discharged, but only after a forcible catheterization, which resulted in Leo crying thereafter every time we changed his diaper.

Truly the worst of our negligence, though, was our failure to tie up the tassels on our accordion window shades in the sunroom. One Sunday, when I was at the grocery store and Ryan was cooking dinner, Fern and Francis played Tarzan and Jane, swinging from the back of the couch, using the tassels as vines. In some fluke fashion, as Fern swung from her vine, she managed to wrap the corrugated strings around her neck just before landing on the sofa cushion. The deep red marks made Fern appear as if strangled, and still, to this day, in bright sunlight, the scars are visible on the soft velour of her neck. When we sent her to school, looking as if she'd faced near death, perhaps at the hands of a caretaker, nobody questioned us except to say, "You're really lucky things didn't turn out worse." Teachers and other supervisors believed our story, but just as easily, they could have chosen to report us to CPS or any other institution of authority charged with protecting the lives of children.

At the preliminary hearing for Carl Schunk, Ryan was given an opportunity to cross-examine Jared Cabot about the beating at his stepdad's bike shop.

"You testified that two people held you down while Mr. Pomeno struck you?"

"Yes."

"But you do not know who held you, correct?"

"No."

"You do not know if Mr. Schunk held you down?"

"No."

"And you do not know what the other two people in the room were doing at the time of the beating, correct?"

"Yes."

In his closing remarks, Ryan argued to the judge that the state was cherry-picking evidence from opposing statements to create a composite charge. The DA used Schunk's statement about breaking up the fight to prove he was at the bike shop, combined with Cabot's statement about being held down by two other men—even though the victim himself did not identify any of his assailants other than his own stepfather—to imply that Schunk was one of those men.

"I don't find in reviewing the transcript in the testimony presented today that there's enough of a nexus between what's been presented here on this record and the charge as contained in the criminal complaint to bind over on a felony in this case," the court commissioner stated, in an unusual turn of events. Cases are rarely dismissed as early on as the preliminary hearing. "So I don't find that the state has met their burden of proof and will dismiss this matter without prejudice."

Outside the courtroom, Schunk took Ryan's hand in his oil-stained grip and said, "Going forward, you're going to be one of the lawyers the club calls upon, son." And sure enough, within the next few years, Ryan would help, among others, a member of Hell's Lovers with his messy divorce. As a payment of gratitude, that biker gave Ryan a large black sweatshirt embossed with the bike shop logo, flames shooting from the Harley's exhaust in a fire-orange blaze—a comical image, to me, as Ryan had only ever driven cars, his first vehicle a little blue Honda Civic.

Wayne Pomeno did not fare as well at his preliminary hearing. With plenty of evidence to bind over his case, he ultimately took his charges to trial, where jurors found him guilty of child abuse. The judge saw fit to sentence him to three years of probation and thirty days in jail, a token gesture of confinement. If punishment in the criminal system were dished out Hell's Lovers–style, surely Pomeno would have preferred a couple of uppercuts and maybe a few broken bones.

Could Liberty Cabot have predicted her son Jared's beating? Should she have foreseen his bloody face and bulging chin in her mind's eye? Pomeno described himself as ballistic, after all, but he was not entirely bad. When their son Vaughn died, and Cabot was charged and found guilty of negligent homicide, Pomeno remained faithful to his wife. He even wrote a statement requesting leniency at her sentencing, reminding the judge of an accidental death by motor vehicle that the judge himself had been involved in as a teenager years earlier. Pomeno was resourceful, to say the least, and he was Cabot's advocate. In fact, before Cabot reported for her eighteen-month prison sentence, he demonstrated his capacity for forgiveness and his readiness to begin anew. Cabot arrived at Taycheedah Correctional Institution pregnant with her third child, a baby girl in honor of the boy they lost, and prepared for the antiquated but still largely practiced process of birthing in shackles.

Celebrated midwife Ina May Gaskin reminds women, when giving birth, we are not lemons, squeezing citrus pulp into breakfast glasses, nor are we machines, even if doctors were trained for centuries to think of women's bodies as apparatuses—(re)productive, unproductive, or defunct—the medical notion of baby-making meant to follow some industrial business model. If not a business model, then birth was a simple transaction. At my first-ever babysitting gig, coincidentally the year my parents divorced and I met Ryan, the two girls wasted little time when I arrived at their house, a young and willing stranger. They begged me to give "pretend birth," folding a soft-bodied doll into a small mixing bowl. "Wear it up under your shirt," Kelsey demanded. I lay back on the kitchen floor and groaned long enough to simulate labor—a minute, I suppose—probably acting out something I'd seen on TV. Kelsey, playing the role of midwife, pulled the baby free and said, "Congratulations, it's a girl."

In real life, ready to birth my second baby, I welcomed that big plastic crochet hook as our midwife reached up inside me to break my water. In the onslaught of amniotic fluid, Leo set fire to my body, and I warmed up in the way of machines, fortifying my sanity and strength for hours of work. Like a blacksmith or a welder, I'd been charged with converting nine pounds of iron into the shape of a baby, using heat and my vaginal muscles like grinding stones. Each painful contraction radiated from my uterine furnace like a convection wave, cranking up the temperature of my belly to what age-old artisans call "forging heat."

When I closed my eyes, entering the dreamscape of childbirth, my insides glowed orange and I could see precious metal softening, ready to be pressed into the outline of my son. Fever could be measured on my forehead and across my breasts. I ripped off what clothes remained on my body and crawled onto my hands and knees, legs wide, opening my torso like an oven door.

When I was pregnant, I spooked myself imagining women drugged, bound, and gagged during labor, based on something I'd read once about pregnant women and Argentina's Dirty War. As birth requires its own form of restraint and attenuated focus, my greatest fear about giving birth was doing so while attached to an IV, a gown, a bed, or any kind of authoritative regimen. In every real instance of childbirth, I was grateful to be free. Nearly febrile, begging for washcloths soaked in ice water, I'd enter the agonizing awareness that the real work of birthing was imminent, and I was free to curl inward, leaning toward the searing middle of my own hearth. Frightened but also snug and happy in my bare skin, I tucked my chin against my chest. "Please make him come," I groaned, as the contractions intensified, my voice sounding possessed by some Brothers Grimm demon that enters a woman's chest cavity for the sole purpose of hammering out a baby. "Get. Him. Out," I growled. Afterward, I realized I was barking commands at myself.

After two hours of sweating against my own hot flames, I could feel my insides turning to embers, and at long last, I passed Leo through the forging press of my birth canal. When he emerged, he'd been stamped by the contour of my "labor"—another word feminist linguists critique—into a baby formed with the same mold, though with slightly less pressure, as Irie.

I could imagine but could not truly fathom Cabot's prison birth. Cabot's baby waited, confined within the walls of her womb. Now that Vaughn had passed away, this baby girl would become Cabot's second living child. She shed grief as her body thickened and Pomeno waited for them both, working long days at the bike shop, transforming burned-out bikes into revved-up ones. When Cabot finally fell into labor, after long months, she was whisked to the local hospital but forced to give birth in ankle cuffs.

She was not free to spread her legs as wide as I was mine. Padlocked to herself, Cabot was deemed a flight risk by the state of Wisconsin, even in the throes of labor. If she was a machine, pressing a baby into existence, the Department of Corrections controlled her operating lever. What shape did she press that burning hunk of baby into, given all those restrictions? Did she nearly burn to death, or did she lose consciousness when it came time to push, as she realized even her muscles were weakened by the chain-link bracelets tied above her feet? Was she allowed to scream or would prison guards have muzzled her? Did she have any idea that, years into the future, her husband would beat the shit out of her first baby, just to teach him a lesson?

She must have wept, but then, I suppose, I did too, not for shame or sadness or even elation but for some small-scale release. Tears spilled from my pressure valve when the baby was not yet ready. Liberty Cabot and I certainly shared one thing in common: our babies were born tethered to our powerhouses, connected to our lifeblood, placentas gleaming like liver, cross-stitched with veins; and surely at both of our births, mine in Madison and Cabot's up the road from Taycheedah Correctional Institution, those umbilical cords were cut to set our babies free.

Upon each of our four births, midwives offered Ryan an enormous sterilized pair of scissors, blades gleaming under fluorescent light, and each time, he declined their invitations to sever that fibrous bond, the cable that kept our children, for nine months, suspended in uterine safekeeping. The same squeamishness that impaired his enthusiasm for a vasectomy likewise stunned him in the delivery room, even though he faithfully stayed, helped, and watched me give birth from his weak and stupefied position. Once our babies were unchained, fully disentangled from the womb, by a nurse, not by their father, Ryan would became a co-provider, those little bundles of nerves and shared blood reliant on more than just my body to flourish and survive. Cutting the cord, as it were, was a moment of truth for Ryan, in which he preferred to be a passive participant, quietly enjoying those final seconds of his fatherly birth-day position, one step removed from the impending intensification of family life.

CHAPTER 6

Stargazers

Our babies were born in lavishly good health, but Ryan, who probably needed more postnatal care than I, appeared like a man subjected to a host of communicable diseases. The anguish of his clients' lives was increasingly contagious. He lived through them vicariously, taking on drug addiction, domestic abuse, and violence as his own problems. Sometimes I felt responsible. Ryan was raised in a conservative, stand-pat, "pull yourself up by your bootstraps" household, whereas I was raised by parents in helping professions who explained away every stranger's mistake. Perhaps I'd rubbed off on him, my über-empathy a symptom of some liberal sickness that was killing him now.

"My parents probably blame you," he'd say, laughing, but he also pointed the finger at his education. He left for college a self-invested future business major but returned an altruist, a political science guy, more benevolent than I ever imagined possible but also frighteningly more vulnerable. Now he left for work sober and returned strung out. In hospital photographs from Francis's birth, Ryan is unrecognizable, hollow and bleary-eyed, a father incapably exhausted.

Years later, I'd look back at photos and see that I was hefty with short hair and swollen, meaty cheeks, but I don't remember feeling self-conscious. All the postpartum and breastfeeding hormones pacified me into accepting my body. But how did either of us ever find the energy required to hang the moon in our newborn son's sky?

In the classic picture book *Love You Forever*, Robert Munsch depicts mother-child love as reciprocal. For most of the book, the boy's mother rocks him to sleep, even when he is a teenager, but when she grows old and sick, the boy, now a man, volunteers to lull her, rocking his old lady as he sings, "I'll love you forever." Linda Duffy's story of motherhood was not picture-book perfect, or even arguably a parody of the Robert Munsch story, if one could muster laughter when listening to Ryan talk, as he did most nights, about his law practice. Did Linda Duffy even rock her son Kevin in childhood, and if so, what kind of lullaby would she have sung? Kevin Duffy, Ryan's client, assigned by the public defender, was a musician, a passion for songwriting having begun somewhere in childhood, but the state of Wisconsin didn't care about all that. Linda's story, not Kevin's, inspired the criminal complaint against him.

According to Linda, in spite of an imminent divorce, she moved back in with her future ex-husband Bob to make a last-ditch effort at reconciliation and caretaking. Bob, long suffering from hepatitis C, was on a waitlist for a second liver transplant. The first transplant was not as successful as anticipated, and Bob was suffering from surgery-induced frontal lobe brain damage, which interfered with his ability to live productively, demonstrate appropriate emotions, and remember details.

When Linda and Bob initially separated, Kevin voluntarily moved home, but Kevin, working long hours in retail, was not an ideal medic. Kevin's father ended up not taking his meds as prescribed or eating sufficiently. When a family friend named Jackie learned of Bob's poor health, she took it upon herself to become his backup nurse, delivering breakfast sandwiches and filling Bob's day-by-day medicine tray.

Bob and Jackie described their relationship as platonic, but Bob's wife, Linda, suspected that Bob and Jackie had become lovers. Upon coming to this conclusion after moving back home, she decided to drop Bob for good. "Reconciliation was out of the question," she said. Linda packed up her bags for the last time, slammed the door, and drove away, but shortly thereafter, she realized she'd left her own meds in Bob's refrigerator. If Linda and Bob shared one thing in common, it was their chronic health problems. Linda was a lifelong smoker, suffering from osteoporosis, once having broken several ribs from coughing too hard. She kept buying cigarettes, against her doctors' warnings that nicotine would deplete the curative effects of her prescriptions.

When Linda returned to the house to collect her osteoporosis meds, she and Bob began to fight again in their typical fashion. Their voices coalesced into caterwauling, which, according to Linda, brought their adult son Kevin up from the basement in a furious rage. Allegedly, when she stormed outside, "leaving once and for all," Kevin, young and able-bodied, chased her down, and before Linda reached the sidewalk, he grabbed his mother's hair, pulled her to the ground, and dragged her backward across the lawn.

"He broke my back," Linda wailed to Bob, who was standing just inside the house. "Please help me. Make him stop!"

"Get that fucking bitch in the house," Bob instructed, according to Linda's testimony. Kevin dragged Linda inside as if her hair were the rope on a toboggan, lifting her over a lip between rooms and dropping her facedown in a heap. Kevin confiscated her cell phone and pitched it against the wall, busting the phone so it could not be used—and thus began hours of torture at the hands of her ex-husband and son, in the form of insults and indifference toward Linda's agonizing injuries.

Apparently, Bob and Kevin took turns lifting Linda's head by her dyed-blonde tendrils and banging her forehead against the floor. Bob spit at the nape of her neck and accused her of ruining the Duffy family name. At one point, when Linda begged for her husband and son to stop beating her, Kevin duct-taped her mouth shut, then ripped it back off, as if waxing her upper lip.

"My back is broken," Linda moaned. "I can't move."

"How about we tie her behind the car and drag her to Lake Winnebago," Bob reportedly said. "Put her out of her misery."

"And throw her in the water when we get there," Kevin replied.

They accused Linda of faking her agony and aired their grievances instead of tending to her pain, bantering over years of pent-up anger like two guys on a radio talk show. They laughed as Bob supposedly unscrewed his Gatorade bottle and dumped its contents on Linda's head. Even when she begged for help getting to the bathroom, the men showed her no sympathy, turning her incontinence into a joke when she soiled her underpants. Then Kevin disappeared for a minute and returned with a ten-pound cylindrical weight meant for stabilizing his telescope. He hovered over his mother, blocking the light as if eclipsing the sun, as Linda once floated over his passive body in a montage of nursery settings: his crib, his bassinet, the flex of her once-strong arms. "If you don't tell me where you hid my gun, I could kill you," he supposedly said, angry his Bushmaster AR-15 had gone missing that week.

He aimed the weight beyond his mom's body before dropping it. The telescope cylinder nicked Linda's lip, settling inches from her hand, clenched into a fetal fist. Supposedly she lay there like that, as time slipped by, excruciating minutes made up of whole hours, like a small helpless child who has not yet learned to walk. When Kevin was little, his dad would smash dishes during marital spats, and afterward he would explain to his son, "It's OK to break things that belong to you."

As far back as my childhood tantrums, I recall breaking dishes, bookbindings, Precious Moments figurines, and my bedroom door. Once I even nicked our dining room table with a candlestick when I spiked it at dinnertime, but there's a definitive line between things and people, even if every family story adheres to patterns of breaking and mending. At Ryan's and my wedding, I refused to be "given away" by my dad but paradoxically kept Baker, my father's surname. Both were misguided decisions I'd later regret. My father did not own me, but together we were equal shareholders in the gift of our kinship. As for remaining a Baker, I needed constantly to assert, for those remaining confused, that the Ulrich children belonged to me.

Did Linda belong to Bob, or he to Linda, as she eventually managed to crawl helplessly from room to room? Unable to call for help from her own phone, Linda convinced Bob to retrieve her cigarettes from the car, but after she'd smoked only half of the first one, he plucked it from her fingers and stubbed out the burning ember on Linda's knuckle. Only by some miracle, she finally convinced Kevin to call for help in the early morning hours. She asked him to call the ambulance service instead of 911 because she didn't want neighbors to see the lights.

The imminence of the paramedics' arrival must have cued Bob to react in some prescribed husbandly fashion, or maybe his brain damage explains his erratic behavior as he collected armloads of pillows from beds and sofas, slowly and carefully fitting them against her legs and torso, as if outlining a dead body in chalk. When the paramedics entered the house, Kevin stood back against a wall, tuckered out and resigned to fate, while Bob began to sob. Curiously, Linda did not immediately indict her husband or son; in fact, she told the ambulance crew she hurt herself by falling down. But hours later, when Bob failed to show up at her hospital bedside, Linda availed herself of a police investigator, divulging a horrifying story of abuse.

Linda's son, Kevin Duffy, was charged with three felonies: aggravated battery, second-degree recklessly endangering safety, and threats to injure with intent to extort. Ryan was admittedly baffled upon meeting Kevin, an acoustic guitarist and an amateur astronomer who possessed the characteristic disposition of a stargazer. He was soft-spoken and contemplative. Although he worked long hours selling furniture, he'd spent countless hours in his early twenties volunteering at Barlow Planetarium and developing his astrophotography skills. In fact, police collected reels of undeveloped film from Kevin—pretty much the only evidence collected in this, yet another, he-said-she-said case—only to discover useless images of star clusters and galaxies in the night sky.

Although Ryan could not imagine this man having committed the alleged crimes, he didn't consider taking Kevin Duffy's case to trial until the preliminary hearing. By now, Ryan had observed dozens of victims on the witness stand. "They almost always struggle to keep their emotions in check," he said. "They can barely finish their sentences without choking on their tears. But Linda was just so matter-of-fact and nonchalant that she came across as a liar. I mean, we're talking about her son allegedly trying to kill her, and she didn't express any anguish at all."

Unlike Joseph Michalik, Rob McNally, or even Aloysius Jungwirth, whose stories explained their wrongdoing, Kevin Duffy seemed to have been entirely forsaken by his own mother with little to no explanation at all. If Ryan didn't take his case to trial, Kevin faced prison for the crime of simply getting sucked into the black hole of his parents' imploding marriage, not to mention their collective poor health—as if Ryan didn't have his own well-being to worry about.

I tried to distinguish Ryan's boyish freckles from the scabs he gouged into his face. He'd given up on regular shaving, instead digging whiskers out with his fingernails. It would have been easy to blame Ryan for his lack of coping skills and his clients for their misery. All doped up on the hedonistic pleasures of motherhood, I didn't imagine indicting myself. But hadn't I been almost entirely self-invested, pushing four babies, back-to-back, without offering Ryan any kind of veto power? And although we had agreed on four children, Ryan had imagined two children, followed by a long recovery break, and then two more—sets of offspring with money-saving room in between.

As a child of divorced parents, I needed to grow into marriage. Throughout the first decade of our betrothed lives, I'd threaten divorce whenever frustrated, relying on dissolution as my model for long-term romance. Parenting further complicated my conflict-management skill set. Our fights became compound chain reactions. My intimacy with our children was so intense, I'd cut Ryan out unknowingly; he'd long to rekindle our physical affection, but in vying for my attention, he'd stifle the kids. Overcome with fierce protectiveness, I'd tug them closer to my apron strings, shooing Ryan to some remote circle, far from the life-sustaining pulse of our mother-child nexus.

"Mom, you love Dad," Irie or Fern would say. We didn't need to dial 911 to solve our domestic disputes as Ryan's clients did. Our children, causing and resolving our fights, were the crux of meaning. They exacerbated Ryan's poor health but inspired him to live longer; they alleviated my depression but crazed me with love and greed. Sometimes I found myself longing for men who yelled less, but I'd created the man Ryan had become, and I could not return him into the world so broken. He'd gone on damaging himself to make my wishes come true.

As I breastfed through each pregnancy, I'd sleep mostly in our children's beds, their bodies like warm loaves of bread, fragrant and yeasty, a nighttime aphrodisiac. Engrossed in the nocturnal static of tending to their needs, I was not dismayed by my separateness from Ryan, but when a friend equated husbands sleeping on couches with the inevitability of divorce, I grew defensive and scared. I had forgotten about my husband, adopting a unilateral attachment philosophy—parent-to-child and rarely parent-to-parent. I squandered all my love on our children. Maybe I was drunk on power too. On rare evenings, I'd stand at the top of our staircase and call out, "Ryan?" This was our signal. How could any man resist the call of affection after spending days or weeks alone in a house filled with people for whom he longed? On some level, I was just a trickster, testing his willingness to continue the baby-making process.

One summer night, as I lay in our only air-conditioned room, on a sheet on the floor, Francis and Fern were both begging for "milky." I could not nurse them simultaneously, and they took turns crying out in the dark. Intolerant of humidity and heat, Ryan was already irritable. He marched back and forth in our narrow upstairs hallway, trying to solve the breastfeeding problem. "Can't anyone go to sleep in this house without a fucking tit in their mouth?" he yelled. He censored little to nothing, such that *shitty* and *fuck* were part of our family lexicon, as in, "I'm so tired of my clients' shitty fucking lives." But of course, though we never doubted his loyalty or love, Ryan was also tired of us. During the day, he fumed about mothers and fathers too doped up to feed their babies; and at night, he wondered when I'd ever stop feeding ours.

"You're so pissed off all the time," I'd accuse him. "Don't our children give you the least bit of joy?"

"Yes, of course," he'd say, softening around the edges. "But while you're soaking up all their physical affection, I've been entirely cut out."

And to an extent, Ryan was right. I relished being objectified by my babies. They'd reach down my shirt to twist my nipples like a spigot for milk. They'd duck under the folds of my skirt, lodging their heads between my legs. I invited their fingers inside my mouth, and I rubbed their saliva into my hands like some ancient salve. As I stared into baby Franco's eyes, lashes fluttering, I finally began to wonder, when was the last time I'd looked into Ryan's? What comes first, Daddy or the child; the family or the marriage? And how many nights during those years did I find my way into the warm dugout of Ryan's body, or he into mine, intent on recreational as opposed to procreative sex? We needed desperately to hitch our wagons to the same star, but aside from our desires for each other, a figment of the past, we differed entirely in our wants.

How much of Linda Duffy's story shone true, and how much did she embellish? When we look at the night sky, we find Orion the mighty hunter, but another stargazer may perceive a different picture in the constellation. Bright stars that appear close together are actually very far apart in the reality known as space. While Linda said she returned to live with Bob in an effort to reconcile, the courts had recently ordered Linda to pay $500 a month in spousal maintenance to Bob, as he was living exclusively on disability monies. Although Linda was in poor health, her husband was worse off, and she'd need to continue working to help support him. She also stood to lose the house and other assets in the pending divorce.

The dissolution of a marriage reduces a family into its own specialized glossary of symbols. In the failed marriage between

Linda and Bob Duffy, symbols included but were not limited to the long-lost Camaro Bob was driving when he sweet-talked Linda into dating him at age seventeen; a 1960 Gibson dot electric guitar with flame top, a Fender Closet Classic Stratocaster, and a Canon Rebel digital camera with f/2.8 lens; a Ruger Mark III pistol and a Bushmaster AR-15, both of which Bob was court-ordered to relinquish after shooting a hole in his wall when his brain damage flared up; the laptop Linda took into her possession, even though Bob, also an amateur cosmologist, had saved his astronomy notes, schematics, and electrical circuits on the hard drive; and the fragments of broken glass tables and dinner plates with which Bob confetti-dusted the house in one or more fits of hysteria. Given his history, one wondered, was Bob a reliable narrator?

According to him, after a long afternoon, the day of the alleged crimes, he awoke to find Linda digging through his drawers and reading his email messages, trying to find something she might use against him in divorce proceedings. In her mad search, Linda came upon correspondence from Jackie, his friend and caretaker, and began reading her sleepy husband the riot act, pacing between rooms and stomping her feet, right there in front of the fireplace.

"I'm no second fiddle!" she screamed. She was disoriented and seemingly rabid.

"Jesus Christ, Linda," Bob said. "You'll break your back."

Before the paramedics arrived, according to Bob, Linda lifted her shirt and asked for help removing three fentanyl patches. Up to one hundred times more potent than morphine and fifty times stronger than pharmaceutical heroin, fentanyl had been prescribed to Linda for pain associated with her osteoporosis. Absorbing three patches' worth of meds, three times prescription strength, would certainly make anybody loopy, and her bones were only growing weaker, thanks to her faithful smokes.

Bob described her as a raving lunatic in and out of the house all evening, yelling obscenities. Kevin admitted that he emerged from his bedroom in the basement in the midst of his parents' fighting, but certainly not to interject himself. An intervention didn't make sense now; his parents had been fighting nonstop his entire life. Guitar case in hand, he was leaving for his Friday night gig when his mother stormed out of the house ahead of him into the dark. He noticed his mother on the front lawn, having tripped by the ditch, but fed up with her prescription drug abuse and other manufactured theatrics, Kevin Duffy admittedly did not help Linda to her feet. Instead, he sped off, leaving his mother in a cloud of dust.

For years, he'd begged her to stop smoking, to stop overloading on meds, to take some small modicum of pride in her body, but as her physical health deteriorated, so too did her mental well-being. From what Kevin understood, his mother had recently stalked Jackie, running her off the road in a crazed high-speed chase. He did not have the time, the patience, or any remaining sense of loyalty to get hooked into what he perceived as never-ending drama. This is where Kevin Duffy and Ryan came into synchronicity. Attorney and client were both growing jaded, both on the brink of complete and total empathy fatigue.

The advent of technology has undoubtedly altered the face of criminal law. While clients are commonly implicated in crimes thanks to emails, videos, texts, Facebook, and Snapchat, defendants have also used social media and their iPhone savvy to exonerate themselves and their loved ones. After Ryan was privately retained by a friend of Rob McNally's facing domestic battery charges, the client's wife, Judy Welch, came forward to admit she'd fabricated the abuse because she was pissed off.

"I'll tell you when to start," she said, instructing Ryan to video-record her demonstration. Seated at his desk, painting a black eye as if dressing up for Halloween, she began with a little mascara, followed by blue eye shadow and rouge. "I can make myself look like a battered woman, easy as one, two, three," she boasted. When Ryan forwarded the video, by embedding it in a text message, to the district attorney's office, the state was forced to drop charges against his client, which should have been a relief, but months later, the guy pulled a pillowcase over his head to contain the debris before shooting his brains out. It's no wonder Ryan was beginning to distrust formal statements, even if the victim, as in Kevin Duffy's case, was the young man's ailing mother.

Until his visit with Judy Welch, Ryan had been deeply sympathetic toward all who claimed to be victims of domestic abuse. Coming forward to report abuse was a sign of courage; the more often victims reported abuse, the more directly authorities might address its traumatic effects on women, children, families, and entire communities. He had his convictions. I did too. My own mom was a founding member of Siena Transitional Housing in Oshkosh, meant exclusively for women rebuilding their lives, often with children in tow, after leaving abusive relationships. But Cali Ziegler and now Judy Welch were two of several self-professed victims on a growing list of women Ryan encountered who were exploiting the lifelines of criminal justice, undermining women's progress.

Evidence told Ryan that Linda was working the system. Kevin, the only unmedicated of the three affiants in this case, never wavered in his version of events, and he had an alibi with a witness, even a set list, to corroborate his gig: "Pride and Joy," "Rude Mood," and "Cold Shot" by Stevie Ray Vaughan and "Manic Depression" and "Little Wing" by Jimi Hendrix. He stopped off at Hardee's for a burger afterward; he returned to his room to sleep; and he woke up when his father called him from the basement.

"I thought my dad was calling me up to see some celestial event," he said. That happened often in the Duffy household. Both men had learned to console themselves by watching for flashes of brilliance far beyond this realm. "Call your mother an ambulance," Bob said, and without hesitation, Kevin did, even if he admitted to staring blank-faced at his mother on the stretcher, his explanation simple. He'd seen her, not to mention his father, in hospital beds off and on since childhood.

Every child receives a summons to separate from his parents. Casually we talk about rites of passage such as kindergarten or the sweet sixteen, but we might be called at any time to step outside our mothers' or fathers' shadows. It's startling how easily our toddlers have already taken turns forsaking Ryan and me. Do you want to snuggle? No. Do you want to hold my hand? No. Don't you love your mama? No. From as early on as Irie and Fern could talk, they used hatred as power, screaming from behind slammed doors, "You're the worst mother in the world!"

In the wake of my own parents' divorce, I'd regularly practice cutting proverbial cords. My mom's women's group, the Ovular Society, comprised mostly of divorcées, celebrated womanhood with stupid-men jokes and symbols of female fertility ranging from chocolate to ceramic eggs, painted deliriously bright. When I began to menstruate, my mom gave me my great-grandmother's diamond-studded seashell ring, which I carelessly dropped down our bathtub drain, but the message remained: women's eggs were cause for celebration.

My mom perched her collectible eggs on precarious ledges, little Humpty Dumpties poised for great falls, and later on in life I'd wonder if all the king's horses and all the king's men might put so many women together again. All around me friends lost babies to miscarriages, bisected uteruses, kidney failures, floating placentas, chromosomal abnormalities, and ectopic eruptions, and I worried my dosage units of suffering awaited me in the future.

Ryan and I were fortunate to birth our full-term able-bodied children in May or June to fit my teaching schedule, so that even chocolate eggs at Easter time racked me with survivor's guilt.

But the Ovular Society, on the brink of menopause, threw epiphany parties in long robes and wizards' hats and cackled through the night, working on their sugar highs. I felt like the little bird in P. D. Eastman's story *Are You My Mother?* My mom laughed and snorted uproariously, like I'd never seen before, and I'd think of the orange-and-yellow digger spewing soot. The excavator is not the little bird's mother, though it does lift the yellow-beaked critter back into its nest.

When Ryan and I were teenagers, we'd don rubber masks on Halloween and trick-or-treat at my dad's, never revealing ourselves, so I could look inside his house from a stranger's perspective. Later, in my twenties, I would drive by my mom's and tell myself, when I resisted beeping the horn, she was just some lady on a street corner shoveling snow. Sometimes, I wished I could have surgically removed my parents from my heart, worth the pain to feel whole. Now when I look at old photographs of my parents—my mom's dark, flowing hair or my dad's black beard, nothing like the gray-and-white-haired figures they are now—I'm not entirely sure I can identify them.

At Christmas in 1983, my kindergarten year, toy stores were selling out of Cabbage Patch dolls at breakneck speed. Shoppers went to fisticuffs inside depots where the plastic-faced, yarn-haired babies were offered on a first-come-first-serve basis. My own mother shopped till she dropped in Appleton, Oshkosh, Fond du Lac, and Milwaukee, to no avail, locating, instead, a lady sewing homemade imitation Cabbage Patch dolls off Highway 21.

On Christmas Eve, I opened up a casket-like box and met Marita Marie. Her limbs were panty hose sausage-looking things filled with polyester stuffing; her face was embroidered into a sinister expression, eyes like slits; and her hair was made from an old toupee, sewn to her panty hose scalp haphazardly. She was wearing a mint-green frock. Within months, her thin skin would rip open, her cottony guts spilling out. I did not feel the least bit of loyalty toward Marita Marie and determined, early on, I'd make a bad mother. Was I capable of discarding my children, I wondered, and if so, what circumstances might incite me to commit such a crime?

Instead of dolls, animals, or other stuffed loveys, Irie preferred to mother faceless objects. When she was three years old, she adopted a soft-sided playground ball, also preferring her babies without torsos or limbs. Perhaps planetary roundness most closely resembled the way my stomach inflated during pregnancies with Leo, Fern, and Francis. Or maybe, in her mind, the baby lay nestled inside the ball like a chick, because entirely of her own accord, Irie named the ball Eggy.

Sometimes we'd be forced to substitute in changelings of Eggy's same texture and size as he was prone to rolling away, but Irie preferred Eggy to any other, even as he shrank over time, losing air with little intermittent gasps. She swaddled Eggy in baby blankets, latched him to her hip with belts, and gave him an old swimming suit for adventures in Lake Winnebago. At times, I'd think of Pascal in Albert Lamorisse's *The Red Balloon* and his helium-filled best friend following him on a journey through Paris.

Once at a park in Milwaukee, Irie and I simultaneously laid eyes on a girl kicking Eggy's twin through the grass, his bulbous body skidding to a painful halt on the pavement. Irie stepped backward and tripped, landing in an openmouthed, unblinking stupor, sick from her first experience with mother bear syndrome.

"That's not your Eggy," I said. "He just looks like your Eggy." How could I explain that Eggy was from a tall open-sided bin at Target, not from some sacred or creative space in which Irie was regaled as the matriarch?

After Eggy came Moony, a stuffed turquoise crescent moon the length of Irie's forearm. This baby, who cost fifty cents, was grabbed with a metal claw from a stuffed-animal pit at a local pizza joint. In second grade, for pajama day, she carried Moony to school but returned home without him. He never turned up in the lost-and-found or in a neighbor's yard; we retraced our school-day walk a dozen times. We never did figure out how she lost him. She cried for nights on end, going limp and ragged even if we so much as mentioned the real moon in the sky. After Moony, by some grace of God, came Starry, a pocket-size turquoise-and-gold stuffed pendant cut loose from Moony by accident before he went missing. Starry, Moony's little baby, slept inside Irie's pillowcase. Never consistently, but randomly, she would double-check for Starry at bedtime, like a mother peeking in on a baby. He went missing after I had changed her sheets one day, and Irie, already nine years old, wept uncontrollably until I found him.

After Starry came a series of babies named Rocky. On a ten-pound chunk of gravel, she drew a face in Sharpie, keeping him under her bed in a special padded box until he was deemed too dangerous to keep inside. Ryan envisioned our children mistakenly or, worse yet, purposely hurling Rocky at each other in a savage sibling feud, so we relegated Rocky to the garden, an "outside baby" much like a barn cat. Whereas Irie's maternal inklings led her to objects, Fern was a human-baby fanatic. From the time she could say "baby," she spied babies *everywhere*: in passing cars, crowded stores, museums; on billboards; hidden away in baby slings; in commercials; in the shapes of clouds; and always in the toy aisles. Fern wanted an entire nursery's worth of baby dolls. She named them and remembered their baptisms with reverence. Babies Wallace, Ashley, Adele, and Dylan were her favorites. I'd say, "You know, GG once owned a nursery," and Fern, who resembled her great-grandmother, Jean, since birth, smiled, her cheekbones like hard little apples.

For Christmas, years in and out, Fern requested babies that cried and crawled, and at long last, she became the proud mother of Baby Alive, who ate green slop and pooped it out into a diaper. Eventually we had to send this doll to the county dump after Fern mixed her peas too thick and the powdered vegetables turned moldy in Baby Alive's food chute. Fern equipped her playroom nursery with a diaper station and every other accoutrement on the market. She learned, early on, to play lullabies on a CD player and, later, on my iPhone. She borrowed report sheets from the UW Oshkosh Children's Center, circling "W" for wet diaper and "BM" for bowel movement; these were the first acronyms of Fern's life. Not only did Fern physically resemble her great-grandmother, but GG owned and operated one of the first licensed childcare centers in the state of Wisconsin, and Fern was following, at least in her land of make-believe, in GG's footsteps.

Fern's infatuation with babies defined her. When we ordered personalized birthday cakes one year, Irie's cake was a swimming pool, Leo's cake was a Stormtrooper, and Fern's was a nursery. Our friend, a cake guru, rolled little diapered babies out of fondant and arranged them on the pastel frosting. For every special event, we'd associate Fern with babies. Even on her birthday, we'd wrap her gifts in paper meant for baby showers. She loved her babies so much, she convinced us they were real, and then, if I found them discarded on the playroom floor, facedown and naked next to a T. rex or a Nerf gun, I'd threaten to call social services, jokingly but with some degree of genuine distress.

When and how do girls learn to nurture? If "maternal instinct" is part of our evolutionary wiring, why do girls in the same family, with the same mother, attach to such diverse representations of babies? For some time, I worried about Irie. Was she not drawn toward human contact? Did she experience less anxiety when she rocked her blank-faced Eggy, as a ball was less likely to spit up or cry or cause anguish, or was Irie just gloriously imaginative, anthropomorphizing the least animate objects? After all, some children invented headless imaginary friends out of thin air. Was Fern more likely than Irie to become an attentive mother, or a mother at all, and did this matter to me, a woman raised by my own staunchly feminist mom? Would the ability to nurture come to Fern more naturally, or was it possible Fern would deplete her supply of fuel early on?

For as different as our girls acted toward their babies, they seemed to be passing at least one litmus test. Years apart, without each other's influence, both took turns converting our least coveted dolls into feminist symbols for their futures. Irie chopped off secondhand Barbie's hair, streaked it purple; painted her face like a princess warrior's; and marked badass rock star clothes on her naked body. Then, to my surprise, Fern used permanent ink to map brain surgery onto Crawly Baby's cranium. Irie wanted a career in the arts, and Fern wanted to be a doctor. Was the jumble of hieroglyphics, in fact, a true set of lobotomy instructions, or was Fern planning another type of brain surgery?

As their siblings grew older, the girls would cry secretly to me, "I wish Leo was little again" or "I want to turn Frank back into a baby." Dr. Walter Freeman, father of the lobotomy, admitted that lobotomies were largely dangerous. He described them as "inducing childhood," forcing patients backward to an infantile state, thereby seriously diminishing their psychic lives. Maybe, deep down, this was what Dr. Fern wanted, some easy, albeit gory, remedy to the constant process in our family of people growing bigger.

She herself often said, "I wish I was a baby again," and then she'd crawl into our laps in fetal pose. Maybe she was fantasizing less about motherhood than we imagined, instead living vicariously through her dolls, becoming baby Fern all over again, all these dolls for Fern being rooted in nostalgia.

How many of us have wished our children would not grow up at all? At the very least, Fern did not have to worry about Crawly Baby, or Wallace, Ashley, Adele, and Dylan. Dolls can't ever become older, stronger, self-possessed, or independent in the way that real children do.

Kevin's trial felt like divorce proceedings from his own parents. As he awaited the big day, Ryan matched his quota of angst. Kevin was sending heartbreaking letters from jail, reminding Ryan that his life was on the line, not to mention pages upon pages of notes on potential legal strategies. On lined papers ripped from legal pads, Kevin jotted down "F = M(V2)" to explain why it was altogether impossible that Kevin could break his mother's back by pulling her to the ground. He made long lists of inconsistencies: no grass stains on Linda's clothing, no scalp damage, and no tracks in the lawn where Kevin allegedly dragged her inside. Wouldn't lack of evidence be enough to raise suspicions about his mom's lies?

The police took statements from all three affiants but never returned to the scene of the crime to collect much of any evidence, such as, say, the bottle of Gatorade and duct tape. Neighbors were not interviewed, nor were family members, like Linda's older son, many of whom would have revealed that Linda often used incarceration as a threat to gain power. "I'll have you locked up," she was known to say.

"Life is hard. You either take responsibility and soldier on, or you pass blame to your kids," Kevin wrote. "Can you imagine how I feel knowing I am in jail because my mother loves getting high more than she loves her own son?" He reiterated over and over that three fentanyl patches equaled "THREE TIMES" what she had been prescribed.

Ryan worked long hours preparing for the Duffy trial. In the weeks leading up to the big event, Linda began to call Ryan at his office. Bob had already been found guilty at his trial of felony counts for recklessly endangering safety and for threats to injure with intent to extort, and he was sentenced to serve two years in prison with five years of extended supervision. Linda was fully aware now of her power. Maybe she regretted it.

"I don't want Kevin to end up in prison," she told Ryan. "I feel like I'm squealing on my own baby, and now he's going to be in the dark for years."

She called repeatedly, asking for advice about what to say when the DA called her to the witness stand at trial. "I can't tell you what to say," Ryan said, reminding her that if she recanted her written statement and prior testimony, she would be impeached and called a liar. Eventually at trial, Ryan was given the opportunity to cross-examine Linda after the assistant DA took her turn, and Linda testified that she could not remember events.

"Is it possible that on that night in October you fell to the ground because the grass was slippery or because it was dark or because the ground was uneven?"

"I can't say for sure," she said.

"And is it possible that Bob, not Kevin, helped you back into the house?"

"I don't remember."

"And is it possible that Kevin left for his gig and didn't return until closing time?"

"I really don't remember."

"And is it possible that on the night of October second because you were under the influence of powerful drugs, self-administered and later administered by hospital personnel, among them opiates, and then Xanax, a downer and mood relaxer, that you misrepresented the events?"

"It's possible."

"You agree, then, that your statement might be colored by the drugs and your emotional state at the time?"

"Yes."

And there it was—the take-back. Linda Duffy backpedaled her way off the witness stand, having retracted significant details in her story. Did she do it because she loved her son or rather because she had lied in the first place?

"This is a case about the dissolution of a thirty-year marriage and how, in that marriage's dissolution, Kevin Duffy became collateral damage," Ryan argued in his closing statement. "Seventeenth-century philosopher Thomas Hobbes believed that humankind is driven by the passions or instincts linked to self-preservation. In other words, humans—people—as much as we may not want to believe it, are inherently self-interested. Linda was recently ordered to pay five hundred dollars a month in spousal maintenance to Bob. Certainly she would have been excused from those payments if the man were in prison."

What else did Linda stand to gain if her husband and son were incarcerated: the house, all of the family's possessions, and some version of revenge? In his statement, Bob said about Linda, "She was always hurting her sons, always wanting them to take sides." In her statement, Linda said much the opposite: "I believe Kevin is a victim because of his dad. The kids were put in the middle a lot."

Before Kevin's testimony, Ryan jotted him a note, right there at the defense table: "Say you love your mother and father." Was this reminder really necessary, and if so, would his efforts to appear sympathetic be enough to convert self-preservation into real tenderness and possibly forgiveness, if not now, sometime in the distant future?

I attended portions of Kevin Duffy's trial. I'd become attached to his innocence too. When he offered us an employee discount on bunk beds at the furniture store where he worked, we arrived, all four kids in tow. Although we sternly warned them not to climb around like monkeys, they disobeyed us. They scaled the sides of stacked beds and mounted them in wet boots. The girls fought vociferously.

"I'm sleeping on top."

"No, I am, you idiot. I'm older and I've earned it."

"Mom, Irie says she's getting the top bunk. She's too big to sleep up there. She'll break the bed and land on me."

If bunk beds provided the illusion of more space in our 1,700-square-foot house on Hazel Street, maybe the kids would fight less, and maybe Ryan would scream fewer curse words at bedtime. With two in top bunks, I'd be less inclined to sleep with them, more likely to climb into my husband's heat.

"My brother and I slept in bunk beds," Kevin told us. He was sweet-lipped and smiley, waving away my apologies as if truly entertained by the kids' antics. It was impossible for me to imagine he ever got angry, much less violent, but I'd also learned nothing is what it seems. Our children were known to hold hands and dole out bloody noses on the same afternoon. Leo, for example, never exhibited violence in public. People found him to be passive and gentle, but his nickname at home was "the angry German." He threw tantrums as if gargling anger, vomiting if the Badgers or Packers lost an important game. He'd throw books at the TV screen and convulse in a language we didn't understand.

Friends and colleagues of Kevin Duffy's responded to his plight with an outpouring of support in the form of letters addressed to the court. His aunt wrote, "I believe the entire incident is a grand fabricated scheme and that Linda let her lies go too far. She has manipulated the system for her own agenda."

After a two-day trial and hours of deliberation in *State of Wisconsin v. Kevin Duffy*, the jury somehow came back with a split verdict. They found Kevin Duffy not guilty of aggravated battery, the first event, and threats to injure, the last event, but despite having an alibi to defend himself against his mother's allegations, confirmation that he was away from home all night, he was convicted of recklessly endangering safety, a charge Ryan refers to as felony disorderly conduct. At sentencing, the judge was also confounded by the illogical verdict and imposed four years of probation with credit for the time served in the Winnebago County Jail while on a cash bond. Kevin Duffy had survived his short-lived time behind bars and would not face prison.

By Ryan's estimation, Bob and Linda Duffy's poor health was the core of their problems, and he became determined, thereafter, to get healthy. His efforts started with a diet and more exercise, of course. He reiterated, time and again, often in a joking manner, that he had "a real nice life insurance policy" set aside in case he died of stress, but he was actually serious, secretly worried he'd give up the ghost and traumatize the children. "Time to get healthy" was naturally one of the strongest arguments he'd make against conceiving a fifth child.

Throughout the intervening months, though, I had become legitimately obsessed with the number five. *Five little ducks went out one day. Five little monkeys jumped on the bed. Over in the meadow, in a snug beehive, lived a mother honeybee and her little honeys five.* According to the Scottish folk song, there was "always room for one more." Somebody was missing, and Irie was leading the pack, getting older every year. As a birthday gift for Irie, my dad and stepmom bought her star number Gemini RA 6h 27m 23s D 20° 54' from the International Star Registry and named it Irelyn Ulrich. Framed on her wall, the certificate is a constant reminder of the way she glistens in our sky. Don't they all?

Stellar nurseries are the special portions of interstellar space where baby stars are born. Especially in the Orion Nebula, the region of star formation closest to Earth, molecular clouds collapse frequently, leaving behind hot, blinking orbs that shimmer, light-years away but seeming to dangle within reach. Like people, stars are born, grow old—if they're healthy enough—and die, leaving a new generation of stars, luminescent marbles tossed against the sky, many of which I wished upon.

But maybe wishing would not, or could not, alter our predestination, whatever fate was written for us in the stars. My dad had told me that motherhood would either make me or break me, but being only a psychiatrist, and neither a physicist nor a psychic, he'd failed to give me numbers, leaving many questions unanswered—like, was there a tipping point? Would a fifth baby make or break my husband, my marriage, or whatever delicate energy had sustained us this far?

CHAPTER 7

On the Lam

Although Ryan's give-a-shit meter was busted by now, finagled, even psychologically engineered, to work only on certain days, he still worried over his defendants, and so did I, asking him all the questions he didn't want to think about or answer.

"It looks like Linda Duffy ran away to Harbor House when the boys were little," I said after reading more discoverable evidence in Kevin Duffy's case. "Do you suppose Bob was abusing them back then?" It remained nearly impossible for me to imagine Kevin's mother exploiting the sanctuaries and shelters meant to save women from domestic violence, even if she later turned out to be a liar.

"Who knows?" Ryan said.

As for Kevin Duffy, after the bunk beds, a resounding space-saving success, he also helped us to score new living room furniture, rooting for us to feather our nest when he'd been permanently booted from his own.

What disheartened me more, I wondered: mothers exploiting criminal justice or mothers exploited by the system? Were police over- or underreacting to women's reports, or, worse yet, both, to the detriment of all families? The nuances of lawyering, smack-dab in the middle of the criminal justice system, were variegated, paradoxical, and altogether impenetrable at times, so far removed from good-guy-bad-guy simplicities that I finally understood what Aristotle seemed to suggest in *Metaphysics*: the more you know, the more you know you don't know. Add gender, social class, family status, and race to the muddy waters, and Ryan's work was impossible to describe definitively.

If I were to have witnessed Lucy Vasquez, for example, on the day California police materialized on her parents' doorstep and handcuffed her dainty wrists, rattling off her Miranda rights with stern grimaces, I might have assumed, based on their attitudes, she was guilty as charged with kidnapping her own son. But upon noticing Callum, peeking out at officers, tucked knee-high behind his nana's skirt, I would have begun to ask questions. If Callum was unscathed and intact, corn bread crumbs and salsa sticky on his chin, a boy fed to his heart's content, had he really been kidnapped? Callum and Lucy had left Wisconsin almost a full year earlier, and nobody ever sounded the Amber Alert or deployed a search party then.

It was just as easy to argue that the state of California was guilty of kidnapping Callum's mother right before his eyes at naptime, a shocking turn of events. When the arresting officer shepherded Callum's mom away, lowering her into the squad car by pushing on the crown of her black, braided hair, I can only imagine, based on my children's way of seeing, that Lucy reminded Callum of a jack-in-the-box. He reached out his hand instinctively, beginning to weep, as if grasping for the crank to release his mother from the dark compartment with its tinted windows. Much to his further traumatic surprise, after officers taxied Lucy to the county jail, Callum was the next to be snatched away from the sunny, piquant warmth of Nana's home, temporarily placed with a foster family. His future placement would be determined once Lucy was extradited to Wisconsin after intake, a process that might last weeks.

As Lucy's husband, Remy, who lived in Green Bay, waited anxiously for news from California, Ryan received tidings in the form of a long-distance phone call 2,500 miles away that Lucy Vasquez needed his services. Lucy's mom, having found Ryan on the Internet, hired him five minutes into their conversation. She begged him to break Lucy free from jail as soon as possible, and to quash the warrant that authorized her arrest, as it had been initiated in Brown County, fifty miles north of Oshkosh. As always, Ryan promised to do his best.

The idiomatic expression *spirited away*, which actually means to be killed, evokes a magnificent spirit bird, delicate beak and wings of pearl, hoisting babies through stratus-streaked skies, not unlike the stork I imagined when the Stark Collection Agency came calling after Leo's uninsured birth. Long ago, in the Eastern world, children who disappeared mysteriously were said to be "spirited away" by deities and then deposited, according to mythology, alive and well, in shrines or temples. Every mother I know fears her children might be snatched or seized and then killed. Many of Maurice Sendak's stories for children were inspired, in fact, by the kidnapping of the Lindbergh baby in 1932. "When the news came that the baby was dead, it was just not to be believed," Sendak said in a talk at the New York Public Library. "I rejected the information because I so badly wanted him to come home alive." *Outside over There* taps into this most innate fear, among parents, of child abduction.

Much as Sendak was forever plagued by the Lindbergh kidnapping, modern parents remember other child abductions hitting the headlines. In 1996, my freshman year of college, I attended the University of Colorado at Boulder, and early on I declared my journalism major. When I returned home to Wisconsin for Christmas break, I was shocked by news from the CU campus.

A six-year-old girl named JonBenét Ramsey was found missing and reported to have been kidnapped by "a group of individuals that represent a small foreign faction," according to the ransom note. Boulder quickly became the eye of a media tornado. When I returned to my post at the *Campus Press* and journalism classes after Christmas break, we had already learned that JonBenét was dead, discovered in her basement. A ransom note accompanying the deceased is highly anomalous in criminal history. Every journalist in Boulder fixated on the Ramsey family. One night, a fellow journalism student and I parked near the scene of the crime, nestled into a neighborhood between campus and the foothills. We traipsed past police tape and peered in the family's windows. I vividly recall monochromatic tiles on a hallway floor.

I marvel still about my close proximity to the site of JonBenét's murder, how I managed to touch her first-floor window with the tip of my nose. Where were the police at this time, and how many other nosy students would trespass there, drawn to her home like fanatics to celebrity graves? Over the years, I've felt relieved by updates on the case. If her pretend kidnapping and real murder were inside jobs, we parents had less to worry about, right?

With four children now to protect, I tried to remind myself that abduction by strangers is anomalous, living, as we were, in an age of paranoia perpetuated by twenty-four-hour television news and social media. Mothers today are being arrested for failure to hover like helicopters, as a mother in South Carolina found out when she was arrested for allowing her nine-year-old to play at a park while she worked. One summer, a couple of Amber Alerts beamed through our iPhones with a shattering frequency and pitch, and we needed to explain them to our children. Of course, when we used the word *kidnapping*, they immediately fretted.

"Am I going to be kidnapped?" Fern wanted to know.

"The most likely scenario is that a parent or family member took the child without permission," I said, and in both Amber Alerts, this turned out to be true, but other news stories ended more gruesomely, as I ended up explaining to Leo.

When he advanced beyond early elementary school, he noticed and lamented the trick-or-treat schedule in Oshkosh.

"Halloween is supposed to be scary," he said. "Trick-or-treating when it's light out is for babies." Indeed the city of Oshkosh had long ago decided that door-to-door candy collecting should be completed by dark, thwarting Leo's designs on fear. He chose increasingly frightening costumes, evolving from year to year in this order: zombie hockey player, wounded Civil War soldier, zombie mummy, scarecrow serial killer. Not only did he want to be scared, but he wanted to scare little kids, not realizing he still was one. Leo was developing a jaded attitude at the age of nine, and finally, after a dozen expressions of "This is stupid," I said, "Well, do you want to know why we trick-or-treat during daylight hours?"

"Sure?" he said, the question mark his favorite kind of punctuation to verbalize.

"Because in 1973, a girl named Lisa French was abducted and murdered by her neighbor while trick-or-treating, and nobody saw it happen." This truth marked the end of his complaints, a cautionary tale not unlike my father would spin, except that Lisa French really was kidnapped and murdered, whereas mole people were science fiction.

The word *kidnap* was first used to describe the action whereby children in American colonies were stolen away from their families to serve on farms and plantations. Today, *kidnapping* suggests that children are mere bargaining chips, often held hostage for ransom or extortion purposes. *Abduction* is used interchangeably but legally means to take away a child without the consent of the child's legal guardian. We might also use other terms loosely—*interference with custody, child theft,* and *trafficking of a child.*

I was beginning to wonder, what was so wonderful about motherhood, anyway? Hadn't it replaced my melancholy with anxiety and fear? At least when I was depressed, all my emotion cocooned inside me. I suffered, but so what? Any and all forms of inherited grief were part of me. I felt safe and calm—depressed and deflated—before I became a mother. Now I had attached my hopefulness and joy to objects that moved erratically beyond my control, otherwise known as children. Of course, I never talked about this aloud, within Ryan's hearing distance. Maintaining my outward position on motherhood remained essential to my pursuit of happiness in the form of children, but even I truly worried about what would happen when the hormonal surges stopped and my kids outgrew their early childhood charms. I'd be commandeering a household full of unruly people, who talked back and begged for money, buoyed not the least bit by oxy but dragged down by age.

The physiological definition of *abduct* is to move or draw away from the axis of the body, whereby one might argue that birth is a kind of abduction, even if medical necessity sets our babies free. When we cut the umbilical cord, the ritual of "taking away" commences. Nurses grab our babies to suction their noses and stick their heels with needles. Siblings, grandparents, and friends demand, "Give me that baby," and we hesitantly hoist our sons and daughters into somebody else's arms.

When I carved out little nurseries around the UW Oshkosh campus to minimize the exorbitant cost of day care, did I also do so for vigilance? I remodeled my office in the name of "home," outfitting the corner between my desk and loveseat with a baby swing for Fern, my constant companion, then later Francis. We were not a wheelchair-friendly institution, I learned, as I pushed babies in strollers to meetings. The first time I applied for a grant from the Office of Grants and Faculty Development at Oshkosh, an anonymous reviewer scored my proposal low because I had admitted, in writing, I'd use the funds for childcare. To speak of motherhood was "distracting," this reviewer wrote. But how else would I write, without babysitting provisions and a quiet room of my own?

Begrudgingly I learned, from seasoned colleagues, I'd need to replace the key word *childcare* with a more scholarly-sounding activity like *travel*. A few of my students practiced institutional mimicry, likewise offended by the permeable borders between my domestic and professional lives. A graduate student in Women Writers once called out, "You're an enabler," when I admitted struggling to walk away from my crying child. I publicly laughed it off; she was not a mother and planned to remain forever "child-free." One of my workplace survival tactics was to design courses on family and motherhood, but still, my smuggest colleagues never failed to belittle me. When I finally got Picture Books for Children, a theoretical and practical approach to writing and illus-trating for ages birth to eight, off the ground, people said, "Oh, how sweet," as if I were teaching a course on doodling. What else would they expect from me? Memoir, one colleague said, was just bad reality TV. When I worked up the nerve to admit I was writ-ing one, the spouse of another said, "What are you going to write about—changing diapers?" Then there was this one: "You're like Mary Poppins," a female colleague said. Was this a compliment or an insult? I was not sure, though certainly Mary Poppins had not chased her brother with butcher knives or set out on a baby bender to cope with her depression.

Despite these frictions, I was grateful to be perceived as a good mother figure at times. Students living on campus, apart from their own families, projected kinship on me, tending to me as they might have tended to their own mothers. They'd bring me cookies, smoothies, sandwiches, warm mittens sewn and quilted by their grandmothers, socks they knitted while studying for exams, felt-tip pens for marking papers when mine ran faint, origami boxes, greeting cards, spring flowers, pages ripped from coloring books, and ambitious revisions. They'd swim upstream just to get here, then stay awhile, rescuing me. One whispered in my ear during class, "You're bleeding through your pants," when I'd begun to menstruate while teaching. Others alerted me to my crookedly buttoned shirts, my static cling, and my exposed bra straps. Once, a male student beckoned me close, then straightened the collar on my dress, as if readying for the family photograph, I the matriarch of the entire class.

Lucy Vasquez was only one of several mothers charged with variations on kidnapping. Another such woman was Agnes Jacobson, who arrived at the Winnebago County Jail to retrieve her son, Wyatt, for a half-day getaway and ended up in far more trouble than she anticipated. She entered the building like a mother authorizing release from school detention. She was slightly ashamed, apologetic, anxious, and clearly oblivious to the stakes. Ryan had helped to secure a five-hour furlough for Wyatt Jacobson, only nineteen years old, in order that Agnes could drive him to a cardiology appointment at the hospital in Neenah. His heroin addiction had ravaged his heart tissue and valves. Even when he was clean, his poorly functioning organs troubled his everyday life.

This was, no doubt, a nearsighted experience for Agnes. When you've been given a five-hour reprieve with your son, it's probably a lot like being granted five hours left to live. Make the most of it, she probably thought, and in doing so, she floated inside a scintillating bubble she was afraid might pop. Wyatt Jacobson was precisely the kind of impulsive, thrill-seeking, blue-eyed boy to be spirited away without warning. Agnes believed this field trip was intended exclusively as a medical precaution, but the cops, at the mercy of the judge's orders to allow the furlough, were concerned the furlough might double as a drug run. Intent to crack down on drug smuggling to inmates, they decided to invest in spying on the Jacobsons.

Agnes and Wyatt emerged from the parking lot without ever bothering to read the rules for chaperoning an inmate, and therefore, right away, she violated those unread rules. Instead of driving Wyatt straight to his appointment, she zipped through the McDonald's drive-thru and parked just beyond the pickup window to let Wyatt eat his triple order of bacon-egg-and-cheese biscuits, its own kind of Happy Meal for adult children.

At Theda Clark Medical Center, in the waiting room, Agnes allowed Wyatt to use her cell phone to send text messages. He barely talked to his mother, but he was active. His finger pads tapping the screen appeared to energize him. He was a young adult connecting with friends. When they left the cardiology appointment, Agnes should have known she was instructed to bring her son straight back to the jail, but two hours remained on the furlough time clock. Like a mother assigned joint custody in a divorce proceeding, she intended to keep her son until 2:59 PM. She drove him the long way to their house on the outskirts of Winnebago County, where she parked in the driveway and shepherded him inside.

When mother and son reemerged, Wyatt had changed his clothing, as if freshening up, and instead of turning, finally, in the direction of the Winnebago County Jail, Agnes drove toward Waupaca County. Agnes and Wyatt's father were planning to purchase a lot and build a home there. She was taking Wyatt to see the plot of land where he might get clean—new house, clean slate. It never occurred to Agnes that the subdivision was across the county line. As soon as Agnes accelerated into Waupaca County, two unmarked squad cars synchronized their strobes, their red lights pale in the afternoon sun. The furlough instructions stipulated that Wyatt was not allowed, under any circumstances, to leave the jurisdiction of Winnebago County.

"It's amazing what becomes of an afternoon joyride," Ryan said.

A failure to comply with the terms of his bond gave the officers the right to cuff Wyatt as soon as he emerged from his mom's vehicle. Having planned this surveillance operation days in advance, officers were equipped with a search warrant, and their K-9 unit was on call, prepared to forage Agnes's car for contraband. Neither Agnes nor Wyatt had any inkling they were being trailed since leaving the Winnebago County Jail. The officers began to interrogate Agnes, irritated that she was oblivious.

"Ma'am, at any point did you allow Wyatt to use your cell phone?" one of the officers asked.

"No, sir."

"Don't you recognize me from the waiting room at Theda Clark?" he said to Agnes, as if she were playing dumb. "We observed Wyatt using your cell phone in the waiting room."

"Well, yes," she said. "He contacted a few of his friends. That was all."

Perhaps most incriminating in the minds of law enforcement was Agnes and Wyatt's fifteen-minute layover at home, sufficient time for Wyatt either to use heroin, to hide drugs (enough for himself and a few jailbirds) in a body cavity, or both. Or was it possible that Agnes Jacobson actually intended to drive into Waupaca County and then right on through to Marathon County, toward Lake Superior and Canada? What wouldn't a mother do for her only son?

When officers took Wyatt into custody well before 2:59 PM, they likewise headed away from the Winnebago County Jail. With a second warrant in hand to search Wyatt Jacobson's body cavities, they drove him to Aurora Medical Center, where they intended to learn for certain, using a CT scan, whether Wyatt was more than just an addict. He might also be a drug mule with plans to pass a balloon of heroin he'd swallowed, and Agnes Jacobson, the young man's mother, might be his accomplice.

Irie was once entered as "deceased" in her pediatrician's database. At her first checkup, three days postpartum, a receptionist stared into our bassinet, trying to reconcile pink vernix-caked ears with the dead baby listed on her computer screen. "What a strange clerical error," she said, mesmerized more by our baby than a woman accustomed to newborns should be. "I'm really sorry," she said. We laughed but secretly prayed against omens, prophecies, and the sloppy typist we'd never met.

"Does it hurt right here?" my midwife had asked when I was new to pregnancy, unaware implantation ached. A metal button seemed stitched too tight against my innards. Everything inside my abdomen felt tender and inflamed. In later pregnancies, I'd feel exactly the same button pinching my uterus, and I'd remember Irie like trial by fire.

"I'm thinking this could be an ectopic pregnancy," my midwife said.

Ryan and I called my mom in Oshkosh and asked her to meet us at the hospital. The midwifery clinic was not equipped with a sonogram machine, so we drove across town and waited for our first ultrasound. I imagined this misguided egg bursting inside me like a baby chick born into a fun house maze with no exit. My mom consoled me on the phone, reminding me of her own miscarriage, which had compelled my parents to conceive me, the second child they still wanted to make the family complete.

But at long last, when the radiologist called us into the blinking, cavernous room, and the technician slathered my still-flat tummy with goo, the grouchy ob-gyn on call said, "That baby looks just fine." She'd been up all day and night. Everything about her was dry—her skin, her humor, and her voice—but inside of me, my baby was apparently moist and healthy and sewn posteriorly into the back wall of my uterus.

"Where's the baby?" I asked. "I don't see it."

"That little bean right there," the technician said. Irie was smaller than the tip of my pinky finger. In just one afternoon, I imagined my first baby dead and then alive. I felt lucky and greedy all at once. Lost and found was a metaphor for life.

The first time Leo died before my eyes, he was two months old. I dropped him on a sidewalk in downtown Milwaukee as I exited a restaurant, the first consequential faltering of my lifetime. Clutching him against my chest, I missed a step on a public sidewalk and fell. Leo's head cracked against the concrete like a ball dropped against the sweet spot of a maple bat, a telltale sound effect for the crowd of patrons dining alfresco. Instead of applause, they responded with silence against my instantaneous begging.

"Somebody help me," I said. My pleas sounded inside my head like child's play, as if real cries can echo something pretend. "Somebody, find my husband." He'd gone into another nearby restaurant ahead of me.

I bent against the grainy slab of pavement. The rough texture matched a small bruise forming on the back of Leo's head. I pulled him into the apron of my skirt, my thighs now bare, the seams of my underpants the only stitches holding me together. An old man with goggles for glasses stood up from a table and limped toward me. "God takes care of the little ones," he said. He cupped Leo's head with his palms, leathery and wide like baseball mitts. Another stranger called an ambulance. I pulled down my shirt and released my breast from the buoy of my bra, an offering to the baby I thought might die. His wet lips parted, and his gums palpated my knot of flesh, his crying muffled by the warm linen of my bosom. By the time paramedics arrived, Leo had breastfed himself back to life. Later at the Brewers game, the sound of bat-to-ball contact reverberated throughout the stadium as I held my baby swaddled in the miraculousness of resurrection.

Later when Leo was two years old, he disappeared at a local school playground. Irelyn was under the supervision of employees from the Oshkosh Recreation Department, and Fern was asleep in my arms. She was the new baby now. A ten-year-old boy led Leo up through the tunnel slides and safely down ladders. He rolled a ball to Leo, and Leo kicked the ball back, his green LITTLE HOO-LIGANS T-shirt to his knees. Under and over the balance beams, and through the open gaps between logs—smoothed, stained, and bolted to the earth—the boys scampered.

I began chatting with a fellow mother about nothing—sixty seconds of banter—and when I looked back, Leo was gone. I retraced the boys' scurrying, then called "Leo" on repeat, growing louder and more panicked, a crescendo toward real fright. "Leo!" I ran toward the school to scream at Irelyn. Fern, the youngest, was a nine-pound bundle of warmth and indifference against the slack of my midsection.

"Help me," I said to the mother I had just met, begging and reprimanding, a tone reserved for immediate family. I broke in every direction like a bird whose clipped wings prevent it from taking flight. A knife split my body wide as I searched, and already I could see the scar forming, vitality ripped from inside me, though I'd be expected to keep living.

My spirit was a coin in his left shoe, tucked away for good luck, its fortune turned against him, like the time he picked up a penny on the driveway and slipped it into the back of his mouth, where it lodged for a minute before he coughed up strings of mucous followed by the money, which shot like a copper stone from the sling of his throat against greater evil.

This time he would be ushered back by a custodian mowing the school lawn with a tractor the size of a harvesting combine.

"This guy yours?" he asked.

Leo's semisweet eyes and whipped-cream skin made me want to eat him with the kind of voraciousness reserved for true relief. He was somehow cut from dual advertisements for fancy cakes, and snakes, snails, and puppy-dog tails.

"You could have been kidnapped," I cried. My heart rate would not recalibrate until Leo was safely in bed hours later. Studying a child as he sleeps can be tranquil but ominous. My childhood friend's mother forbade her from sleeping on her back, hands clasped across her chest. "It looks like you're dead!" she'd admonish. Indeed, beds are shallow graves, and certainly every mother has studied her baby's chest in the night: *Is it rising, and is it falling?*

When Francis was born two years later, my friend Angie referred to him as "Leo's backup," funny for its various meanings. We could imagine Franco as a backup singer or dancer. Irie was given the gift of voice and Franco the gift of rhythm. Franco was Leo's understudy, and true to definition, he learned to play many roles by watching Leo—brother, son, and wiseacre. Frank was and still is a performer, his big brother's stunt double and mimic, his thespian's eyebrow peaked in the shape of constant, enthusiastic expression.

But of course, when Angie referred to Frank as Leo's backup, she really meant that he could replace Leo if anything bad happened. When Leo was afraid of being ejected from the Zippin Pippin roller coaster at Bay Beach, she said, "Don't worry. Mom's got backup." She said the same thing if Leo hit his head or took a spill. Frank could take his place as the firstborn son; no big deal. Deep down, I would actually think in these provocatively old-fashioned terms, as if I were matriarch of a family farm and relied on child labor to sustain our existence.

As I listened over the years to fellow mothers in academia, I realized I was potentially less evolved than they were. If I wasn't a throwback to midcentury rural America, then I operated like lesser mammals, maybe a fox, but more likely a rabbit or mole. To legitimize my investment, so as not to waste a full breeding season, I craved a cumulatively large litter of human babies. A larger brood increased the chances of their partial survival. This explains why birds and fish lay so many eggs; they are optimizing their chances that a portion of their eggs will hatch, even if the remaining portion is slurped up by some carnivorous beast.

Even lower in the animal kingdom are ants and bees, making millions of potential babies in one lay. Maybe Fern and Francis really were backups, and if so, my protective animal instinct refused to shut down or shut up. I intuitively felt I could better protect my babies if I kept on making more. Power in numbers was my strategy for self-preservation, a shield against all manner of abduction.

When Lucy Vasquez was charged with kidnapping—or in legal parlance, interference with custody beyond visitation, in the state of Wisconsin a Class F felony—she had a good explanation. According to Lucy, her husband, Remy, was an abusive father. Once he choked Callum, who was strapped into his car seat, until the baby's lips turned blue. Another time, he taught Callum to grab a man's balls in self-defense, but when Callum grabbed Remy's family jewels in the midst of a father-son wrestling match, Remy slapped him across the head. And when Lucy found porn on her husband's cell phone, Remy blamed his two-year-old son for hacking into his account.

Lucy and Remy had met and married a few years earlier in California, where Remy, a Wisconsin native, was serving in the US Marine Corps, but upon his discharge he convinced her to move with him to Wisconsin, under the guise of landing a plum job. When Lucy, Remy, and Callum arrived here, the employment opportunity turned out not to be lucrative, at which point Remy declared he would collect unemployment benefits for a year and catch up with old friends instead. This was the first of many red flags. As Ryan put it, "Lucy had buyer's remorse." She wondered how to be reimbursed for this bad mistake of marrying an ill-equipped father.

The worst of her co-parenting experiences happened not long before she left for California. When Lucy returned home from work one day to find Remy asleep on the sofa, she nearly gagged on her own galloping heart. Why wasn't he watching Callum, or better yet, where was Callum? The wide-open refrigerator glowed, a fluorescent rectangle in the kitchen, like an exit to another territory. Mayonnaise and jelly jars had been tipped from the shelves; a loaf of bread without a twist tie had been shaken loose into a mound on the linoleum. Velveeta slices had been crumpled into cheese-and-cellophane balls.

"Callum," she called. "Come out wherever you are!"

She followed Mickey Mouse boxcars and Hot Wheels into Callum's bedroom, only to find he'd yanked the mini blinds from the window and bent the slats. A bottle of nail polish remover was empty next to a wet spot of ethyl acetate. This was not a cheerful game of hide-and-seek. Callum was not in his closet. He was not hiding in his dirty laundry pile or behind the shower curtain in the bathroom.

"Remy!" Lucy screamed at her husband. "Wake up, God dammit! Callum is missing!"

"No he's not," Remy said. "He's not fucking gone."

"He's not inside," she hissed.

She ran out into the communal play yard at their apartment complex and began screaming demands at six-year-olds kicking a ball. Had they seen Callum? Were they playing with him earlier? They stared at Lucy blankly, baffled by her hysterics, and when a squad car pulled into the parking lot, Lucy was just as confused because she intended to call 911 but hadn't yet. The officer parked in front of the maintenance office, and Lucy immediately chased after him, crying now and muttering her son's name. Remy never bothered to join in the search, arguing the little shit was probably hiding out behind the trash heap or something.

When Lucy entered the maintenance office, she barely recognized the boy sitting on the desk in just his diaper. It was like a scene from a movie—barrel-chested little boy flexes his muscles and giggles for the audience. Lucy's tongue had gone numb; she could hardly pronounce his name. "He was found about a half mile from here, just wandering on the side of the road," the maintenance guy said. "We didn't know whose kid he was."

"My husband was supposed to be watching him," she whimpered.

Callum hugged his mother, heaving his bare chest against her lips. She kissed his belly button, and he squealed with delight. His diaper was soiled and beginning to shred but he was otherwise unscathed. The police officer ended up talking sternly to Remy, who was assigned to write and sign a statement of events for the police department, but the incident was never referred to the district attorney's office.

Another time, against Lucy's demands, Remy planned to take Callum fishing. "I'll just leave him to sleep in the truck while I fish," Remy said.

"You can't just leave him on the side of the road!" Lucy shrieked.

"Watch me!" he shouted, then loaded Callum into his vehicle and sped off for an entire day, unreachable by phone.

"He could have been kidnapped," Lucy said to Remy over and over in the wake of these scares, no doubt imagining the worst of America's notorious abduction cases, as her husband slouched on the sofa, the click-toggle of the video game controller his only response. Maybe kidnapping became such a concrete reality in Lucy's mind that she began to fantasize about absconding with her own child. She couldn't be arrested for that, could she? And couldn't she improve the circumstances of their lives if she were to leave behind Remy and all of his inadequacies—his short fuse, his vulgarity, and his laziness?

Lucy's favorite ritual in Wisconsin was hunting season, when Remy would disappear into his Northwoods deer stand for a full week. During Lucy's first year as "a deer hunter's widow," our local way of describing women temporarily abandoned by their sportsman husbands, she had invited her family to Wisconsin, but this second time around, she planned to visit them in sunny California, with Remy thousands of miles away, not just a hundred, and Callum right by her side. Lucy Vasquez's homeland was calling her name.

On the plane trip to California, she held Callum in her lap, and together they peered out the window at mountains and cerulean skies. Once she was back in California, in the safety of her childhood home, she began to confide in her mother about fears of remaining trapped in Wisconsin, subjected to Remy's bullying. After a week of mother-daughter conversations, Lucy decided the only solution was to file for divorce immediately, in California, documenting for the courts in an affidavit all of her reasons. The final step in formalizing the divorce was to serve Remy divorce papers, though she didn't anticipate Remy's reaction, which was to file for divorce in Wisconsin and ultimately to report Callum abducted. The battle of homelands began, Remy already imagining that he'd have the upper hand again, once Lucy was behind bars.

Parenting was rife with inconsistencies. I was protective but permissive, vigilant but lax. Sometimes I wondered if oxytocin had over-tranquilized my brain. All doped up, I'd react to crisis in a daze like a kid on weed. On one occasion, Irie was chasing Leo around the backyard. The kitchen window did not afford me a view. Ryan was loading up the car for the Experimental Aircraft Association fireworks display, much to his annoyance, when a yowl, followed by a short whistle, exploded in the backyard.

Leo cried out, "Help!" From my blind spot in the kitchen, I stood still, huffing the hot air, calm to the point of fecklessness. Many seconds passed as he called out again. The other children chimed in: "Oh my God, oh my God!" As if playing a child's game of Statue, numb to his calling, I did not rush to his rescue as a mother should. Instead, I waited for Ryan's voice, deep and reassuring. After four babies and nearly a decade of hormonal overload, I was useless.

"Laura," Ryan called out. "I need to take Leo to the emergency room."

I edged around the corner toward the back door, squinting, as if trying to spot some faraway bird. Leo's knee looked like it had taken the sharp end of an axe. A wide gash cut to the bone. Apparently in running from Irie, he had tripped on a shepherd's hook and launched into the tree stump near the sandbox. Who knew the remains of our maple tree were so dangerous?

Ryan carried Leo to the van, loaded him like delicate freight, and left me flanked by my remaining children, who would make Leo get-well cards and insist on buying him chocolate before we met him for the fireworks, an event to which he'd arrive with eight stitches right where his knee was supposed to bend. Two years later Frank would fall face-first into our front door. When our babysitter, Gabby, called us at our favorite restaurant, Ryan looked at me and said into the phone, "I'm sure he's fine."

We both remained calm, but maybe too calm. Gabby consulted our neighbor Betty, who worked for years in pediatrics, then called us again, insisting this might require stitches. Sure enough, our little Frankenstein was slashed deep on his forehead, right between his eyebrows.

On another occasion, Ryan and I squabbled over taking the children to an event sponsored by the Fox Valley Herp Club. Snakes made him uneasy, but in my characteristic fashion, I encouraged him to live a little. "This is the kind of thing I do in the summer while you're busy working," I said. "The kids love it."

And at first, they did. The red-eared slider turtles and painter turtles were fun to examine, but most impressive were the ball pythons of varying colors and sizes, from babies to big mamas. Volunteers permitted the children to wear the constrictors around their necks or to brandish them as bracelets. On several instances, Ryan excused himself from the room, feeling nervous.

"They're typically pretty docile," one of the Herp Club members told us.

"See," I told Ryan. "Everyone is doing it."

And then, after nearly an hour of parading around with snakes as jewelry, Fern walked toward me, caramel skin gone white. "This one bit me," she said.

"What do you mean?" I asked. "Are you sure?" Fern began to weep, and looked faint. A volunteer grappled the python from Fern's cradle hold, and stuffed her into a potato sack "to calm her down."

"Maybe she's getting ready to lay her eggs," one of the other snake experts said before she rushed into the nature center lobby to collect first-aid provisions.

Little pinpricks of blood on Fern's forearm showed where the snake had punctured our daughter's skin. Although the snake was not venomous, scabs from Fern's snakebite lasted a week. We kept the wound sterilized, but a bandage was not necessary. As we walked to the van in the July heat, Fern's entire body blanched to the bone, I realized that Ryan's professional life had helped to fine-tune his intuition. On the other hand, I'd not felt the rush of adrenaline in a dangerously long time.

Lucy Vasquez and Agnes Jacobson felt longing I hate to imagine, both separated from their sons by police intervention, forced to look at their sons through plate glass. Was Wyatt's image, ever so slightly, refracted or bent, as police chauffeured him away, back into the breadbasket of Winnebago County? Did he lift his hand against the light and wave to his mother? The only photograph of Wyatt Jacobson in his ever-expanding case file was a disembodied image of his forearms, palms up, junkie scar tissue fastened to his skin like pink metal clasps.

Aurora Medical Center was Jacobson's second hospital of the day, fair excitement for a guy otherwise stuck awaiting sentencing in the Winnebago County Jail. He'd been struggling with heroin addiction for several years now, and every crime he'd committed was a quick fix. He was originally charged with theft of movable property. He seemed always to know somebody with guns, be it a .22 caliber handgun or a Winchester .30-30 rifle. He smuggled these from a friend's home and pawned them for dope.

Derek Green never needed a middleman. If he stole tornado rolls, he ate them. If he stole Gerber Onesies, he was attempting to clothe his daughter. But Wyatt Jacobson stole only the kinds of possessions for which pawnshops would pay. While on probation for the first felony, he racked up pawn tickets the length of his forearms: more guns—a Remington Arms rifle, an AK-47 rifle, and a Taurus .357 stainless steel revolver pistol; a pressure washer; a RotoZip Rebel spiral saw; a Showtime rotisserie; Ray-Ban sunglasses; and his mother's jewelry, including her rings and a gold cross necklace.

If he was stealing from his own mother, why didn't she confront him or report him to police? Maybe she was waiting patiently for her son to clean up. In the end, a friend's sister was the whistleblower. She discovered that her brother and Wyatt were stealing her blank checks, forging them, and cashing them at a local bank in amounts of $120 or $150. With police guidance, she agreed to a traffic stop in a designated location while her brother sat shotgun. They led police to Jacobson, who consented to be searched. His addiction was little secret to anybody, it seems. He stored a tourniquet, alcohol prep pads, and a syringe in his front jeans pocket. Police cuffed him and carried him away, each arrest like déjà vu. Not only was his probation revoked, but Jacobson also tallied three party to the crime of forgery and possession of drug paraphernalia charges. From jail, he began writing letters to friends, begging them to smuggle smack to visitation hour. His mail could be opened and read at any time, and his letters gave credence to investigators' suspicions that he might try to smuggle heroin himself.

When technicians in Radiology laid him on the gurney, maybe they hoped they'd find the balloon-tied finger of a latex glove or a condom-wrapped baggie of smack. They studied his stomach and intestines for anomalous white shapes, but they were disappointed to report that Wyatt Jacobson was clean. Maybe they were relieved. But good news for Wyatt was bad news for the cops. Their suspicions were unfounded, their surveillance wasted.

In the following months, Ryan negotiated with the district attorney, explaining Agnes's good intentions, and neither Agnes nor Wyatt was charged with bail jumping. In totality, though, Jacobson was sentenced to twenty-four months in prison, and Ryan assured Agnes that Wyatt could get out early if he completed his treatment plan while incarcerated.

In the case of Lucy Vasquez, the state of California refused to extradite her, a judge stating he was shocked and disappointed in Wisconsin's actions, given court orders in California, and considering that Lucy made a good-faith effort to follow those California orders awarding her custody of Callum. She was released from custody, but in turn, the judge ordered her to return with Callum "of her own recognizance" to resolve these matters on Remy's home turf.

When Lucy's family had retained Ryan, he wrote a letter to the district attorney in Green Bay asking for dismissal of criminal charges against her, documenting the fact that Lucy filed for divorce in California, that Remy was served, and he never appeared. Even though that order was overruled by Wisconsin, Lucy had relied on it to guide her actions.

"This is a civil matter now. Ms. Vasquez has retained my office to sort it out in family court, which is the proper venue here."

Ryan's request was granted, and therein began the epic battle of territories, the Land of Milk and Honey versus the Cheese State, each volleying for jurisdiction in Callum's fate. From time to time, Ryan would joke that this case required "real lawyering"—in other words, that he couldn't rely on his quick wit and storytelling to "save a client's ass," usually the only gadgets in his toolbox when his clients looked guilty as charged.

"Things aren't looking so hot for my California kidnapping case," he told me. I knew his casework by crime, label, or nickname.

"What's the problem?"

"Well, by my legal research, it looks like Wisconsin will win on jurisdiction. She will definitely lose the home-court advantage."

Ryan was ultimately proven correct. Despite his recommendation that the California divorce and custody order remain in effect permanently, Green Bay was the final site for resolution. Mysteriously, though Lucy had fled with Callum to California to keep him safe from Remy, when the guardian ad litem, appointed by the judge to represent Callum's best interests, recommended fifty-fifty custody—that is, equal parenting rights and privileges for Lucy and Remy, so long as Lucy stayed in Wisconsin—Lucy opted for California instead. She eventually left Callum behind to be raised primarily by the very father she'd accused of recklessness and abuse.

"What?" I asked Ryan. Why on earth would Lucy Vasquez travel such an enormous distance, risking criminal charges, if she would give up the fight for her son's well-being? Wouldn't she want to remain close to oversee his safety? Was it possible that, like other mothers we'd met through Ryan's work in criminal defense, she had exaggerated the fear factor, or more disheartening yet, had thrown in the towel, exhausted by her fruitless attempt to fight the system?

One day, right after Fern was born, I forgot eggs on the stovetop, left home, and almost torched our Hazel Street house. When Ryan arrived home from work, smoke hung from the ceiling like black petticoats. He grabbed the plastic handle of our stockpot with an oven mitt, ran it outside, and sprayed it with the hose. What remained of the eggs looked like shriveled black testicles, and he stared into the pot for a moment before remembering our dog, Mr. Owen, not yet deceased. Ryan called out several times before the curly black beast tumbled like a charred effigy from upstairs. He had been hiding in our closet and had survived.

"What the hell were you thinking?" Ryan screamed when we arrived home from the YMCA. "There could be twenty thousand dollars worth of smoke damage inside. The furniture, the curtains, the clothes—it's probably all garbage. We might as well haul it out to the curb." He vomited on the driveway, orange strings like the hems of his organs unraveling. We spent the night at my dad and stepmom's, and I remember privately wishing the house had burst entirely into flames. Arson sometimes seemed like a possible solution to the escalating problem of our small old house. Slash and burn, I thought, and then move on. But the relative humidity over the next few days was low. We left our windows open and boiled vinegar on the stove until the stench of burned eggs faded into the broom pantry.

As for Lucy Vasquez, she crashed, burned, and moved back to California. For the duration of all upcoming school years, according to court orders, Callum would live in Wisconsin with Remy and his girlfriend, a new mother figure in the boy's life. Callum would see Lucy for major holidays and summer vacations, and at the final hearing, Lucy earned Mother's Day weekends with her son, in Wisconsin or California, her choice, every year going forward. I began to realize that maybe Lucy needed her own mother, still a pretty young woman herself, more than she needed the responsibility of raising the next generation.

Some days Ryan could not switch out of his lawyering mode. Even on dates, when we'd sucker a babysitter into supervising our four kids, he'd itemize his thought processes, presenting them to me as if I were the judge or jury. One early summer night at Koreana, as we waited for the chef to roll our sushi, he circumstantiated all the reasons we'd reached our limit with four children, and for the first time ever, beleaguered by the anxieties of motherhood, fearful of bad news, loss, or spiriting away, I was willing to hear him out.

He might as well have begun with "Your Honor," or "Ladies and gentlemen of the jury," laying out his focused and convincing argument *In re the Family of Ryan Ulrich and Laura Jean Baker*, advocating for "enough already." He repeated all the evidence of our case, a bulleted list for me to consider, as our fate remained in my hands. "Just think about it. We've already achieved the full experience of both sexes, a family with gender equality—two girls, two boys. What more do we want?" We might even be able to afford a more spacious house one day. At this point, piano lessons and sports team fees wiped our bank account clean, resulting often in overdraft fees, but we could dream more freely and realistically if we stopped at four children. True, occasionally we were saved by an impromptu visit to Cash in a Flash, where scratch awaited us, having been sent Western Union from some client's crony eager to settle his street debt by contributing to the legal fees—someone who needed to be on good terms when Ryan's client was finally released—but was that the kind of stability on which we wanted to hang our family's future?

"Our little house is overflowing with noise, people, and those people's junk. Let's not be those parents who just keep kicking the can down the road. Honey, Your Honor, we aren't getting any younger."

We were sitting beside a half wall in the middle of the restaurant. Ryan was looking at me and beyond me, through the window onto Wisconsin Avenue, and beyond that into a forthcoming decade. I ordered a martini and drank it faster than normal. We may have even toasted to our future before eating sushi faster than advisable, the wasabi burn a much needed palate cleanser. Maybe Ryan was right. Maybe four babies were plenty.

CHAPTER 8

Sawdust Days

When Rob McNally, our junkie magician incarnate, finally resurfaced in our lives, he seemed more like a genie than ever, even if methamphetamine was the opposite of magic. Out of curiosity—cursed as I was with intense desires to possess knowledge, otherwise just plain nosy—I studied and cross-referenced online instructions for "how to make crystal methamphetamine" as if researching recipes for scones, and I wondered if "chemist" were just as fitting for McNally as labels like "drug user," "career criminal," or, as he called himself in a message to his parole officer, "street scum."

I'd not been in the mind frame of reading instructions for a science lab since high school. From what I gathered, patience and precision were just as necessary as other required supplies like measuring spoons, scissors, rubber hoses, empty soda bottles, Energizer batteries, rubber gloves, books of matches, coffee filters, engine starter fluid, Sudafed, distilled water, a big old tarp, and a little bit of lye.

McNally's meth method was "shake and bake." He fashioned a lab at his latest girlfriend's house where he went to work unrolling guts of batteries in order to extract lithium strips, agitating bottles with solvents until the cloudy parts dropped out, and using a hair dryer to harden white smoke into crystals, all the while using a replica of the air-filtration systems he once sold over the phone, his only arguably legitimate day job.

Of course, back when Ryan first knew McNally, the guy was proud to have stopped drinking alcohol. "I picked up a pretty bad heroin habit, though," he said, laughing in a wry and lugubrious way. This time around was no different. He admitted to Ryan, equal parts sardonic and sad, that he'd devolved from heroin to meth, the most toxic drug around. And McNally wasn't just using meth. He was manufacturing the dope, running it to places like Illinois and Indiana, true entrepreneurship. "Addict" was a label he owned, free and clear, and making his own drugs proved, at the very least, he was a self-made and self-sustained American. Pull yourself up by your bootstraps, son, and make your own meth.

If you were to have passed McNally on the street by this time in his life, you'd look twice, even if your gut instinct was to look away. His face was tattooed now with permanent sideburns of ink. Very little of his Matthew McConaughey good looks remained. He seemed more pathetic, less human, self-destruction having fully diluted his charm. Doctors say meth addicts pick at their faces because they feel bugs crawling and scuttling beneath the surface of the skin. Did McNally imagine fleas or cockroaches under his former glow? He also smiled now with rotting teeth. Meth mouth was such a blatant reality that Ryan nicknamed the worst of his meth addicts by the condition itself, as in, "Meth Mouth wants to give me money to help her boyfriend, Low-Level Con Man."

When Ryan's clients nicknamed themselves with monikers like Crash and Face, he shot back, in echo effect, with his own designators, such that I often knew them only by their crimes or physical attributes. There was The Troll, The Pathological Liar, The Wheelchair Pervert, and Pothead Betty Crocker. Nicknames were symbols of their hard living.

Meth Mouth and McNally might explain why Ryan got disproportionately angry about our kids' toothbrushing habits and dental bills, especially after Francis required surgery for his putrid and rotting baby set. The longer Ryan worked in criminal defense, the more he pinpointed differences between us and his clients. They let their teeth rot; we would not anymore. Teeth grinding, cotton mouth, a general disregard for hygiene—these are just the visible symptoms of meth use. Never mind what it does to the brain.

But no matter how much McNally had begun to resemble the kind of scourge from whom parents avert their children's eyes, Ryan continued taking him back like a wayward brother. Police were always taking McNally back too, even in other counties, where any pretext to pull over a dude with face tats was sure to prove justified. Was he traveling over the speed limit? A taillight burned out? Registration expired? Any excuse would work with a guy like McNally behind the wheel, and ditto for probable cause. McNally himself might as well have tattooed CONFIRM YOUR SUSPICION OF CONTRABAND on his forehead before hitting the highway between Oshkosh and Milwaukee, his girl, Shelby Drake, riding shotgun. One glimpse of McNally through the windshield led to a routine traffic stop, then a search of his car, the cop discovering, without much effort, 120 ephedrine pills crammed into an empty hard pack of cigarettes. Upon further searching, he also found a drug he believed to be meth, later confirmed at the state crime lab.

Drake, still married to a different convict, who was incarcerated for homicide by intoxicated use of a vehicle, must have felt eager to see McNally back behind bars too—a quick and easy way to dispose of a lover, I suppose. When police escorted Drake to the nearest station, she consented willingly to a two-hour interview with police, laying out details of McNally's meth lab in the garage of her Oshkosh home, where she lived with her father and seven-year-old daughter. When police obtained the search warrant for Drake's home, her ailing father answered the door and welcomed them onto the premises, where evidence of methamphetamine production proliferated beneath their fingertips—empty soda bottles with eyeholes punched out for tubing, empty Sudafed and cold-relief packages, fuel, fire starter, charred remains on burnt spoons, and the innards from batteries splashed against the backdrop of card tables like the intestines of fish.

In each photo taken as evidence, accoutrements of a young girl's life made cameo appearances—a booster seat, a pin-striped umbrella stroller that matched one in our own garage, and a bright pink bike that was likely the fastest and only ticket out of the girl's septic existence. Were homes evacuated, as they often were, upon discovery of meth labs, neighbors hoping for clean-up crews to finish their job before precursors required to manufacture meth erupted into a fireworks display of toxic waste, hopeful their own front porches and gardens wouldn't also burst into flames? Eventually a letter from a federal agent would be delivered to Drake's address, and it would read: "A clandestine drug laboratory was seized at this address." Nobody was home to gather and read the mail, so what difference would it make for the obvious to be noted?

Lives were in turmoil. Shelby Drake sat sixty days in jail while her daughter was taken into child protective custody. It seemed everywhere McNally went, CPS followed along behind him, picking up children as if on a bus route, the sons and daughters of women who fell for McNally, his drugs, or both. As Mama McNally's apprentice at the age of thirteen, learning to concoct meth in the bathroom of the Hells Angels clubhouse, how could he have predicted all the kids who'd fall in line behind him, a processional of his former selves? What had this little girl witnessed? Did she carry crystal meth in a medicine pouch around her neck, convinced, as my children would be, she'd found a magic rock?

They say each pound of meth makes six pounds of toxic waste. How many pounds did the special agents find at Drake's house during detox, and how many months passed before this defunct home fell into foreclosure, its owners now in separate big houses in separate counties? Ryan visited McNally at the jail. He squinted and scrunched up his nose, trying to literally read McNally's face through the glass. The digits 1488 were scrawled to match the arch of his eyebrow. Homage to white supremacy and Hitler, it was a common, if despicable, prison tattoo.

"Hey, bro," McNally said.

"What's with the face tattoo?" Ryan said.

"I know, I know," McNally told him. "It's stupid. I'm going to fix it. I promise."

"What the fuck, dude?" Ryan shook his head slowly, trying to loosen fragments of disbelief stuck inside. "You're not exactly making my job defending you any easier."

What, exactly, was his sense of obligation to Rob McNally? Watching him fry his brain, year by year, was like watching a person's body rot before it expired, yet Ryan had been summoned there by some sense of unspeakable loyalty they shared. After all, McNally was the first of his clients to make jailhouse referrals. A lot of Ryan's early business came from word-of-mouth recommendations straight from McNally, at a time when money was so tight that Ryan often muttered despairingly about blowing out his own brains.

"There's nothing I'd ever be scared to tell you," McNally wrote in a letter to Ryan from jail on one occasion. "I could not ask for more of a friend." Even so, there were always limits, and Ryan was trying to draw firmer, more boldfaced boundaries, as part of his plan to improve his own overall health.

"I can't keep you out of prison this time around," Ryan told him. "There's just no way around your record anymore."

"I get it," he said. "Yeah, man."

But did he really?

McNally convinced the judge in Washington County to lower his bond to $1,000, and then convinced another former girlfriend to post his bond. He was set free for a full week before charges were filed in Winnebago County against McNally for knowingly possessing methamphetamine precursors and waste. Inside this small window of time, our favorite lowlife performed another one of his magic tricks. He went up in a cloud of smoke, disappearing entirely from the face of the map. Just like Lucy Vasquez, and so many other clients Ryan represented, Rob McNally was on the lam.

This happened in September, and after that, he didn't even contact Ryan, at least not until New Year's Day, when he called from an anonymous number. "I'm down South, working the carnival again," he said. "Got myself a new name. It's Robin Marks. As in 'robbing' the easy 'marks,' playing the carnival goers till they're broke." A buddy fixed him up with a fake ID complete with a criminal record to match all his prison tattoos. But nothing too serious, just a few battery convictions—you know, beating the shit out of a few guys, no big deal.

I could see in Ryan's face that McNally was on the line, and I could hear his voice as if he were right across the street at our Menominee Park against the blinking lights and stench of fried cheese curds.

"We'll set you right up here. Come on now, don't be a cheap date. Go for the big prizes. Get yourself a jumbo. Take home a teddy bear, come on now!"

When Sawdust Days, an annual Fourth of July festival featuring a flea market, historic village, music stages, and a carnival, descended upon Oshkosh, we increased our vigilance, locked our back doors, and refrained from playground visits. Our least favorite side effect of living on Hazel Street was Sawdust Days. On a daily basis otherwise, Ryan's life in criminal defense tainted his attitude toward our neighborhood, but Independence Day festivities amplified his angst epidemically. Thousands of people, including the carneys, penetrated our facade of a safe haven, drinking, smoking, and fighting on our sidewalks until we called the police or closed the windows and fell asleep. We awoke to firecracker and cigarette butts in our gardens, air smoldering inside empty Faygo bottles on the terraces. In the historic village, Civil War reenactors blasted a cannon every hour or so, starting after breakfast. "Drummer Hoff," we joked, "fires it off," quoting from the children's book by Barbara and Ed Emberley.

"We're not taking the kids over there," Ryan warned. "My clients are working the rides." During his first full summer in criminal defense, while waiting in line for the Ferris wheel, as Irie and Leo flushed with claustrophobic heat, Ryan noticed a sheet of paper adhered with packing tape to a rickety fence post holding up the queue. The name of one of his clients—Willie Gago—appeared in bold print above a black-and-white xerox of his face. Somebody had written "RIP" in smaller print beneath.

Less than a year earlier, Willie Gago and his wife, Lucia, had frequented Ryan's office, after Lucia drank too much and stabbed Willie at a park with a small knife on her keychain. They both regretted the public disturbance and were still in love. Ryan essentially offered them marriage counseling for free, and now that Willie had died, Ryan wondered, where was Lucia? He was a loyal attorney but not enough he'd want to acquaint our children with the drunk and disorderly.

That same year, Ryan glimpsed half a dozen former clients either working or chilling out at Sawdust Days. A lot of them were deep in the heroin scene. In fact, each year, the list of clients born from this days-long holiday celebration expanded, to include a classic case in which an overzealous security guard roughed up an intoxicated patron. Since our teen years, we'd referred to the crown jewel of Oshkosh festivals as "Dirtball Days," a designation fully confirmed in our adult lives by Ryan's work in criminal defense.

But we did feel a patriotic duty to observe the fireworks display at Menominee Park. We would begrudgingly take turns, every other year, chaperoning our kids through a maze of sparklers, glow-in-the-dark wands, and bottle rockets to the best viewing site up the block. Only one of us was lucky enough to remain home with our youngest child, whoever that happened to be. The other gritted his or her teeth against the missile launches and slow-burning punks until the air burned to a crisp and it was time to come home.

The summer Francis turned two years old was Ryan's year to attend the fireworks. He set off on his journey with Irie, Leo, and Fern, leaving us behind in the boys' room, a smoking porch converted to a bedroom. The air conditioner rattled as I rocked little Frank. I hummed with the machine, blocking out the festival music and heat. The greenhouse effect of this summer had reduced all of us to inanimate potted plants, sweaty and swollen with no energy stored up for anything else like talking or eating. We lived on a diet of Popsicles. It was like being trapped at the equator, sick with fever and nerve damage. The real temperature that day was 93 degrees. The humidity cranked temperatures even higher to a heat index of 106, cooling to 101 at 9:00 PM, shortly before the fireworks were to commence.

Breastfeeding in summer sundresses and tank tops afforded us easy access but was sticky and warm, even more difficult during a heat wave and overstimulating as Frank gnawed on my nipples, sending little painful injections into the surface of my hot skin. We sweated together, sweet and sour, salty and sapped. Although I could have fallen asleep in the rocking chair, I knew if I could transfer Franco's body into his lower bunk, I'd finally be able to confirm or refute my latest worry.

I'd been taking my birth control pill haphazardly. Before I'd birthed children, the pill had little negative effect on me, aside from its obvious purpose of preventing conception, but since Irie was born, every prescription made me feel queasy. The synthetic hormones, as opposed to the natural ones, deadened my libido and my sense of self; I'd feel depressed and numb. I experimented with new pill-popping patterns, hoping to avoid nausea—at bedtime, in the morning, with lunch—but now I wasn't menstruating either. I wish I'd tracked how many pregnancy tests I bought between the first time Ryan and I had sex and now, at which point I was buying First Response mega boxes, just to keep the sticks on hand, like Band-Aids or tampons. My body was in a constant state of hormonal adjustment with the nonstop breastfeeding and postpartum recoveries. Although on one hand, my textbook cycles never betrayed me, on the other hand, I was continually permutating. I'd ultimately give up birth control altogether and resort to the rhythm method, natural family planning that seemed to work.

When the fireworks began, I could feel them detonating inside my rib cage. As I carried Francis to his cool sheets, he threw his arms over his head, sleeping, as babies do, to air out the soft pleats of their armpits. Our house rumbled. I imagined we were inside a nuclear fallout shelter. Half the population of Oshkosh, right outside our windows, sacrificed their lives for some short-lived but radiant pleasure.

I'd peed on so many tests, I never bothered anymore to read the directions. The urine spread through the little window quickly as if somebody had pulled the shade. Any sighted person in the world can decode two pink lines. They crawl slyly into view with perfect lineographic certainty like two styluses across an Etch A Sketch.

I was pregnant.

Worry was not the honest word, except that I was worried about Ryan's reaction. I'd knowingly been imagining another baby—a fifth load of laundry, a fifth twang of laughter. Our lovemaking was no accident either. It still felt purposeful and creative as opposed to recreational. And hadn't I been harboring baby clothes since that fight over Goodwill donations in the basement, claiming ridiculously we'd save some special baby clothes for Fern's baby dolls or our future grandchildren? Sure, he'd convinced me of his position at Koreana, and sure, I'd concurred, but no number of "Your Honors" prevented me from changing my mind.

As the last pyrotechnics rocked our house, rendering us deaf and numb, a titanium salute that resounded till morning, I stood alone in the bathroom, holding a proclamation: we were going to be parents again. I was afraid Ryan would feel betrayed, and I was already dreading the first twenty weeks—sickness and exhaustion. During every previous first trimester, I'd fallen asleep against my will by dinnertime, leaving Ryan to cook, clean, and bathe the children alone. But I also realized that taking birth control pills was just a ruse, all along. I'd opened my mouth and swallowed inconsistently, and in my heart, those little tablets were just placebos.

A cavalcade of people trudged by our house, children balancing on the short retention wall holding our garden in place, and at long last, the front door yawned. Ryan carried Fern up to bed. We marveled how children could fall asleep at concerts and basketball games and fireworks displays. Irie and Leo were itchy and hot. They footslogged upstairs without being asked twice. They closed their eyes; lights out.

"I need a quick shower," Ryan said. He was filmy with bug spray and sweat. I waited for him at the foot of our bed, knowing he'd cranked the water cold. After his shower, he walked into our bedroom, already sweating again, wrapped at his waist in a towel. Droplets of water clung to his skin like transparent little scuttle bugs.

"So, I have to tell you something," I said.

"Don't tell me you're pregnant." Maybe he was waiting for a fifth baby too, the inevitability of my need and desire like a footnote in his vehement case against it.

"Yes, I think so."

He unknotted his towel and stood there naked. Then he grabbed the towel by the corners and tightened it, as if he were going to whip or snap the bath sheet, aimed at me, but he didn't do that either. He dropped the towel and began to laugh. He walked toward the door and closed it, so that he could laugh harder.

"We're fucked," he said. He perched, though with gravitas, on the edge of our bed, bare-bottomed and thick around his waist, clutching his thick, wet hair in white-knuckled fists. The dusty ceiling fan whipped in variables over his head, Ryan's laughter rising and catching in the old brown propellers. "Oh, honey," he chuckled. "We're totally fucked."

The very next day, we were scheduled for the rare luxury of dropping the kids at my dad and Nancy's house. We were headed to Summerfest to see the Avett Brothers in concert. I imagined the worst, Ryan haranguing or scolding me in the comical but overbearing way he castigated our children, pulling his Ryan-isms from a deep, dark bag of tricks. "I'll give you something to smirk about," he'd admonish, if Leo or Fern covered their lips, smug beneath their little five-fingered fig leaves. "You'll be sorry," he'd say, or "If you don't watch it, I'll spank you so hard it'll send you into next week." Of course, he was all bark, no bite. The barking was expressly what I dreaded.

But on the drive to Milwaukee, he was calm, humming to himself, and I could feel my husband closer emotionally to me than earlier in the summer. He reached for my hand, and somehow, we reinvented electricity. To what did I owe this pleasure: my husband suddenly, surprisingly, more lover than lawyer? I remembered that defense attorneys, by judicial design, are losers, no matter how cogent and emphatic their arguments. This was a man accustomed to defeat. Most of his clients served time. That was just the way criminal defense worked. To his credit, he never once argued a fifth baby wouldn't make me happy, and that day, having accepted his fate, he allowed me the unforeseen gift of basking in motherhood.

We ate lunch at a patisserie in Wauwatosa and shopped at a specialty boutique, where Ryan insisted on buying me two dresses. One was gingham with ruffled sleeves and flowing lines; we imagined I could wear it until my third trimester. At the register, I found a pair of thumbnail-size earrings embossed with the image of the Madonna and child, which he purchased so I could wear them to the lakefront, where we swayed together, a man with his lady, about to embark on advanced maternal age. I could still dance and sing out loud. Growing this surprise baby was as nostalgic for me as listening to "Kick Drum Heart" would be a decade later.

The air at Summerfest smelled of beer and dead Lake Michigan fish, but knowing I was pregnant was like wearing rose-colored glasses. Everything looked pretty, even the polluted walkways, as I remembered what I loved about early pregnancy, always a secret, hidden away in a specialized pocket. It's the pumpkin seed you've planted that has not yet sprouted. It's the poem you've memorized but never recited out loud. We made love twice, before the concert and again in the morning, and I readapted to the mysteriousness of sex, my baby and my husband inside me at the same time. Ryan seemed resigned but accepting, less fearful of a fifth baby in practice than in theory, ready to adapt with me.

When we returned home to Oshkosh, we didn't tell the kids about the pregnancy, but they must have noticed I was higher than usual, floating through summer in a helium-filled balloon. Whenever I was pregnant again, parenting seemed, at least for a short honeymoon period, to be easier. Maybe my capacity for love was expanding but not yet filled, or maybe, because babies are blank slates, mothers can't help but feel inspired. They are brand-new, never-scribbled-in notebooks with lily-white pages; they are new houses to inhabit. We'd probably need one of those too, if we could ever afford it.

Although I was expecting to feel tired, instead I felt like I'd swallowed some uppers. Soldiers during World War II were given crystal meth so they'd stay up all night and avoid death by surprise in the trenches. This new baby galvanized me against the grueling task of nurturing four children through the heinous July heat. I counted their heads on bike rides, adding an invisible fifth. A neighbor boy accompanied us on outings to the library and the pool, and I pretended he was mine.

Two weeks later, when Ryan and I got away for dinner at an Italian bistro in Appleton for our wedding anniversary, we asked for a hidden table, where we huddled close on our iPhones, searching for early twentieth-century gender-neutral baby names. Fern had been born exactly a century after my dad's mom; we called them "the '08 girls," a lovely coincidence that ultimately made us superstitious about numbers and the passage of time.

We ordered Benedictine cheese with bread and Whistleberry Farm's pork chop with apple *marmellata* and smoked bacon jam. We had conceived this baby in June, a month named for the Roman goddess of fertility, so we would christen number five "June," a boy's name back in 1912, exactly a century before he'd arrive. If our June were a boy, he'd be the third in our Ulrich trifecta: Leo-Franco-Juno. I was about seven weeks along, and I'd scheduled an appointment with my midwife, the same who'd delivered Fern and Francis.

The summer continued to rage hot, and a draught had turned the grass brown, but as far as my eye could see, our landscape was brimming with color and life. When a mother-to-be is pregnant, she is never alone. Throughout the month of July, June remained inside me. I didn't need champagne or lyricism to feel buzzed. Then, for the third time in a month, Ryan and I were on a date at a wedding. Our fifth baby was with us but not yet a third wheel. He or she was quiet, discreet, and without the power yet to interrupt our conversations.

The bathroom off the lobby was narrow and dark, and I needed to adjust my eyes inside the dark stall. When I finally hoisted up my dress and sat down, I could feel that my urine was clotted. I spread my legs to look between them, and that's when I saw the thick brocade of bloody mucous. I wiped several times, hopeful to be imagining my period, having a flashback to an earlier month or year. Each time I pressed down with tissue, more blood appeared. I felt very little cramping, which baffled me, as I realized, right then and there, I was bleeding out a baby without any contractions. I felt suddenly stupid and naive, the embarrassment of having secretly celebrated just one emotion, in a string of them, meant to ward off instantaneous grief.

I didn't want to return to my seat. I didn't want to feast on love and marriage. I didn't want to dance or eat or applaud or tap a fork against my crystal glass. When I found Ryan, I whispered into his ear, "I'm bleeding," and although the blood was plentiful, I pretended it wasn't.

From the cavernous lobby of the banquet hall, I called the answering service at our hospital, and one of our midwives called me back. She said I should come in the morning to have my hCG levels tested to determine viability. She was an especially religious midwife, and although we did not share that in common, I felt comforted when she mentioned God because I wanted to share this loss with somebody else who might, conceivably, be in on the secret.

Whereas Rob McNally had creative control over his meth lab, messy and toxic as it was, my body was its own chemist. I could not force my baby to adhere to my womb. My body had a mind of its own. Between my first hCG test in the morning and a follow-up one three days later, I kept thinking there must be something I could do to help the egg thrive. What if I rested more than usual or remained horizontal—self-imposed bed rest, forcing the blood not to drain? What if I prayed to God or the gods? Whenever I found a spare moment, I'd read blogs about women whose successful pregnancies were riddled early on with heavy spotting. If a criminal like Rob McNally could cook up his fix with a few items from Walmart in his girlfriend's garage, why couldn't I work my own magic to keep a baby from sliding out of me?

My pregnancy hormones were supposed to double every three days. Although I suspected my numbers were dwindling, as I was still bleeding and feeling neither nauseated nor exhausted, I was still secretly hopeful. Seventy-two hours after the first test, I returned for another numbers check. When my midwife called with results, the upside-down lilt of her voice revealed my miscarriage.

The hCG in my blood had diminished, though traces remained—twenty-nine mlU/ml, in fact. If you look this up online, a calculator will say, "Congrats, you're pregnant!"

In my case, however, my baby was growing backward, from an embryo back into a zygote. Within a few hours or days, my baby would be just a wasted egg, absorbed into pads and the breaches of my underpants. Some of my baby would be flushed away through pipes beneath our house toward the water-treatment plant, awash in other kinds of waste we speak of only in private. Perhaps I'd jinxed our chances, naming our fifth baby too soon. Worst of all, I feared I'd been presumptuous in asking Juno, goddess of fertility and childbirth, for protection.

Pregnancy and childbirth helped me record time just as sundials helped the Romans. After the miscarriage, Irie was about to embark on her third-grade year at our neighborhood school. She failed to make close friends, and when the principal asked why, Irie said, "All the kids' parents are drug dealers." The principal politely admonished me as I tried to explain, "There's some grain of truth." Ryan knew more than he wished about other school families.

Our house on Hazel Street, that great albatross, was shrinking in size as our professional burdens intensified. Many mornings, I'd wake at 4:00 AM, pack four lunches, lay out four outfits, line up four sets of winter boots, then head to my office in the dark to grade and prepare for class, leaving Ryan to commandeer the morning. He would work late, and I'd repeat this process in reverse. We lacked the time to air workplace grievances, so we never bothered censoring what little we managed to spit out, over the bows of our ships, passing in the night. All the kids' parents were not drug dealers, of course, but this was the nutshell version that Irie had gleaned. Like my dad, who censored nothing, I told too many horror stories at home.

Eventually Irie spun the stories thick, telling them to her younger siblings on car rides. She'd point at houses with Confederate flags for curtains and heaping mounds of garbage on dilapidated front porches. "If you're naughty, we'll drop you off over there," she'd say. According to these ever-evolving tales, not as tall as they seemed, parents smoked "ciga-rats" and crushed ashes onto steep landings where children slept without mattresses, the nightmare of free-falling so real they ground their teeth into petrified corn kernels. "You'd better listen, Leo," Irie warned. Her words emerged slow and muffled like backmasking on old cassette tapes.

When I regretfully volunteered during Irie's third-grade year to lead a Girl Scout troop, I lasted only two months before quitting, safeguarding my mental health but causing the entire corps to disband. I'd feel uneasy, nauseated even, as I organized activities. One girl's toothless mother scared me too stiff to function. Was she a meth addict, buying the junk from a guy like McNally, or was she just an impoverished woman without proper health insurance coverage, as I was once? After meetings, the toothless mom smoked cigarettes outside, and I'd wonder, would she grind that butt into some steep landing? The line between truth and fiction was blurry; I preferred simply to close the book. As Ryan increasingly resented his clients, the proximity of our neighbors' crimes, though real, grew distorted. Sometimes I felt trapped inside a video game, waiting for the most innocuous humanlike cardboard cutouts to detonate.

When our children initiate their own risk-taking—climbing tall, crooked trees; petting pit bulls; attaching ropes to skateboards and pretending to water-ski—my gut instinct is to allow them, but I've been taught by Ryan to step in and say, "My job is to keep you safe." For as grouchy and irritable as Ryan can be, ever beat down by the stress of his job, he possesses the air of a protector. He is Dr. Daddy, the man who held both boys during their

ER visits for stitches. He premeditates about safety precautions around the house. Bouncy balls are choking hazards; suckers, sticks, forks—you name it—might impale our children. Although he has gained weight, softening in the middle, his shoulders have remained broad and naturally muscular. He can bench-press two hundred pounds, even when he is out of shape. He worries about me if I don't call, come home when expected, get enough sleep, or if I begin to show signs of depression, inwardly or outwardly, ever attuned as he is to my states of suffering.

Sometimes I think Rob McNally and I shared the same kind of need for Ryan. Although fortitude for his clients was depleted, I hoped his patience for me never would be. I tried to behave, to respect moral decency, to want less, to count my blessings, and I hoped he'd never express disappointment in my choices as he did with McNally. A few months passed after the New Year before McNally called Ryan again, this time with somewhat surprising news. He'd met a girl, fallen in love, and was living on her hog farm in Missouri.

"I quit the junk, man," he said. "I'm clean." Whether McNally was clean or not and, if so, for how long, we'd never know. Shortly after this phone call, he turned up back in the Winnebago County Jail. According to him, an "associate" down in Missouri threatened to turn McNally in to the cops if he didn't keep supplying him with meth. When the cops showed up at the hog farm, they were able to quickly identify Robin Marks as Rob McNally. A warrant was out for his arrest. Now he faced the meth charges alongside charges for violating the conditions of his bond. He'd end up serving two years in prison with three years' extended supervision upon his release.

Conversations about prison center on the likelihood of rehabilitation and recidivism rates. McNally was certainly the quintessential revolving-door criminal. I've often wondered what kinds of pleasures kept him afloat when he was serving time. Was it possible that this girl in Missouri had fixed him, at least temporarily? They say meth and love both manifest as euphoria. They release dopamine in the brain and signal pure felicity.

"Would you ever think about ending the pregnancy?" I had asked Ryan, shortly after the Fourth of July, worried still that he might be mad or resentful, holding back his anger for some surprise attack. Of course, nobody I knew used the *a*-word. Abortions were not something we admitted to considering, even among liberals and women's rights activists. People did not imagine such procedures; they simply performed them in secret.

"I would never want to destroy something we made together," he said, as if the line had been scripted, but I also knew he meant his devotion to me. In that moment, love was an elixir, a magic potion, a drug, and whenever we expressed it openly, I felt like I'd popped a happy pill or begun to buzz with warmth.

But when my miscarriage was complete, when the summer of love failed to produce a viable baby, Ryan was also relieved. His heart could always clear space for another baby, but nothing in his rational brain had budged regarding our responsibility tally. Children were stressful, expensive, and exhausting. My midwife told me to wait a few months before trying to conceive again, believing we'd planned our June conception, but I knew I'd struggle convincing Ryan to "try again" when we hadn't tried in the first place.

I rejected the recommended waiting period, fretfully aware of women in the world who'd lost babies after much greater investment and bided their time. The urge to replace, repair, redo was stronger than the urge to make a baby from scratch, and in those few weeks of viability, I'd been reminded of my baby cravings. I'd been hooked back in, and I admittedly felt desperate. Whatever happened to the woman at Koreana, ready to move on in life, to bigger, less sacrificial things?

Then Ryan said, "Maybe it was a sign we're not meant to have another baby."

In other words, he would love whatever we made but was not sure he could knowingly do it again, aware as he was, the transcripts of his arguments still logged in recent memory. My miscarriage had consumed me with self-indulgent grief while it had freed him from the burden he was willing to but no longer required to accept.

My purple Avett Brothers T-shirt would become the garment I'd associate with miscarriage. I had imagined the thin fabric stretching over my abdomen, that convex dome where my baby would incubate until early spring. In Milwaukee, only twenty-four hours after confirming the existence of a baby we imagined keeping, I had leaned against Ryan and faced the music, just as Ryan faced the unexpectedness of our fifth pregnancy with love and willingness. But by August, Summerfest became a distant memory, and I had become unwilling to face the sad song my body played. My heart was beating, but my stomach was not. Ryan's job was convincing his clients to face the music, in a courtroom, before a judge or jury. "You've committed this crime," he'd tell them. "The only way to take matters back into your own hands is to accept responsibility and the kinds of conditions that will help you turn your life around." If he could convince the most obstinate, drug-addicted, mind-altered of his clients, could he convince me too?

At one point, after Agnes Jacobson "kidnapped" her son from the Winnebago County Jail and drove him across county lines on their afternoon joyride, Ryan had assured Agnes and his client, Wyatt Jacobson, that as part of his two-year prison sentence for all his heroin-related offenses, he would be afforded the opportunity to shorten his stay in the big house by participating in a rehabilitative program designed for nonviolent drug addicts. In fact, Jacobson was accepted into the St. Croix State Correctional Center, known for its Challenge Incarceration Program, where physical activity, military training, and manual labor, along with drug counseling, might rehabilitate him.

But more than halfway through his effective completion of the program, he and two fellow convicts escaped from the minimum-security facility. We saw it on the news, Jacobson's mug shot pressed up against the TV screen. He'd shaved his head. He looked angry and strung out, blue-green prison-issued shirt bringing out the color of his eyes—ethereal but indignant. Together the three inmates stole a car and drove to three different locations where they hid separately with their own sets of friends. Schools in the area were canceled to keep children safe in the unlikely event that the prisoners plotted violence.

After all that time in rehab, eight months or more, how desperate must Jacobson have been for a fix? What kind of drugs did he procure and shoot up—crush, snort, ingest—between his escape and his apprehension the following day? And was it worth the additional years of incarceration he might now face? Did he pop some slow-release tablets, the chemicals still coursing through his veins when he pleaded guilty to the charge of escape?

Before I conceived and lost baby June, how close had I come to being rehabilitated myself, to giving up my addiction to pregnancy, and was it safe to say Ryan and I were now right back where we'd started? Conceiving a fifth baby, despite the loss, confirmed what I already knew. Every time I counted the kids—Irelyn, Leo, Fern, and Francis—to ensure they were safe, I'd feel an uninhabited and unnamed void. For the first time in my childbearing life, my body had failed me. But now I knew a fifth baby was exactly what I wanted and needed, my grand finale, one final star-spangled season of rapture.

CHAPTER 9

Ultrasonic

Patience is a heavenly virtue but certainly not one of mine. To cope with my miscarriage, I categorized my bleeding as menstruation and began to calculate when I'd ovulate next. One month of summer remained, and if I could convince Ryan to release his genetic code on the day of ovulation, I might officially be pregnant again by our last-hurrah summer trip to Door County. Within nine months, I was determined to be cradling evidence of our sex in my arms. I wanted to catch "the birds and the bees" and hold their buzzing but delicate wings between my hands, inoculating me against the onset of sadness.

We'd need to love quietly and covertly, the intimate parts of our bodies deciphering each other, without speaking. Lovemaking and parenting in tandem had altered our sex rituals. When Irelyn was still little, she would wake us in the morning and say, "Your sheets smell like wet grass." Over the years, identical voices would call out ambiguously from the darkness in the midst of our trysts—"Mama," spoken like a question, as if I might be gone. We'd be half-dressed, under the sheets, listening for the flutter of footsteps. But now that I'd revived my mission for a fifth baby, I worried less about being caught in the act by our children and more that the pressure to conceive would paralyze Ryan into choosing celibacy over sex. What's the old joke: children are their own form of birth control?

They say before the uterus bears babies, it's the size of a small pear, but postpartum, it never returns to its original dimensions, one of many ways in which women are never the same after childbirth. We're like old houses in which the wood is warped by the load of its inhabitants. Even in the throes of lovemaking, my bones seemed to emit a low-pitched hum. During the month of August, Ryan and I copulated once to the murmuring of my body, which I hoped was enough, even though my midwife had downplayed the chances of conception this quickly after miscarriage, as my body needed to recalibrate. I had used this biological unlikelihood to seduce Ryan.

But why else was he willing to climb into bed and make love without a net? I've wondered in hindsight. Maybe he saw that unprotected sex was staving off my depression. He vividly remembered my volatile and explosive side, the woman I was pre-motherhood. Although he loved me then, he preferred me now, mellowed out on hormones. He must have considered the trade-off: a few more years of an enchanted existence with his otherwise moody and never-satisfied spouse in exchange for a fifth baby.

When we arrived at our rented cottage in Ephraim right across from the kids' favorite beach, warm and shallow for hundreds of yards, Ryan was proud to unlock the door. Wasn't the location specifically what I'd requested? In previous summers, we'd stayed farther north on the peninsula, but I'd strongly hinted about wanting to stay in a more central hot spot. The kids galloped across the sloping floors and darted between the three bedrooms, jumping on the springy mattresses.

Everything was bare-bones, including the indoor-outdoor brown carpeting and the glorified card table in the kitchen. I felt gravely and unexpectedly disappointed. The cottage smelled like cigarette smoke and mold, nothing like the maple-syrup scent of my own childhood cottage on Rainbow Lake. I sat down in an ugly gray chair as the kids escaped into the yard, and I began to cry.

Since becoming a mother, I had cried very little. Even upon learning of the miscarriage, I carried the grief like heavy rocks in my stomach as opposed to releasing sadness in the waterworks. But now, stuck in the mind-set of wanting a nest egg, I could not bear the thought of sleeping in a dump even for a few days. I knew how selfish and ridiculous I was acting, but in the moment, I could not help but feel sorry for myself.

"Oh, honey," Ryan said. He was laughing again but wounded too. "I tried. I'm always trying." I was crossing my fingers, looking for omens that I would not menstruate, while Ryan was rooting—half-joking, half-serious—that I'd be able to join him in a celebratory drink as soon as I began bleeding.

There was nothing like taking four small children on vacation to remind us how noisy, chaotic, and unpredictable our lives were. We warned the kids we'd be expelled from Door County for a public disturbance. Between the squabbling, teasing, laughing, whining, complaining, begging, singing, fighting over snacks, and stumbling over their own feet, we believed, at times, we were the loudest family in existence. Even on little trips like this, we'd often divide and conquer in order to survive and advance. Ryan preferred the terminology of warfare to represent the joyful but exhausting day-to-day struggle of our lives. With two full-time careers and extracurricular activities galore, leisure remained, counterintuitively, the hardest part of raising a family.

One of those late vacation afternoons, Ryan dropped me, Irie, and Frank off at a beach in Fish Creek, and he headed to Peninsula State Park with Leo and Fern. Their plan was to fish for an hour with hopes of catching and releasing anything with scales and fins. In our corner of the lake, Irie and I collected smooth rocks and stacked them on big boulders, pretending to construct lakefront spas. We took turns massaging our feet with handfuls of sand, pushing stones between each other's toes.

Across the bay, we could see Ryan fishing with the other half of us. The depths of Lake Michigan separated us from each other, and although I knew our separateness was temporary, I could feel myself sinking into the quicksand of sadness. The cold water pushed bright shards of earth onto the matrix of my foot, and minnows flicked around my ankles. In precisely that moment, another baby seemed like the only solution to my loneliness, a bridge or lifeboat that would unite the halves of our family, making us whole again.

Over the previous decade, I'd watched the EKG of my mental health spike and return to its baseline every fourteen months, but this time around, I'd waited twenty-six months, and I was beginning to plummet far below my functioning threshold. I knew a final pregnancy would lift me up toward happiness one last time before I returned to the doldrums where I'd spent most of my life before becoming a mother.

When we lived in Ann Arbor, I picked fights with Ryan daily. During a snowstorm once, I threw open the kitchen door and launched my wedding ring outside into a snowbank. "Fuck you," I said. "Fuck this marriage." Back then, I was crazy, and Ryan was calm. He pulled on his winter boots, trudged outside, maneuvered our vehicle from the carport, cast headlights over the snowy dunes, and traced a tiny hole to my ring at the bottom. This kind of behavior was normal for both of us back then. My depression would rise like reflux; he'd contain it with his patience.

When I was feeling most unhinged, in my early twenties, my suicidal fantasies were linked to symbols of motherhood. I'd close my eyes and ball into fetal position, a child inside an anonymous womb, maybe my own mother's, as this vessel of a woman hurled herself from balconies into cold Wisconsin waters.

How strange that motherhood itself temporarily cured me. When Ryan began his law practice, people asked, "How does he defend guilty people?" I'd think to myself, if Ryan knowingly combined his DNA with mine in the spirit of new life, setting aside my problems in mental health, he could defend just about anybody.

On our last full day in Door County, the kids and I walked to a candy store, where we handpicked our favorite saltwater taffy from a repurposed claw-foot bathtub. From there we meandered to a toy store, where I excused myself to the restroom. I hung a plastic shopping bag filled with a pound of taffy on a hook. A cool breeze filtered through the window. Sunshine and fluorescent lighting cast me in the spotlight of the public toilet, where once again I sat down and realized I was bleeding. Disappointment stuck in my throat. I never ended up eating anything sweet on that trip, neither taffy nor pie, not even s'mores. Eat your heart out, they say, and I did. Back at our rented cottage, I told Ryan bluntly and plainly, "We didn't make a baby." I remember vividly that he started to dance across the gold-and-beige pattern of the peeling linoleum.

When my dad said motherhood possessed the power to cleave open or to heal old wounds, to ameliorate or to exacerbate my depression, he was specifically referring to my perfectionism. Submitting dozens of unnecessary extra-credit assignments in middle school, pushing bedtime to midnight; counting my foot-steps and paces, long before Fitbits were invented; and washing our atrium floors until they gleamed, on my hands and knees, when I should have been outside playing—just a few examples from my former obsessive self. People I'd known since mother-hood probably couldn't imagine Laura Jean the fusspot, the purist, hair slicked back into a ballerina's bun. Motherhood transformed me into somebody blithe, easygoing, and filled with laughter; although Ryan, who'd known me forever, said my seriousness remained tangible, a long thread whipping blind stitches.

Raising children stimulates the dreamlike pleasure of déjà vu. My children seem to have emerged from old film reels, appearing and acting like me but slightly varied, restored, fully embodied, as opposed to remembered fragments. Nothing comforts like familiarity. A kaleidoscopic gene-scape—that recombination and redistribution of my traits and Ryan's—is just part of the magic. Children also quickly master the art of mimicry. My neighbors' girls, adopted from Ethiopia, resembled their mother more than my own daughters resembled me. They had studied her facial expressions intently. They were quick understudies, motivated by love. I'd have gambled on their affinity.

I could easily have suffered postpartum depression, but instead, with children underfoot, I began miraculously to appreciate messes, unfinished business, and the unlucky odd number of muddy footprints on my kitchen floor. With a psychiatrist as a father, imagining the worst had come easy, and my perfectionism was a talisman against bad luck. My parents' divorce had proved to be a coming-of-age event, grooming me to hear awful true-crime stories. My mom chronicled my father's alleged solecisms and sins, and in turn, my dad upped the ante on storytelling too, phasing out the mole people and the Grow-Up Lady (a magical woman who was said to descend through a hole in my ceiling to steal babyish attachments like blankies and dolls), replacing them with real characters.

One of my dad's favorite keepsakes was a bureau handcrafted by Ed Gein in the woodworking shops at Central State Hospital for the Criminally Insane, where my dad met the soft-spoken but infamous Wisconsin murderer. The bureau drawers provided perfect storage for my dad's ties, rolled into little polyester wreaths. Waushara County, adjacent to our home county, will never escape the legacy of Ed Gein. Fanatics still lurk around the courthouse, more than fifty years later, pestering cops and lawyers. According to the district attorney in Wautoma, the no-man's-land where Ryan ventured to expand his criminal-defense practice, the Gein file has been completely pilfered, winnowed down to nothing, "scholars" chewing away at its literal and moral fiber. Of course, Ed Gein stories revolved around his mother, Augusta, a religious fanatic who kept Ed isolated from worldly influences and convinced him that all women, except a boy's mother, were impure. After she died, he tailored costumes from women's corpses, believing his corset of rib bones and flesh leggings might bring Augusta back to life. But even without celebrity-level crimes, there were plenty of real women in and around Oshkosh who gave Ed Gein a run for his money. Several of my dad's female patients at Winnebago Mental Health Institute experienced motherhood-induced madness that landed them in courts of law in the 1980s and '90s, decades before Ryan would build his career.

Brenda Lund was the most famous, at home and in the *Oshkosh Northwestern*. The oldest of four children, Lund went by "Granny," for she nurtured her siblings with the firm hand of an old matriarch. But when she became unexpectedly pregnant in college, she hid the truth, admitting to her "condition" only after making adoption arrangements. In an unexpected reversal, however, after she gave birth, Lund's attachment to her baby blossomed and she canceled the adoption. Her daughter's cues, through skin-to-skin contact and spikes in oxytocin, obviously triggered a neurological response, nudging her toward nurture.

But when Lund conceived a second baby, three months later, she mysteriously decided to hide this new pregnancy also, restarting the same tight-lipped cycle. When her boyfriend, Nilus Walker, arrived home one day to find Lund bleeding through her clothes as she shuffled, hunched over, from their bathroom to the living room sofa, he had no reason to believe she was expecting. "Just a heavy period," she told him, and he believed her, but when Lund tried to rise from the couch later, she fainted, was revived, and fainted again. She was more than pale, her face blanched to match the color of her veins. Walker drove Lund to the ER, where doctors discovered, protruding from her insides, a placenta and the remains of an umbilical cord.

Suffering from dehydration and blood loss, Lund was in a disoriented and anemic state, but she was alert enough to speak. She denied giving birth but was admitted to the hospital for blood loss. When Walker returned to their house later that day, he investigated the scene more closely, this time around discovering bloody towels wadded up in the sink and red splotches leading from the hallway to their basement, where he found an old five-gallon bucket stained with runnels of purple blood. A towel had been carefully laid over the opening as if it merely contained bread dough rising.

"I couldn't bring myself to look inside," Walker told police after driving the bucket back to the hospital and submitting it as evidence. A baby was swaddled inside.

With no further way to deny the existence of her second child, Lund claimed the baby was stillborn, cord wrapped around her neck, but doctors still suspected she was withholding the truth. A test on the contents of the pail—that is, an autopsy report—would quickly confirm that Lund's baby was born alive. The baby's lungs showed evidence of having drawn air, and the bleeding of her wounds was consistent with a live birth.

As it turned out, Lund's baby had been stabbed four times with a sewing scissors, puncturing her soft skull. Although she arrived two months early, she had probably been kicking, alerting Mama to her existence. Bruising to the baby's body was not consistent with childbirth but with some other less sacred struggle. A revelation of this evidence led Lund to revise her statement. "I must have did it, didn't I?" she said to the investigator. "I was the only one there." She relayed a tale of fear, not unlike stories told by Linda Duffy or Lucy Vasquez. "What if Walker became furious about the baby?" she said. Brenda Lund feared abandonment. She could never support a family on her own. Her version of events, late in coming, was either truthful but troubling or faulty and fabricated.

Did Brenda Lund truly forget butchering her newborn baby, or was she a heathen? We think of infanticide as pathological rather than adaptive behavior. Any mother who kills her baby must be uncivilized—a savage, but was she really? Historians have shown that most of the earliest Christian mothers abandoned at least one child, either to avoid shame or to avoid stretching their families too thin. By the fifteenth century, foundling homes in Europe were accepting thousands of infants per year, abandoned by their mothers. Most of these babies died before their first birthday. Until as late as the early nineteenth century, infant mortality rates in Europe were as high as one in every three babies, in part because they were deserted. One must wonder, how many of these same women bashed their abdomens, bathed in boiling water, or heaved weights beyond measure to extract their babies before reaching this point of no return?

On the front lines of modern mommy wars, mothers engage in bloodthirsty battles over vaccinations, breast- or bottle-feeding, and organic foods, but I must have been assigned to the fringe wars, comparing myself more often to moms falling apart than to those keeping their magazine-cover lives intact. Regardless of the battlefront, though, I'd forever known that mothers were targets. When my best friend Mandy's mom was murdered by Harold

Franz, I saw myself as Laura Chapman's namesake. My name was earmarked for this momentous turn of events. Mandy grieved for her murdered mother, Laura, and as ten-year-old girls in cahoots, believing every coincidence mattered deeply, we wondered if I was sent to Mandy as an emissary from heaven. I selfishly shared in Laura's afterglow, long after she died.

Laura Chapman's love of music lived on in Mandy's piano fingers. I'd often stare at my friend as if she were cut from stained glass, sacrosanct, golden, and godly. On the treble clef of my existence, a never-ending fermata lodged itself like jealousy. This girl had it all, except, of course, she did not have a mother, and I did. My parents often banned Christopher and me from their bedroom, the site of what they called "P and Q time," for peace and quiet. On several occasions, though, my mom invited Mandy to stay and talk, Mandy accepting my mom's generous offer. My friend suffered real pain, horrific compared to my annoying neediness and seemingly contrived emotional wounds. I left the bedroom, surrendering my mother to Mandy, the deafening click of the door blotting out my generic sadness.

I was born into a world in which fathers killed mothers, and mothers killed children, and further yet, intelligent and well-intentioned adults provided stories to explain these acts. Brenda Lund brutalized the baby her body had painstakingly created, and I was painstakingly obsessed with regenerating a baby from the one my body dispensed of too quickly. But even if Brenda Lund and I were flip sides of the same hot coin, I suspected we shared common ground in the crepuscular depths of our womanhood.

Between the day we returned from Door County and the day I began teaching my fall university classes, Ryan and I coexisted without speaking much, mostly out of necessity. We needed to buy school supplies, attend open houses, wash and sort school clothes, and worst of all, as usual, I needed to draft and post my syllabi. As if by osmosis, separated from me only by some permeable membrane, Ryan absorbed my emotions, disappointment and hopefulness, until we reached equilibrium.

Throughout our lives together, since sixth grade, he'd been making me laugh, often with such turbulence that I'd pass gas or wet my pants, but much to his disappointment, I had taken my period, and his celebratory jokes, not with the smallest dose of levity. Rather than tilting my head back, smiling wide, all gums and teeth, I curled inward, doubled over, ministering to myself, consumed by a covert longing for that fifth child. "It was easy to measure your sadness," he later said, and whenever I could not soothe myself, Ryan would become my healer, if not with jokes, stories, and funny accents, then with something much deeper beneath the surface of tomfoolery and wisecracks.

Ryan had taken up recreational hockey to bond with our sons. Leo played beautifully and Frank could skate backward by the time he was two. Hockey was also indispensible to Ryan's health-management plan, ever in flux. Once he began to shred ice, he also managed to cut pounds, progressing, gradually, toward a lower number on the bathroom scale. The league he played in ran late Tuesday nights, the only slot for which they could finagle ice time. He texted me after my first day back on campus: "Off the ice. Hitting showers." He'd be coming home fresh, clean, and ready for bed, just before ten o'clock.

I nursed Franco to sleep and slipped out of his bottom bunk before Ryan's keys jangled in the back door. As he climbed our creaky stairs and probed our room in the dark, we were strangers, my husband just a dark shadow having come by special request to my bedside. His skin was supple and moist from bathing. I could smell his cleanliness. Without notice or hesitation, he undressed and poured himself into the mold of my body.

Ryan and I talked about making a baby less explicitly since the miscarriage, but he'd been telling me for years, "A boy is the only way I can ever think of another baby." Although we tried not to gender our children, inevitably the girls, like me, were emotive yet mercurial, intense but elusive, and because he himself had been raised in the absence of girls, Irie and Fern caused him greater anguish than Leo or Frank ever did. Our children took turns asking how babies were made, Fern the most earnest. When I described intercourse, she followed up by asking, "Do you do it in the bathroom?"

That narrow tiled space was where we most practiced intimacy, I suppose. It was where Fern had climbed into my bubble baths, or stood naked by the toilet, leaning over to touch her own toes so I could wipe her bottom from behind. She once caught me removing a tampon and gasped, "Is that a bone?" as if I'd reached inside and magically plucked a rib.

"No, we make babies in bed," I said. "We like to be comfortable."

Under perfect conditions, the male sperm, which are fast but fragile, will reach the egg faster than the female sperm, which are slow but hearty; this works, though, only if the egg has just descended through the fallopian tube. On that night, all signs pointed to "yes." I imagined it dropping through a secret tunnel like a gumball in a machine. In my mind's eye, it was sticky and translucent. We began in missionary style and never switched positions, rocking as quietly and as purposefully as ever. Though Ryan was nearly twice my weight, he felt weightless against me. Then, as my body swallowed his DNA, I closed my eyes and could see the sperm swimming to meet my egg as if illustrated for some kind of sweet children's story about tadpoles.

Neither of us spoke before falling asleep. It wasn't until two days later, while we were drinking our first cups of coffee, that

Ryan said, "Who's going to be the first to mention our liaison the other night?" I would have danced across the worn wooden floorboards if our kitchen were big enough.

A day before I was due to menstruate, I left campus early and returned to our messy house. It was Friday afternoon, our weekday housekeeping energy long since depleted. Children's Nutella-stained T-shirts and dirty balled-up socks were bundled with blankets and stuffed animals in piles on the couch. Half-eaten bagels with petrified cream cheese lay discarded on end tables. A baby doll was facedown on the back of the toilet. Bald plastic heads attached to soft, forsaken torsos—on cutting boards in the kitchen and in carpeted corners—reminded me of my brother's year-round efforts at running a haunted house for other neighbor kids. His favorite accoutrement was a hanged baby that shared a rope with a hatchet, strung from the pipes in our childhood basement. Babies, and their various forms of demise, had long been programmed into my brain.

This time, when I peed on the pregnancy test, I set it upright on the bathroom counter and walked away for a minute. When I returned, the pink lines were darker than on the last test. They did not appear erasable. I called Ryan on the phone to tell him, and he was surprised I'd taken the test so early, without warning him first.

"How do you feel?" he asked.

"Complete," I said, and I sat still for a while, calculating my due date—another May baby. Gratefully, I could again avert having to request maternity leave. Although I'd learned through a small whisper network of academic moms that I could also petition for a "pause" of my tenure clock, I'd long since been discouraged from demanding my rights. By May 2016, the university's Family Policy Action Group would make a formal recommendation to UW Oshkosh for more fair and civilized family leave policies and practices, but even by baby number five, I was still three years ahead of my time. Alone on Hazel Street that September day in 2012, tapping a little e.p.t. ditty against my palm, I was too happy to be mad, already drifting into the dreamscape of pregnancy, wondering how long I'd have to wait to feel the metal button of life stitched to my insides.

Brenda Lund's attorney advised her to plead NGI—not guilty by reason of mental disease or defect, the insanity defense. Her trial was postponed so that she could be rightfully examined by psychiatric professionals. My dad was one of two psychiatrists who testified at her trial.

During jury selection, attorneys asked panelists about their attitudes on abortion, childbirth, postpartum depression, and premarital sex, running the gamut of nerves they'd hit as they unveiled the tragic story of how Brenda Lund murdered her baby. The prosecution and defense selected a jury of ten women, many of them mothers, and only two men. Was Brenda Lund fully aware of the wrongfulness of her actions when she plunged a pair of scissors through her baby's skull? Did she realize she had killed her baby as she lumbered down the basement steps to hide the bruised and gouged body? Where was her first daughter, now a toddler, on the day of the crime, and would seeing her mother, in the hospital or behind bars, have scared her?

Fern once returned home from my dad's house giddy on tales of Lizzie Borden. My dad and my stepmom had recently returned from a tour of the Lizzie Borden crime scene in Fall River, Massachusetts. Nancy had photographed my dad lounging gruesomely on the divan in the Lizzie Borden Bed & Breakfast, the exact coordinates where Andrew Borden was discovered bludgeoned to death. I helped Fern find videos about Lizzie Borden with documentary voice-overs of pigtailed girls jumping rope to the well-known rhyme, skirts flouncing and grainy on the screen.

Fern memorized the words:

Lizzie Borden took an axe,
And gave her mother forty whacks.
When she saw what she had done,
she gave her father forty-one.

We read about the bloodstained dress that Borden burned to hide her crime, or so historians believe. I caught Fern studying the folds of her own dress, decoding secrets revealed in the ketchup stain or the dirty flocked hem. Then, in the middle of the night, Fern sidled against my pillow and raked my hair with her tiny hands.

"Mom," she whispered, her voice granular but soft like a flurry of talc, "I'm afraid Lizzie Borden's ghost is going to use my body to kill you and Dad." Streetlights illuminated the bedroom and Fern's *Miss Spider* sleeping bag on our floor. I held her hand for a sleepy minute, dismissed her worries, and muttered some variation of "You need to sleep." Fern seemed the least likely of our children to perpetrate a violent crime, but was she? Could anybody determine our penchant for madness from the outside looking in?

"Brenda Lund does not look like your typical criminal," the DA argued to the jury during her trial for the murder of her baby. "A lot of people feel that when someone like Brenda does something like this, she had to be crazy, and that's not necessarily true."

But my dad, in his role as Dr. Ralph Baker, believed she was inherently good. He would have resuscitated her old nicknames if he possessed such power—little old "Granny Brenda." Along with a colleague from Milwaukee, he testified that Brenda Lund suffered from dissociative disorder at the time of her baby's birth. His medical opinion was she had detached involuntarily from her awareness and actions, behaving in ways entirely inconsistent with her value system. The physical stress of birth had even caused short-term amnesia. Brenda Lund, he testified before the jury, was not competent at the time of her crime and therefore could not be held criminally responsible.

In my world, my dad was the clatter of salted peanuts on ice cream, the clink of a spoon against the sink, as he polished off a gallon of ice cream every week, never gaining a pound. Sheathed in Patagonia long underwear, no matter the season, he'd skulk through the house, a lanky cat burglar, double-checking locks on windows and doors, finding his way with a flashlight. My father was a floating orb of light. But in the public sphere, my dad, like Ryan, was helping to exonerate people for their oftentimes heinous crimes.

When the jury found Brenda Lund not guilty by reason of mental disease or defect, the DA was furious. Having built a reputation for himself as tough on crime, he could not accept defeat. When the judge sentenced Lund to an undetermined amount of time at Winnebago Mental Health Institute, he railed against moral depravity. Even more specifically, he punished my father by refusing thereafter to accept him as a credible witness in any criminal case in Winnebago County. My dad had been blacklisted, but his exile would not last indefinitely, as years later this same DA would face his own litany of criminal charges for accepting bribes to go easy on drunk driving. Hidden away in his federal prison, maybe he thought about Brenda Lund or other mothers he had prosecuted. Maybe he watched an internal film reel of all his burned bridges raging like wildfire.

I was ten years old the year Brenda Lund slashed her baby and tucked her into a five-gallon pail, eleven years old when my dad told me the vivid details of her story. I remember once asking my brother, Christopher, "When you're with the family, do you ever feel like you're floating?" "Yeah," he said. "It's called dissociation." Sometimes my bones turned to liquid and I felt myself side-stroking through time. Newborn babies are nearsighted, able to focus short distances, six to ten inches, the distance between our eyes and theirs, but eventually their eyesight expands. They begin to see color, texture, and greater distances over the course of their newborn development. Growing up, coming of age, and developing a keen awareness of the world are similarly developmental. Brenda Lund was my first lesson in the complex tale of mother love and maternal instinct. Like certain species of birds or water bugs, even some mammals such as polar bears and sloth bears, maybe we were evolutionarily predisposed to devour our offspring in certain extenuating circumstances. We could not predict which urges or primal instincts would emerge from our human selves, and maybe the mysteriousness of motherhood is precisely what elevated it to the level of sacred in my eyes.

For all the glory I attached to motherhood, I could admit that sometimes I grew overwhelmed, as if parenting were a big millstone of which I'd become physically aware, heavy and awkward, in my numb baby-bearing arms. What would happen if I dropped it? Ryan and I rarely, if ever, planned our lives more than two days in advance. We could not look farther into the future than forty-eight hours. "Living in the moment" was equal parts philosophy and necessity. It would have been unbearable to think of school supplies lists in June; never mind middle school, high school, car accidents, sickness, college applications, weddings, and all the meltdowns, crises, and sleepless nights in between.

Some days, when our kids were hyped up on fructose and YouTube, because I was teaching new classes or because Ryan had a trial, we'd come suddenly to a breathless halt and wonder, with self-accusation and immense guilt, whether we'd ruined our children. We'd cope by telling jokes about their brains oozing from their ears from "too much screen time," and we'd say something like, "You're going to turn into a donut if you don't drop the iPad immediately and eat these carrots."

We were far, far away from being perfect parents, in some realm we could not name. Leo's fingernails were black with dirt, and I'd swear I'd just bathed him. "I'm going to find that pot of soil you've been digging in," I'd joke, to make it all OK. How often, I'd ask myself, do good mothers change the sheets on their children's beds, and if I sprayed ours with lavender mist and simply changed the pillowcases instead, would that suffice? If I followed up candy binges with fresh grapes, might I be reinstated to good-mother status? "We're keeping it together with spit and baling twine," we'd say, only the twine was often unraveling or rubbing our skin raw.

Mothers like Tina Last continued to lurk on the periphery of my existence, so when Ryan called to say this woman—the neighborhood voodoo doll, my darkest possible alter ego—had been appointed by the public defender's office as his latest client, after four years in criminal defense, I felt entirely responsible for her fateful emergence in our lives. She was my evil twin, my doppelgänger, the worst-case scenario for how motherhood might end, and she had finally and officially debuted in our lives, as I'd always known she would. The state of Wisconsin had charged Tina Last with child neglect after a neighbor observed her children without any signs of adult supervision for days on end and reported the family to CPS. I wondered how truly awful the criminal complaint would be, hopeful that as many degrees of bad parenting as possible would separate us.

Upon reading the initial observations, I remained a bit worried. Tina Last fed her kids Pop-Tarts for breakfast and PB&J for dinner, relying on the free hot lunch from school for their midday meal. That didn't seem like child neglect. Hadn't Ryan and I resorted to PB&J for dinner dozens of times, and although we packed four-healthy-food-groups cold lunches for Irie, Leo, and

Fern, hadn't we threatened hot lunch—the dreaded "pulsing heart" chicken breast—when we'd been too tired some mornings to stand at the counter, using the food pyramid as a checklist? What else did investigators expect from a mother of four, collecting $800 in disability and only $260 in food stamps?

But like all case files, this one revealed truth to me in layers. In subsequent investigator reports, I was able, finally, to see beyond the broken windows, patched up with cardboard and duct tape, into Tina Last's house. The front sitting room was a Dumpster where garbage bags filled to bulging were piled halfway up the walls. Fruit flies congregated in slow-moving hordes, wafting about like schools of baby fish on the air. Beyond that, in the kitchen freezer, lumps of frozen indistinguishable meat without packaging gathered ice fuzz. For years, Irie had been telling Dickensian tales of what happens to naughty children—"You'd better listen, Leo," Irie had warned—and all the while, she'd been conjuring up the horrors of Tina Last's house.

Three varieties of feces had hardened in the corners of all the first-floor rooms, the broom cupboard, and the sink: cat poop, dog poop, and human poop, shaken free from dirty diapers. Missing ceiling tiles were like punched-out teeth, plumbing and electrical fixtures exposed and dangling. Upstairs in the bedrooms, the mattresses looked the same, springs having popped through the upholstery like sharp tendrils of hair. Worst of all was the free flow of pills, scattered like shrapnel on makeshift nightstands, mattresses, and shit-splattered carpeting—guanfacine, Metadate, lamotrigine. The marijuana was the least of Tina Last's problems. By her own admission, she had been overdosing her son on his ADHD medicine, hoping to drug him into submission.

Perhaps a mother like Tina Last is grateful to be exposed. When authorities become involved, maybe she even feels relieved. An entourage of responsible adults will decide, by law, in the best interest of her children. Hundreds of years ago, mothers lacking in resources were the most likely to drop their children into the safety deposits of foundling homes. Was neglect a cry for help, I wondered, not so different from my mother's and brother's suicide attempts years earlier, a small price to pay for rapid intervention?

"What was she like in person?" I asked Ryan. "Did she seem upset?"

"She was completely vacant," he told me. "She's like a shell of a person."

"But she must have shown some emotion," I persisted.

"It's not that she didn't show emotion," he said. "She just didn't appreciate the seriousness of the situation. She had a really hard time pleading to child neglect, even though she admitted to everything in the criminal complaint. The kids had a roof over their heads. She got them to school every day, and I think she thought 'neglect' meant that she didn't love them."

I had just begun to wonder how Tina Last could even afford her rent, albeit in the most run-down corridor of town, on the fringes of our neighborhood, and that was when I found the answer, buried at the bottom of her case file. Years earlier, Tina Last had filed a wrongful death lawsuit, seeking compensation for the death of her three-month-old son who died in foster care. She was awarded enough money to purchase the home, which would end up condemned in the months after she ultimately pleaded guilty to child neglect. She was losing children left and right.

In the district attorney's and public defender's offices, just like at Ulrich Law Office, attorneys are like ER docs working triage. They learn to repress their emotions and to cope humorously with scandal and trauma. Twenty-eight years after Brenda Lund murdered her daughter, some of Ryan's colleagues still remember Dr. Ralph Baker's testimony and Brenda Lund's murder charges. "Of course I remember the case of Bucket Baby," one of them recently said. If Tina Last made even the smallest impression, how might they nutshell her efforts at motherhood? I wondered. Would she become the mom who lived in the Brick Shithouse or the Dumpster Dwelling?

Becoming something of an armchair lawyer myself, I'd argue Tina Last suffered from an ongoing, unrelenting form of dissociative disorder. The only mystery, for me, was how far back one might trace her mental collapse. Was she ill-equipped to become a mother in the first place, or did motherhood sabotage her delicate health, fanning the flames of her ineptitude? Whenever I'd fall into bed without enforcing our toothbrushing routine or put off dishes until morning and wake to a small cloud of fruit flies over my sink, I'd think, *I can do this. I can be a good mom today.* Most of the time, I was able and counted myself lucky, part of a prayer for continued strength. Tina Last would remain imprinted on my brain forever.

In spite of my miscarriage, I'd always refer to *this* pregnancy— the one that "took"—as my fifth, unless I was in a doctor's office, answering questions about my health history. And *this*, the fifth time around, was the charm. I'd figured out how to endure sickness. Fountain soda on ice would carry me through mornings, followed by a huge meal at lunch—soup or chili, crackers, cheese, and sometimes eggs. By midafternoon, I'd be too sick to eat again and would fast until the following morning. I felt as though I'd earned a degree in dietary science and could meticulously measure my intake to maintain my weight, avoid vomiting, and continue teaching and parenting. In fact, I was eating a more well-rounded diet with my fifth pregnancy than during any of my previous ones, even taking prenatal vitamins, which I'd been unable to stomach the first four times around.

As always, we endlessly brainstormed names. I felt nostalgic about names from my grandmother's social circles. The name I most remembered was the ultrafeminine and diminutive Bunny; another gal she talked of was Sweetie, such that all names in this spirit appealed to me in a romantic but ironic way—Kitty, Foxy, Fawn, and Wren. My great-grandmother, whose bangle bracelet and dishes I'd inherited, was Nellie, a name equally possessed of daintiness. I imagined these kinds of names, alluding to animals or nature, being assigned to strong, modern daughters.

Our boy's name, quite decidedly, as no other contenders materialized, would be Gus, but I was insistent his name be longer. Never mind Fern, our monosyllabic daughter, or Leo, our son who was neither Leopold nor Leonardo. Gus was the name of my mother's German shepherd before he was sold to the Manitowoc Police Department and became the "wonder wog," a nickname bestowed upon him by his trainer. The single syllable seemed perfect for a dog but not substantial enough for our son. People suggested the Scottish variant Angus. Despite my penchant for animal names, I could not name a child for the kind of cattle used in gourmet hamburgers. In a past pregnancy, we had considered August, and it seemed appropriate this time around, another fifth baby named for a summer month, but a family on our street, whose name rhymed with ours, already claimed August for their son.

When the day for our twenty-week ultrasound finally arrived in January, we were excited to learn the sex of our baby, but I was also nervous in the face of this anomaly scan. I was about to turn thirty-five years old, and we had not waited as long as recommended to conceive after my miscarriage. I also worried that, statistically, four healthy babies was the most I'd be allowed. Why would I be granted yet another robust child?

At the appointment, I tried to be friendly, even neighborly, with the technician, but like all the previous techs, she did not smile much, having been dutifully trained to take but not interpret data.

Instead of chatting, she focused on taking my baby's measurements, as if appraising a room for carpet installation, apparently bored but also painstakingly precise. I tried to study her facial expressions, the way in which she measured or remeasured certain organs, and the pace with which she tapped digits into her system.

I lay back, sea-blue jelly warming up beneath the tech's ultrasound wand. Occasionally she printed a photograph, a long stream of perforated photo paper flapping from a machine behind her computer. In the small, dark room, lit only by screens, I longed for a soundtrack, perhaps the first CD Ryan ever burned for me—Mazzy Star's *So Tonight That I Might See*.

"If we have another boy, we can probably stay living in our house," Ryan said. Aside from holding my hand and watching our baby roll and stretch, he too wanted affirmation. "There's room for another bed in the boys' room, though just barely. There wouldn't be space for other furniture, of course. But if we have another girl, we'll have to buy a new house, unless we want the baby to sleep in the bathtub or something."

The technician smirked finally, a sort-of smile, and said, "Are you sure you want to know?"

"Yes," we both answered in unison.

"Looks like you won't have to move."

"It's a boy?" I asked, wanting to ensure nothing was lost in translation.

"Yup, I'm ninety-nine percent sure," she said. "I'm not allowed to guarantee more than that."

Ryan had given me a baby; and I had given him another boy.

"What about Gustav?" I asked Ryan. "As in Gustav Klimt, the painter. I've always loved his work." There was also Gustave Flaubert, of course. Not to mention, as my musician friends pointed out, Gustav Mahler and Gustav Holst. I was ready to argue my case.

"Yes, absolutely, I love it," he said. I was surprised, as I'd mentioned this name in pregnancies past and Ryan had quickly dismissed it as "too Old World." By now, though, Ryan, having become a hockey aficionado, was deep into the NHL season, and one of his favorite players, Gustav Nyquist, was having a big year for the Detroit Red Wings.

We continued to play with variations on Gustav, simply for nickname purposes, thinking that Gusto would complement Leo and Franco, names that ended with little halos. We practiced using his nickname in silly sentences like *Gusto hugged us with gusto; he lived life with gusto.* From what we could discern, the technician had found all of our baby boy's body parts and organs. Throughout my previous pregnancies, I'd often dream my babies were born without hands or feet, but there seemed to be confirmation here that nothing was missing. But when my midwife called the next day, she hesitated to speak, just as her colleague had dithered during my miscarriage. "Everything is fine, except . . ."

"Oh, no," I said. "Just tell me."

"The baby's kidneys are measuring larger than they should," she said. "It's a condition called pyelectasis. If it were up to me, I wouldn't even alert you to it because it usually resolves itself before the baby is born, but I'm required to tell you."

"Well, what's the difference between what his kidneys should measure and what they are measuring?" I asked.

"Between four and ten millimeters is the range for pyelectasis," she said. "And your little guy is at 4.6 and 4.8. Not nearly as serious as it could be."

As in all stories about medical diagnoses, we'd need to wait to learn more. In four to six weeks, we could repeat the ultrasound to remeasure Gustav's kidneys. If his kidneys were increasingly dilated, this might indicate a urine backup; my amniotic fluid might even be low. But if his measurements diminished to four millimeters or smaller, we would be free to assume a normal pregnancy. As luck would have it, pyelectasis was much more common in boy babies than in girls.

Who in their right mind would wait six weeks when four weeks was the minimum? I asked my midwife to transfer me to a receptionist, who scheduled our follow-up ultrasound exactly four weeks from that morning.

The Internet is a dangerous place for anybody playing doctor. Pyelectasis might indicate all kinds of problems, ranging from a blocked ureter to malfunctioning valves in the urinary tract, all of which, if still present at birth, might warrant surgery. This seemed like an outcome for which I could brace myself, but upon further research, I began to see references to "soft markers" for Down syndrome too.

Renal pyelectasis was one such indicator for trisomy 21. Reliance on soft as opposed to medium or hard markers for Down syndrome was openly debated everywhere online, but a specific study quantified my fears. For a thirty-four-year-old woman with an isolated finding of kidney dilation, the risk of giving birth to a baby with Down syndrome increased by nearly 50 percent. This was me.

None of the other soft or medium markers for Down syndrome were noted in our anomaly scan, my midwife reassured me. Little Gustav did not seem to have calcium deposits on his heart, abnormal fingers and toes, or any fluid-filled spaces in his brain. Nevertheless, like all mothers in this position, I studied his ultrasound images as closely as possible, trying to determine from his pixelated profile whether his face was characteristically flat; what about the shape of his eyes or the folded palm of his "hello, goodbye" wave?

"No matter who this baby is," Ryan said, "we will love him."

Surprisingly, he was calm when I could not be, and in the face of his composure, I realized that my fear was not about raising a child with a disability but rather about feeling guilty and self-ish. I was nervous people would say, "Serves her right," and then sneer or laugh lightly. "She was so greedy!" My amniotic fluid felt spiked with my colleagues' insults—"If your family were a micro-cosm of the world, you'd have more than doubled its population." Another one joked, his dry sense of humor like the shock of static electricity, "Haven't you ever heard of birth control?" I could hear their voices: "Who does she think she is?" Was I being punished for my crimes, and if so, with so many words to describe those crimes, which came first? How would my own father testify, if I were charged in a court of law? Did boring old depression count as a mental disease or defect, and was this enough to explain why I'd continued to ladle Ryan into the pressure cooker of childbirth?

Around this time, I was still breastfeeding Francis to sleep. I'd remain on the edge of his twin bed most of the night, my belly bloated between us like an extra pillow. In the morning, he would tell me about a recurring dream, with variations. The dream always began with Gustav escaping from my womb. Sometimes he'd cut his way through my belly button; other times, he'd climb up and out of my throat.

"What did he do then?" I'd ask.

"He tried to kill me," Frank would say. For nights on end, he awoke to images of my baby emerging able-bodied but violent, seeking some indescribable vengeance. Frank seemed neither scared nor emotionally wounded. More than anything, he was mystified; he was not yet three years old.

We were all nervous about baby Gustav but for different rea-sons. I wanted Gustav to be born healthy and so-called normal, but I realized that was every mother's wish. I marveled at moth-ers in our community raising children with special needs. They rose elegantly and heroically to the occasion, but could I? With all our latent fatigue, could we do the same? Only so many wishes or prayers could be granted. During this waiting period, I convinced Ryan and Irie to paint our walk-in closet a delicate blue and green. We'd remeasured and realized another bed would not fit in the boys' bedroom. I knew our baby would likely never sleep in the closet, as all my infants and toddlers had always slept with me, but I felt he deserved a proper space.

"I can't believe we're making a bedroom for our baby in the closet," Ryan said.

"It has a window," I reminded him.

"Yeah, but it doesn't open."

I felt a sense of familiarity roosting in the small cubbyholes of our small house. Real Wisconsin birds, robins and sparrows, nested on all the exterior nooks and crannies: inside the downspouts, in the bushes, above the garage door, and on all the hanging ledges. A realtor told me birds' nests are good luck; you should never knock them down, even to put your house on the market. From Colorado, my mom sent two hand-knit baby blankets for Gustav. All the traditional baby colors had been used up: pink (Irie), blue (Leo), yellow (Fern), and green (Frank). Gustav's tiny afghans arrived by mail. They were pale orange, the color of sherbet.

In one of my all-time favorite picture books, *The Carrot Seed* by Ruth Krauss, nobody believes the young boy's seed will grow. "I'm afraid it won't come up," his mother and father tell him. His older brother predicts definitively that it won't, but the boy tends to it anyway until it sprouts. When he finally pulls his carrot from the dirt, it is nearly too large for his wheelbarrow. It grew, "just as he knew it would."

For four weeks, I tried to embody this kind of faith, telling myself, *This baby will grow as he is meant to grow.* And when we returned to the same ultrasound technician in the same room in the women's clinic, she reported the measurements of Gustav's kidneys—4.0 and 3.9 millimeters. Although she could not tell us that he'd "measured normal," we openly expressed our relief. We had arrived at our appointment knowing exactly what the technician was scanning for.

"Have you picked out a name yet?" she asked.

"Gustav," I said. "Little Gussie." His feminine nickname leapt from my lips as if he were a character in some gossipy story my grandmother was telling, and I'd known it all along.

CHAPTER 10

Boiling Over

Storytellers spin tales, endlessly, of third, fourth, fifth, and sixth babies "just falling out"—in cars, on sidewalks, in elevators—in what is called "precipitous labor" or "birth without warning." A family friend was born on her driveway before her mother could even be hoisted into an ambulance. Wombs are known to open wide, dropping amniotic sacs like water balloons, newborns the trinket prizes inside.

I started contractions in the night, and our babysitter, Gabby, picked me up for the hospital. She was more nervous than I, running a stoplight, convinced, like everybody else, that my labor would be fast, but by ten the next morning, my progress had slowed. My midwife agreed to break my water "to get things going," as I had reached forty weeks, but I still had to walk laps to coax Gustav's head toward my cervix, where eventually he latched on like a suction cup.

I endured two hours of intense contractions and nearly fifteen minutes of pushing before he even crowned. Toward the end, in hands-and-knees position on the hospital bed, I performed the impossible task of flipping over, Gustav's eight-pound, eight-ounce body wedged inside my birth canal. Two nurses grabbed my feet, bent my knees, opening my clamshell as wide as humanly possible.

Only then did Gussie emerge. His eyes were big and wet like those of a little boy who opens his eyes underwater without goggles.

In an updraft of energy and relief, Ryan turned away as midwives lifted him from between my legs, umbilical cord stretched like a silver sash between us, braided and swaying. Some water-filled chasm, Ryan's own amniotic pouch, split open at the sight of our fifth child. He'd never cried during my births, but now he pirouetted toward the window, sucking air. Later, he confessed to fear over Gustav's health. He and Gussie experienced simultaneous relief as our baby released himself, or I him, from the vice grip of my body.

May became the most celebrated month in our household. Irie, Leo, Fern, and Gustav were born on days 23, 14, 13, and 30, respectively, each birthday marking the end of winter. Maia, Roman goddess of growth, actually means midwife in Greek, some explanation for why we celebrate Mother's Day in May. My only objection to May was that Francis was born in June. Waiting to officially honor him felt like an eternity.

On Mother's Day, the year Gustav turned two, Ryan was not expecting a phone call from Reginald Price. Mother's Day was like a national holiday, and even Ryan's clients had moms to celebrate. In this, the seventh year for Ulrich Law Office, Ryan had taken on a handful of reckless homicide cases, including one for a guy named Terrell Knight, charged with selling heroin to a user who died from injecting the dope. Reginald Price, on the phone that sunny day, was one of Knight's associates. He'd previously delivered small down payments to Ryan toward Knight's fees, but now he was handcuffed to a hospital bed at Aurora, where I'd birthed our third, fourth, and fifth children.

His voice pulsed, muffled but urgent. The guy was about to face his own attempted homicide charges, two counts in the first degree, and Ryan, still running his law practice as a ministry, agreed to see him. Price was soon to be received by the Winnebago County Jail. For seven long years, Ryan had mistakenly relied on criminals, who otherwise showed little to no responsibility in their lives, to follow through on payments. I wondered, would Reginald Price be the last customer on the pro bono bus?

"I know you're good for it, Reggie," Ryan said. But did he really?

Price and his longtime girlfriend, Autumn Krumenauer, had broken up in the preceding weeks, but Mother's Day also happened to be her daughter Delilah's fourth birthday. Price had purchased gifts for Krumenauer and Delilah, wanted to see them in person, and needed a lift to the Greyhound bus station because he planned to visit his mother in Milwaukee that afternoon. According to the police report, Price was later found to have two bottles of perfume on his person. Unforgivable Woman Parfum Spray by Sean John, perhaps; the police report failed to specify.

Price and Krumenauer ended up running errands together, stopping off last at Walgreens. Surveillance cameras showed them, along with four-year-old Delilah, at the checkout, purchasing flowers, three greeting cards, and prescription medication. When they emerged into the parking lot, Price climbed into the driver's seat of Krumenauer's nearly brand-new Chevy Traverse despite his suspended license. Price commonly drove Krumenauer's vehicle when they dated, and probably without much thought, she handed him the keys. According to one version of the story, Price told Krumenauer he wanted to stop at a nearby junkyard to check on the reupholstery of his Camaro. The clock clicked 1:30 PM, time for Delilah's family birthday party. No matter what happened, they would arrive late or never at all.

As they headed west on Highway 21, one of the most dangerous two-lane thoroughfares in Wisconsin, they began to argue, barreling at least sixty miles per hour away from town. Price accused Krumenauer of being jealous about his new girlfriend, and likewise she accused him. At some point, as their argument escalated—Chevy Traverse galloping like a horse for the stable, faster, faster—Price wrestled away Krumenauer's cell phone. According to Krumenauer, she was texting her boyfriend, Price growing furious; but according to Price, he confiscated it, speedometer up to eighty miles per hour now, because she was wielding it as a weapon, beating him over the head, screaming, "You need mental help, Reggie!"

As their fight mounted, so did their speed. Although Reginald Price had reclined his seat so far back it touched Delilah in the rear seat, and he appeared in full-on leisure-driving mode, somewhere between Oshkosh and Omro, he yanked on his seat belt and buckled himself in. Then, without slowing down, he swerved south on County Road FF and floored the gas pedal as the speedometer needle ticked up—107, 108, 109.

"I'm gonna die, and you're gonna die with me!" he is alleged to have screamed.

"Stop, Reggie!" Krumenauer screamed back. "My baby is in the car!"

County Road FF is far more narrow and uneven than any highway, surrounded on both sides by farmland. Reginald Price would later tell police Krumenauer yanked on the steering wheel, so he lost control. While she would admit to grabbing his leg and pulling it from the gas pedal, she said Reginald Price veered off the road, on purpose, in attempted murder. Whatever the cause—a blip in the road, a tussle, a fit of rage—the Chevy Traverse pivoted from its forward course, caught the country air, laid rubber in the clover grass, hit a telephone pole, rolled three times, and landed upright a hundred feet from FF. The engine and the transaxle were ejected from underneath the hood, and from the outside looking in, three eyewitnesses, a family of three in their rural oasis, reported the windshield instantly shattered. Beyond that was an empty chassis, its passengers banished.

"What did you grab the fucking wheel for?" Price was yelling.

Krumenauer was not answering. Eyewitnesses called 911 immediately, then converged on the scene and found Krumenauer sitting in the grass, holding Delilah. Both were alive but dazed, bleeding but not profusely. Later that day, when an accident reconstruction expert showed up, long after the victims of the "accident" were transported to separate hospitals, he discovered strands of Autumn Krumenauer's hair stuck to the sharp edges of the popped-out windshield. By the time paramedics arrived, Delilah, whose forehead was gashed and swollen, had fallen asleep in her mother's arms. Although she survived the accident, she'd be rushed to the hospital for a thorough examination and would miss her own fourth birthday party.

Flowers meant for her grandmother lay scattered nearby in the field. When Francis was little, he loved to pick dandelions or daisies from our garden. "Mama had a baby, and her head popped off," he'd sing, then laugh uproariously. Beheading flowers, imagining my head flung into the dirt, never got old for my son. Mother's Day would forever be such a combination of wickedness and joy.

Packed tight like little cured meats into our saltbox house, a family of seven in barely 1,700 square feet, we began to indulge fantasies of moving in spring 2015, a few weeks after Reginald Price skyrocketed from County FF, nearly killing his passengers. Gustav's "room" in the closet was repurposed for storage again, and our tape measure stopped lying. On the kids' last day of school in June, Ryan and I drove hopefully around neighborhoods on the other side of town, a Sunday drive on a Tuesday. Ryan's work in criminal defense had fully drained us both, and he hated our Hazel Street house like it was a living, breathing entity.

Irie had attended a charter school for fifth grade, free at long last from our neighborhood school, and we'd applied for Leo to do the same. Fern remained baffled by her school life, as her first-grade teacher routinely ran from the classroom in fits of tears, horror-struck and dumbfounded by the kids. When Leo intercepted a football at recess, a kid stomped on his rib cage until he was bruised but not broken—common practice. With Francis and Gustav queued to join these ranks, we dreaded the next decade. Irie, Leo, and Fern referred to their alma mater, that two-story brick schoolhouse, like it was Alcatraz.

We knew the main barrier to moving would be conquering our credit score. Ryan met with the quirky mortgage broker in his building. He examined our situation and assured us we could secure a loan, so by midsummer, we decided to spend every penny on moving. A realtor pounded a deep hole into our front yard, and two days later, plugged it with a For Sale sign. Every time I'd turn the corner onto Hazel Street, I'd get heartburn.

The years between Gustav's birth and his second birthday in 2015 were as sacred as all the other two-year waiting periods between babies. Wet diapers, the polypropylene and orange-scented wood pulp soaked with urine, smelled good to me. Baby saliva and snot were salves I relied on. I loved the way Gustav's fists stayed clenched and how blue threads twined behind his closed eyelids when he slept. I would breastfeed him longer than any of my other babies, until well after his fourth birthday, marveling that my ducts still filled and released milk.

"This is our last one, I promise," I'd say to everyone we met. No baby gifts, showers, or blessings on a fifth baby. Instead, I was expected to offer assurances to family, friends, colleagues, and strangers. "We're done after this—really, truly." Here he is: our last baby. Ta-da!

When people I'd never met learned of my five children, they'd ask my race or nationality, "because around here the only families with that many kids are Hmong." When one of Ryan's clients learned about our five children, she looked him straight in the eye and said, "All from the same baby mama?"

Strangers assumed we'd amassed them with multiple births. They'd say, "Do you have triplets or something?" For a time, Francis caught up with Fern in terms of size, and we called them "the twins," which fit perfectly the narrative others crafted. For a while, families we knew casually through the YMCA wondered if we were a blended family. One mother was shocked to learn that ours was not a second marriage. Irie once cried about lying to a friend who wanted to know what church we attended because "big families are always religious." She told her St. Raphael, the biannual site of her piano recitals. But we had absolutely no intent to deliver our children into some larger stereotype or social movement. We were most likely to describe them as our citadel, protecting me from suicide and the sieges of sadness, as they buoyed my spirits and fortified my desire to live.

By this, my fifth child, I thought I might possibly let go a little easier, but as McNally said, an addict is always an addict. Fortunately, that summer, Ryan and I experienced such an intense pileup of stressful surprises that for the first time in my childbearing life, I came suddenly to my own conclusion that five babies had to be enough.

The first eye-opener came in the form of a phone call. I was on campus, grading quizzes from Women in Literature, during an intensive three-week semester, teaching three hours a day and preparing lessons and discussions the other five or six. We were reading *The Prize Winner of Defiance, Ohio: How My Mother Raised 10 Kids on 25 Words or Less* by Terry Ryan. I was awestruck by

Evelyn Ryan's tenacity and positive attitude in rearing twice as many children as I, in the 1950s no less, alongside a husband who was certainly not her equal partner in parenting.

"Hi, honey," I said, as I picked up my end.

"You're not going to fucking believe this," Ryan said. Usually when he began our conversations this way, he was gearing up to tell me about one of his clients.

"What now?" I asked.

"The kids are being sent home because their heads are infested with lice," he said. Rather, he screamed, he barked, he yelled.

"No," I said. "Oh, God."

Although my worst maternal fears were of death, disappearance, and drugs, on the level of everyday family operations, head lice was a childrearing reality I had long dreaded. How would I eradicate them? Was the protocol as onerous and horrifying as all those urban legends about the annihilation of super lice suggested? Mothers at the YMCA showed up to swim lessons with their boys' heads shaved bald, regaling me with horror stories of mondo-monstrous lice that refused to die. I knew cockroaches were difficult to kill, and I imagined Fern's and Leo's heads ravaged by bugs in coats of armor.

I headed to Walgreens, where I quickly discovered that RID is expensive. I spent $120 on Complete Lice Elimination Kits, which included the shampoo, gel, and nit combs, all the while wondering how the families who qualified for free and reduced lunch at our elementary school would afford treatment, if, in fact, this was the epidemic Ryan described. A long line of contagious children greeted Ryan as he and other parents arrived, early from work, swearing under their breath. Some of the children had nits, but according to our crusty (and trusty) old school secretary, "Leo had some live ones."

"They'll have to fumigate the entire school," one of the teachers said, and a cluster of them laughed in the hallway, joking about how itchy they felt, down to their feet. None of the children would be allowed to return until cleared by the school nurse.

At home under the bright kitchen light, I sat Leo on a kitchen stool and parted his curls. I was startled to see adult lice scurrying against his scalp. They scuttled fast between the hair follicles like little bugs in a video game. I gasped, Leo started to cry, and Ryan glared. At nine years old, Leo was attached to his hair. It attracted him attention wherever we went. Other mothers and grandmothers often stopped to comment on his curls. "Look at that beautiful hair," they'd say. "Boys have all the luck, now don't they?"

"I'm sorry, buddy," I said. "I just got scared for a second. It's going to be OK."

Leo was the first I treated with the chemical shampoo, working RID into his scalp. Our eyes burned as we stood in the steamy bathroom, Leo hiding behind the curtain. Afterward, he sat on his bedroom floor, towel around his waist, as I drenched his hair with gel and combed in every direction—front to back and vice versa; left to right and vice versa—raking the terrain of his skull. I managed to extract whole bugs with identifiable body parts. Some were still moving, their nervous systems giving in to paralysis as I watched.

I then began to wipe each foaming comb full of gunk against a dry paper towel, amassing hundreds of brown unintelligible specks. They looked like sesame seeds. I wasn't sure if these were the eggs or little dead lice; they were nearly microscopic. The next evening, I used an even stickier conditioner to repeat the nit-combing process. I'd confidently killed the bugs but was warding off new babies with regular combings. Nestled into the warmth of his head, the eggs might still hatch.

No matter how many times I combed, I'd preen dozens of eggs with careful and meticulous swipes of the metal teeth. My job was not yet complete. At midnight, I became a phrenologist examining the bumps of my son's skull. We rarely shared intimate space anymore. Leo was aloof and casual about our mother-son love, but for several nights in a row, he rested his face on a pillow in my lap, and I remembered him crowning inside me years earlier.

The lice on Fern's head were not nearly as active, but we killed them anyway. Her problem was the abundance of eggs clinging to the shafts of her long hair. On the third day, when I believed I'd eradicated them all, our neighbor, Betty, took one look at Fern's head and said, "Oh, poor baby. You've still got hundreds of nits." I honestly thought the nits and casings were flecks of light or dust. Betty came over to our house, where we removed the shade from our reading lamp, and she taught me how to pull nits with my fingernails. Together, we nit-picked until Fern fell asleep. Betty's was the truest sign of love, in place of disgust, that anybody ever showed us.

At school, Fern and Leo felt stigmatized. Two sisters returned with shaved heads after nearly a week, and they both blamed their new dos on the Ulrich kids. What could we do but remind them how insidious and shrewd a louse could be?

In Francis's hair, I found the biggest louse of all, and when I showed it to him in the bathtub, he just shrugged his shoulders and kept playing with his army guys—classic fourth-child nonchalance. We treated him and Gus, and their short hair made constant monitoring easy. Ryan was convinced he never had any lice at all.

Irie and I both found nits in our long, thick hair. We treated ourselves and combed our scalps relentlessly, convinced any tingle was a bug. We washed all our bedding in hot water. We bagged up the stuffed animals in thirty-gallon lawn-and-leaf bags. The literature on lice prevention recommended suffocating the lice out of the bunnies, kitties, bears, and dolphins for just two weeks, but many of the kids' best stuffed friends never returned from their basement exile, landing instead, still bagged up, at Goodwill months later—donated alongside my maternity clothes, all that pent-up longing finally relinquished.

Irie and I stood together, singing from *Les Misérables*. As mistresses of the house, whom could we charge twice for these little pests? In the bathroom together, we practiced horrified expressions, as we blasted the blow-dryer. Lice could not withstand high heat, so as an extra insurance measure, I set my flat iron to 450 degrees, and we took turns clamping down on our roots until our follicles sizzled, then pulling the straightener the length of our hair. I imagined louse eggs cracking and frying between the hot ceramic disks. I'd never been so passionate about murder.

Every night, I'd soak the nit combs in hot water to kill off anything contagious before reusing them in the morning. We were more tired than usual, as I was still teaching Interim, and the last day of public school had not yet arrived. We'd lost hours of sleep grooming our heads, but instead of feeling soft and luxurious like hair in shampoo commercials, our hair felt like corrugated plastic. One evening, eager for even more control, I decided to boil the combs in our stockpot, thinking it would be a more effective way to sanitize our anti-lice tool kit for future use. After turning up the dial, in the distracted madness of the bedtime routine, I lay down to nurse Gustav and fell into a trance.

In the middle of the night, Ryan woke up beside us and said, "Something isn't right." Possessing the magic powers of Miss Clavel from *Madeline*, who awakes with the foreboding of the girl's rupturing appendix, Ryan sensed danger and was roused from sleep. "It smells like burning rubber." The room was not smoky, but the air reeked of chemicals and heat. Ryan climbed from bed and plodded down the stairs, where he found a toxic cloud, like exhaust from an old car, rolling across the stovetop. Inside the stockpot, all the water had evaporated, and the red plastic handles from my nit combs had burned into hard, waxy puddles. The heat was still cranked to high, and the pot looked ready to explode.

For the second time in our lives, I'd almost burned the house down. I began to seriously wonder if these were Freudian slips in behavior. One Christmas between the births of Fern and Frank, or maybe Frank and Gus, a house around the corner *did* burn to the ground. Our realtor had shown it to us twice, before we offered on Hazel Street. Firemen diagnosed the knob-and-tube electrical work in all these old houses. Signs from the universe threatened us from every margin.

I realized, fully awake by now, the rank stench of sterilization permeating my brain, that five babies was probably all I could handle. A sixth baby might lead to a third incident and the likelihood of our home on Hazel Street—or any other future home—going up in flames, melting to the ground, and leaving us charred, homeless, and, as Ryan had often predicted, living like the old lady in a throwaway shoe.

That spring and summer, the pileup of stress grew relentless. In early June, when I was done teaching for the summer and had taken all five children to Leo's baseball game, ice cream seemed a good idea, but waiting in a long line at the Dairy Queen drive-thru, I received a call from Ryan. He was playing hockey at the YMCA in the "old man's league."

"Honey, don't panic," he said. "But I need you to meet me at the hospital. An ambulance is on its way to get me."

"What happened?"

"I went into the wall pretty hard," he said. "I'm pretty sure I broke my ankle."

This was one of those fortunate moments when Gabby answered her phone on my first try. She would meet me at our house, where, joined by Betty, they would hunker down and wait for news from the ER, where I arrived even before Ryan did. When paramedics wheeled him in, I could see they'd unlaced his skate and removed his hockey sock with a scissors. His foot was bent and swollen. Our children all boasted brown eyes, so I'd forgotten the sea-glass green color of Ryan's. His needy and distressed expression reminded me instantly of our boys begging for the comfort of breast milk.

The first order of business was pain relief. The nurse grabbed her tourniquet and went to work installing a port on his left arm. She shook her little vial of Dilaudid—hydromorphone hydrochloride. "You'll be feeling pretty good in a few minutes," she said. She unwrapped a needle, filled it from the decanter, and then she pushed the plunger into his port, filling his veins with relief. They call it hospital heroin for a reason. We could not help but think of Rob McNally and all the other addicts we knew.

The ER doctors X-rayed his lower leg, and the image revealed a fracture that would need to be mended with surgery in the morning, but more pressing was his dislocated bone. As the staff prepared to realign his ankle, they asked me to recuse myself, probably standard operating procedure, unless they surmised I'd be especially squeamish. Dilaudid was so powerful that I could hear the staff repositioning Ryan's ankle without him ever vocalizing pain. The ER doctors admitted him to the hospital overnight to ensure the earliest possible appointment with an orthopedic surgeon.

X-rays soon revealed he'd need extensive surgery, including the installation of a plate with screws. And once the doctor had delved beneath his skin, he discerned he'd also need to reconstruct Ryan's tendons, which had been shredded like the hairs of an old rope. As Ryan awoke from the stupor of his anesthesia, I kept thinking of Francis gaining consciousness after his dental surgery. My husband and my son, both naked under crookedly tied hospital gowns, curled into fetal poses.

When Ryan arrived home, the first thing Fern noticed on Ryan's toes, peeking out from his cast boot, were stains from the iodine solution. She would always say, "Dad's toes look like Cheetos!" Having learned from him the value of humor, we tried to laugh about our newest invalid. One day when Irelyn really pissed him off, he chased her up the driveway, hopping on one foot, aiming the rubber cap of his crutch at her butt. He wanted me to join in reprimanding Irie for mouthing off, but I was too busy laughing. We were living in some TV sitcom.

By this summer, Fern had developed a kind of psychosomatic vomit reflex. We didn't want to attribute her puking to stress, but after evaluations from our pediatrician—who ordered a CT scan to rule out anatomical anomalies; a close look at food allergies; and regular consultation with a speech pathologist, who ruled out tongue and palate abnormalities—we noticed Fern rushed to the bathroom under any kind of duress. Her stomach developed into a barometer of Ulrich family stability.

Most remarkable of all during Ryan's two-day stay and his summerlong recovery was his reaction to the pain meds while hospitalized. Every two hours, as the chemical cure waned, he'd find himself impatient for the next dose, as if he'd die without it. When the nurses injected Dilaudid into his system, a languid happiness billowed up under his skin. By the twenty-four-hour mark, his pain was so expertly managed that he could focus on the sweet rush of meds instead of the easing pain. He knew now how effortless it was to fall under its spell. When the surgeon prescribed

Vicodin upon his release, he weaned himself from its grasp before he'd finished half the bottle, all too aware of how ugly addiction could get.

By Gustav's two-year-old summer, I had run off my baby weight—four pounds per baby for a total of twenty pounds. Pregnancy comes with its own superpowers: a woman can sleep but remain physically productive. Babies exercised inside my womb, satisfying my need to be active, but now I needed to move again all by myself. I was running twenty-five miles per week, and I was relieved to remember that the hormonal blitz from exercise resembled, though to a lesser extent, that of pregnancy and birth. The high I felt from the endorphin, dopamine, and serotonin highs was, at least for now, a short-term solution. I hit the pavement the way alcoholics attend Alcoholics Anonymous meetings. Running, a kind of sobriety, carried me through the summer of Reginald Price, the summer of head lice, the summer of Ryan's broken ankle, and the many months set aside for leaving Hazel Street.

But I was not always careful to hydrate, especially in the heat. Despite breaking his ankle and hobbling after five kids on crutches, Ryan carved out time for me to log miles. The first time I went out after his surgery, I was determined to make up for lost time, setting out on my eight-mile route at noon. My mouth was parched, and I needed to stop to stretch for leg cramps a few times.

When I returned home, I collapsed onto the toilet. I was not menstruating but I was bleeding, and although I knew something was wrong, tending to one's symptoms is not always doable for parents. I needed to make lunch, nurse Gustav, chase the older kids up and down the block while they scootered, help Ryan ice his ankle, throw in a few loads of laundry, break up a couple of fights, and maybe—if I could find the time—bathe.

That night I woke up with a fever. I thought I might throw up, but I controlled my nausea with cold washcloths. My lower back was cramping. Something was not right. Ryan was sleeping downstairs still, on a bed Betty had loaned us, because of the injury, and I sought him out.

"If you hadn't peed out blood earlier today, I'd say you could wait," Ryan said. "But you need to call the doctor right now."

And sure enough, the nurse urged me to the ER. I left my disabled husband and five children at midnight and drove to the hospital, where the same nurse who had tended to Ryan five nights earlier greeted me. Based on my Internet research, I believed I had a urinary tract infection, and I convinced Ryan I'd be home in a few hours with an antibiotic. When the nurse asked me to rate my pain on a scale of one to ten, I didn't want to be dramatic. Lying down in the cool room felt good.

"About a four," I said. "Maybe a five." She inserted a caret between the numbers and jotted "4.5" before leaving the room. A young doctor stopped by shortly thereafter and said, based on my symptoms, he thought I'd be passing a kidney stone. I texted Ryan, "They think it's a kidney stone. Doubt it. Be home soon."

Initially I snoozed, listening to the light traffic in the hallway, but then I woke up cold as a cadaver. Nobody was around to help, so I helped myself, scavenging the drawers and cupboards, finding a thin blanket. My back pain spiked quickly, and I realized the pain, not my temperature, had awoken me. I opened the door and called out for assistance. When nobody came, I crawled onto my hands and knees and balanced on the rickety bed in my room, trying to stretch away the agony. Unlike birthing contractions, this ache was unwavering, like a long screw being drilled in and out of my muscles. I hated myself for choosing "4.5" on the pain scale. I'd reached a nine or a ten, symbolized on the pain scale with a face that cried big confetti tears. I'd never once felt this frightened during any of my natural childbirths.

"Help!" I screamed. "Somebody help me!" All numbers fell away. I could not have rated my agony or how much time passed as I waited for a staff member to arrive. When the nurse found me, she apologized but ran away; I thought she'd never return, but of course she did, shaking up a vial of Dilaudid. She helped me to lie down, pulling me toward the pillow with her muscular hand. She quickly tied off my blood circulation with her stretchy rubber truss.

"There, there," she said. "It's going to be OK. Just make a fist for me." She spiked my arm with birdie powder, and I rose up, leaving the ER for brown-sugar skies. Being loaded onto another gurney, being wheeled away for a CT scan, and passing a three-millimeter stone from my kidney through my ureter and out the tiny pinprick hole of my urethra were the easy parts.

"It will be a little gritty and sore for the next couple of days," the doctor told me. It was 4:00 AM by now, and I was on my second dose of pain meds. I was not allowed to drive due to the potency of my medication. We called on Gabby once again as chauffeur. That Sunday, neither Ryan nor I could drive anywhere, and we tried to imagine what life with five kids would be like if we were permanently as sidelined and powerless as we were then. In the evening, I read my discharge report and discovered my kidney stone was one of many calcified little eggs hiding inside my vital organs.

"Supposedly passing a kidney stone is like giving birth," people said. "Is that true?"

"It's worse. After birth, you have a baby to show for your trouble, and after this, all you have is a pinch of sand."

Much as I inherited depression from my mom's side of the family, my dad had long since suffered kidney stones. The most I could do to prevent them was to hydrate. My biggest fear was that passing more stones would make me wish for the productive pain of labor and the five babies I wanted to birth all over again. But by the end of June, I was so tired from the lice-broken-ankle-kidney-stone trifecta, I didn't want another baby for the moment, and this was something new.

Sometimes, as a joke, I'd roll over in bed and whisper to Ryan, "How did we end up with all these kids?" We were exhausted. To make matters worse, Reginald Price had not paid Ryan a dime, offering up instead a pair of one-carat diamond earrings complete with a certificate of authenticity appraising them at $8,000 as collateral for his legal fees. All he'd need to do was sell or pawn them, but Ryan quickly found the markup on diamonds in retail is so exorbitant, he'd be lucky to get $1,000. He set aside innumerable hours that summer, driving as far north as Green Bay and as far south as Milwaukee to present the diamonds to jewelers. Nobody would pay much more than the cost of gasoline he spent showcasing them. Pawnshops wouldn't take them either. It wasn't that the diamonds weren't worth $8,000 in the retail market, but Zales, and other jewelry stores, could purchase these rocks wholesale for a fraction of the retail amount.

From June until August, as Ryan, loyal to a fault, worked on Price's case, we spent our scant savings paying off car loans and other debt, at our mortgage broker's suggestion, in order to bring our credit up to a manageable score before securing our new mortgage. We invested every penny in paving the way to move, eager to sell our house. When Ryan finally sold Reggie Price's earrings on eBay, he earned only $1,800, the single payment Price made, even though his case remained at the top of Ryan's docket for nine full months.

The deal Ryan procured involved Price pleading to two lesser felonies, reckless driving causing great bodily harm and recklessly endangering safety. Attempted homicide charges would be dismissed. I'd never seen Ryan argue so tenaciously or file so many motions leading up to the plea deal. The assistant DA seemed almost intentionally vague on his definitions for reckless driving and endangering safety.

"Just tell me where you allege the crime took place," Ryan said to the DA. "Was it recklessly endangering safety when he drove off the road? Was it saying, 'We're all going to die' before jerking the wheel? Or was it simply driving a hundred miles per hour with passengers in the car?"

Ryan was confident that if he could pin the state down on when exactly Price crossed the line from speeding, which would result in nothing more than an expensive traffic ticket, to recklessly endangering safety, he could convince a jury that Krumenauer's SUV ending up in a ditch was an accident.

"If Reggie Price was just speeding, and he also happened to be a white guy, with a professional job in the Oshkosh community instead of a criminal record, we'd probably call this an accident, right?" Further complicating the case was that Autumn Krumenauer was white. Whom would we more likely forgive: the driver or the passenger; the ex-boyfriend or the mother; the black man or the white woman?

Ryan felt the same mixed bag of emotions as always. Price was needy and emotionally manipulative. "You're the only chance I got, Mr. Ulrich," he'd say with pleading eyes, but unlike his associate Terrell Knight, Price had nobody surfacing to help pay his bills. Ryan imagined survey questions he'd ask potential jurors: "Raise your hand if you've driven over the speed limit before. Now raise your hand if you've been in a heated conversation while driving over the speed limit." Only liars wouldn't lift their arms high. They call jury selection voir dire, from Old French—literally, "to see, to say"—and derived from Latin for "to speak the truth."

"It's also called planting seeds," Ryan said, when he explained his jury-selection strategy to me. "That's my job when interviewing a jury—planting the seeds of my story, as true as I can make it." When a different kind of seed is planted and a baby is born—or adopted, taken in, baptized, loved—a little wrinkle forms between then and now.

Once I rode in the passenger seat of a boy's car out on Vinland Street in Oshkosh. He wanted me to see the speedometer tick past one hundred miles per hour, and it did. Another time, on the way home from my freshman year at the University of Colorado, driving across Nebraska late at night, I began to weave across the centerline. A friendly police officer issued me a ticket for reckless driving. As I recall, it was cheap to pay off, something like thirty-seven dollars, but, of course, a child wasn't paralyzed with fear in my back seat as her caretaker yanked on my leg from shotgun, screaming, "Stop, please God, stop the car!"

Ryan and I found our refuge, across town, in a new school district, a stone's throw from my childhood home, a house with four official bedrooms and plenty of space to bunk. As Ryan and I meandered through the house separately, we were speaking in synchronicity. The end of summer was upon us.

"This is it," I said.

"We're making an offer," he said.

Old maple trees and wild buckthorn circled the lot, a protective barrier, Mother Nature's blinders. "The only kinds of criminals out here," our realtor said, "are the ones living in your own house," which we took to mean skeletons in closets—things like drug addiction and abuse, middle-class secrets—rarely if ever sprung loose or publicly vetted in courts of law. Bourgeois crime was just as ugly but less visible, we realized, so many of us retreating to houses in the suburbs with plenty of room to hide. At least when we moved, we'd leave the scenery behind: the Carriage House, hot spot for "domestics" and infested with cocaine; the BP, where confidential informants orchestrated drug deals; the condemned houses, among them Tina Last's, where porches sagged like old, rotten jowls; and the police strobes and sirens, ever present, like bombs threatening explosion, suspended from the sky. We made an offer on the new house, and the offer was accepted. In a series of phone calls and a tension-riddled meeting with the superintendent of Oshkosh Area School District, we secured approval for our children to attend new schools until we officially moved.

The only roadblock we failed to anticipate was our mortgage broker's incompetency. For reasons we'd never fathom, he missed appraisal deadlines and failed to submit paperwork to the appraisal management company. With his broken ankle, Ryan was gaining weight again. We'd spent every penny to pump up our credit score, depleted after a full decade of just scraping by, to secure the loan, and now Ryan found he'd entrusted himself to the hands of a charlatan.

A few nights before the move—our belongings boxed up, kids sleeping on the floor, as we'd dismantled their beds—I floated in and out of dreams, skimming the surface of rest. Our old house rocked and swayed in bad weather, and I wondered if the wind had whistled me awake. The sonorous whimpering was almost melodic, like an old lady humming, but I could faintly discern that somebody was weeping. I rolled from bed, accustomed to children calling from distant, nightmarish places. Standing near the top of the steps, I followed the noise downstairs. I plodded slowly, unsure, afraid of what—or whom—I'd find, even though I wanted to be heroic. We say the heart breaks, and mine did. Ryan was sobbing from his bowels, strewn across the sofa, beyond comfort, awash in his own saltwater.

"How could I be so stupid?" The act of cradling a lover twice your size is physically hopeless, but I think I rocked him anyway, desperate to be mother and wife in the same soothing motions. "We're going to end up homeless," he wept over and over, his voice stuck inside the grooves of this mournful refrain. He was petrified.

"He promised we were approved," Ryan said. Every assurance was part of the mortgage broker's ruse. Although I tried to reassure Ryan, his premonitions were confirmed the following day. It was the Tuesday before Halloween. Our broker waltzed into Ryan's office, as he too worked in the First National Bank Building, and said, "It's just not going to happen, buddy. You're not going to close on Friday." He didn't know when—or if—things would work out, never mind the family of four scheduled to replace us on Hazel Street in three days.

"What do you want me to tell my family?" Ryan yelled at him, and therein began just another upheaval of our lives. Ryan and I camped out in his office, calling around the world for solutions. We had relied on our broker's promises, his seemingly genuine representations of professionalism, and his pledge of loyalty.

We moved our five children, and our stuff, temporarily into Ryan's parents' basement, grateful but shocked by their invitation, as paid babysitters—college students, poor like us—almost exclusively comprised our support network. Ryan and I amended our offer to purchase, requesting another thirty days and a shot at securing the new loan. Fortunately, the sellers agreed. With the help of a community bank, we ultimately managed to save the deal after weeks of uncertainty and precariousness. The kids cried a lot, worried they'd be ripped from their current schools midstream. The pressure to afford a bigger house, after the patchwork effort to pay off debt and make a down payment—with newly earned and borrowed monies—was colossal, added to the weight of the broker's ineptitude.

The loan was on a five-year adjustable rate mortgage, followed by a balloon payment. Basically, this was what Ryan called a "prove yourself loan," or a PYL. We'd need to demonstrate financial stability. We reasoned, with only one child still in childcare, and that financial burden being lifted for the first time in thirteen years when Gustav started kindergarten, we might, *maybe*, be able to pull it off. Nevertheless, we weighed our future, deadly and hefty, a tombstone wedged against our chests. We were not yet forty, but some nights, Ryan and I were ready to crawl into our graves and die.

"If anything," Ryan later said, "I learned, right then and there, that my family needed me to be less compassionate in this world." His wide-eyed quest for social justice finally looked naive. He'd trusted the broker, in spite of his quirks and idiosyncrasies, just as he'd trusted violent offenders, addicts, and other scofflaws. He'd helped hundreds of indigent people, admirably, but in the process, at least in his mind, he'd nearly failed us. His hourly need to micromanage our finances just to keep us solvent, combined with the broker's fraud and Reginald Price's deadbeat shortcomings, was the wake-up call he needed. The money could be dirty, sullied, laced with the sad and sordid details of his clients' lives, but, so long as he collected more of it, retainers or advances, we could selfishly make our lives better.

Ryan settled a small personal injury case, long in the making, and invested the earnings into completely revamping his criminal law practice, vowing never, ever, to repeat the first seven years of Ulrich Law Office. He called the public defender's office. "Load me up on cases," he said. And from that moment on, he refused to accept any private clients without the money up front.

One day, a referral showed up at his office, unannounced. "I heard you take merch," he said when Ryan asked for $3,000 up front.

"You heard I take what?" Ryan asked, not at first understanding his slang.

"The guy who referred me said sometimes you'll take merchandise for your fee."

"He did, huh?" Ryan said, chuckling. "Well, once upon a time, maybe, but not anymore. It's all up front or nothing." This was the end of an era. No more donuts or keychains or Green Bay Packers memorabilia. It was money or nothing.

When Ryan told me about the guy hoping to use merchandise as a retainer, I asked, "What do you suppose he did when you didn't agree?"

"Hell if I know," Ryan said. "Got a public defender, maybe. All I know is it ain't my problem."

Reginald Price ended up sentenced to four years in prison, followed by seven years parole, after Ryan spent nine long, fruitless months defending the guy. Even though Price was a "huge pain in the ass," he was essential to Ryan's rehabilitation. Before Reginald Price, Ryan was a pushover, a guy running an outreach program, legal aid nearly free of charge, a philosophy of the heart. But after Reginald Price, Ryan was more hard-hearted than ever before, which is exactly what we needed him to be.

CHAPTER 11

Criminal Procedure

Unlike his, my heart remained soft as wet chalk, even if, in our story, I was the bad guy. When the crime is sex, only women are caught red-handed. The body is evidence. Exhibit A: our bellies inflating like Chinese lanterns, small fires suspended, flickering DNA, waist-high above the dirt. Although teased to some extent for the proliferation of our kids (and their carbon footprints), Ryan, my partner in crime, had been fingered by eyewitnesses and investigators as mere accomplice, subjected to lesser guilt for the same crimes, as if he were just the lookout assigned a post in the alley behind a bank I robbed at gunpoint.

I was the one to blame. Half a year into our new lives, Ryan still hadn't scheduled a vasectomy—awaiting my blessing, he said—so I was responsible for carefully charting my cycles, the rhythm method of family planning our fail-safe since Gustav, now a mischievous and wicked three-year-old, was born. Even at thirty-eight, advanced maternal age by three years, my cycles were as predictable as the Advent calendar; we anticipated those smiling eggs from behind their perforated paper windows. I'd mark menstruation monthly, a delicate red X. Every four weeks, bleeding confirmed my textbook body. How else would we have made five spring babies (timed to match semester's end) so decisively?

Ryan was working a lot—*a lot*—of hours in the summer of 2016, but still, to continue affording our new home, we sought creative money-earning opportunities such as renting our house during the Experimental Aircraft Association Fly-In, the largest of its kind in the world. Oshkosh hotels could not accommodate a half million tourists, so Oshkosh residents rented their properties. We'd be renting ours to an aerospace engineering company for ten days, and in exchange, we'd rent a cottage in Waupaca for a small portion of the cost. I vacuumed, mopped, scoured, and laundered bedding in preparation, a lot like nesting before the birth of a child, only I didn't get to stay. I jam-packed bags, laundry baskets, and suitcases with clothes, swimming gear, books, games, and food. I did not pack the calendar, though. Did I really need it?

At the cottage, we would relax, or so we thought. Gustav refused to wear a life jacket on the boat or in the water. When we insisted, he'd kick, bite, and scream with Herculean might at whomever tried to teach him about water safety. In response, Irie suffered panic attacks about his safety. His favorite game was hiding in stores, neighbors' yards, and restaurants—even in Waupaca, which was foreign territory to our kids. Convinced he'd be cached, forevermore, in the weedy bottom of Long Lake, Irie would hide away in her room, headphones clamped to her ears, reassuring herself with music that Ryan and I were attentively supervising the younger children. Thanks to Gustav's rowdy disposition, she'd developed phobias of kitchen knives and forks, knitting needles, paintbrushes, hockey sticks and baseball bats, any common household or recreational implement that might lead to his death. Danger hankered to devour her youngest brother.

Even at home in Oshkosh, Irie spent most of that summer in the basement, drowning out the sounds of our family with white noise and Broadway tunes. I'd been worried about passing depression on to our children, but in the psyche of our firstborn, those family demons manifested as anxiety instead, just another click-click permutation in the kaleidoscope of genes. She needed medication and counseling. She worried about us, and we worried about her.

Francis's unusual hyperactivity did little to help. On the second vacation day, he leapt from the bow of our pontoon, sinking underneath, before we killed the motor. By the third day, Gustav refused to wear clothes, even to play mini golf. Our only relief was from the puppy we'd bought as a surprise for the kids—Archibald Moonlight Graham. Archie was a pooch as wild, unruly, and voracious as Gustav, but fortunately relegated to doggie day care during the vacation. Ryan and I fantasized about the upcoming weekend. Both sets of grandparents had agreed to babysit a percentage of our children—the only way they could be managed—so that we could celebrate our fifteenth wedding anniversary in Madison.

Friday, our first night alone, was day twenty-one of my twenty-eight-day cycle, wasn't it? Confident, cocksure, verifiably certain—how else might I describe my obliviously unintentional miscalculation? Ryan knew, and I knew, we could not safely raise another baby from scratch, but assuming Friday was the twenty-first and not the fourteenth day, we made love with the kind of freedom reserved for infertile times of the month. In the morning, I ran six miles through the UW–Madison Arboretum, and Ryan biked alongside me, idly chatting, cheerfully nostalgic about his law school days. We even visited the Memorial Union Terrace and walked through the Law School building, fantasizing about our growing independence, as if we were children seeking freedom from our parents, now that Gustav was walking, talking, and blowing bubble gum.

When we finally returned home, our aviation guests had kindly stripped our mattresses to wash our bedding, thereby exposing my menstrual stains, brownish-red stigmata, where I'd leaked, as if opening my veins too many times in the bed. I worried frivolously they'd want a refund for the tainted trundle. Then about ten days later, in that same marriage bed—our wedding gift to each other fifteen years earlier, where we'd conceived all our children—Ryan rolled toward me in a sweat-drenched panic in the blue-black hours of morning, and said, "You're pregnant."

Drowsily I reassured him, "No, I'm not. I'm already bleeding." I wanted to remain in my safe, sleepy existence, and I had been spotting. For two more days, I tried to convince him I was beginning to menstruate, as if I'd been trained to lie, deflect, and deny. Maybe my body was clogged. Bleeding would arrive. The days of August were pliant, putty I could shape and reshape until it suited me, but had I consulted the calendar upon our return, retracked my cycle, and taken a test, I'd have confirmed what three tests told me forty-eight hours later. I was pregnant; I was pregnant; I was pregnant.

Fifty years from now, doctors will probably prescribe "doll therapy" for me, alongside other female residents in assisted living facilities. We'll swaddle fake babies, round plastic heads peeking out from beneath bundles, and among the grizzled women, veteran mothers, I will rock and sing, comforted beyond the effects of medicine or human interaction. Sometimes in a game of make-believe, I cradle Fern's baby dolls and pat their backs, feeling silly but comforted. Gustav's favorite YouTube channel showcases Surprise Egg toy reviews; in a trance, he watches endless unveilings. What surprises are embedded inside? Pregnancy would forever fill me with childlike wonder, and now a test designed by scientists indicated that my empty stomach had been replenished with a magical little novelty.

But when I called Ryan to confirm his suspicions, I felt worried—for *him*, for *me*, for *us*. Since the beginning of time, women have ended pregnancies, and I thought immediately of termination, my only contribution left to this family. What might be a better word—*sacrifice* or *atonement*? Evidence exists of abortifacient herbs in ancient Egyptian documents onward—pennyroyal, black cohosh, brewer's yeast, bitter melon, and tansy. Sometimes women tried to poach their eggs, pry their babies loose, or fall down stairs—what wouldn't they do? And what would it mean to become part of this legacy, a modern woman at the comet's end of this astronomical trajectory? "We don't need to keep it," I said to Ryan, and for a long time, both of us remained enveloped in that ominously dark pocket of silence.

Fern, Francis, and Gustav were enrolled that day in a summer program, and Irie and Leo were with friends; I was free to drive downtown to see Ryan in person. By the time I'd arrived, he'd conducted his research, having prepared phone numbers of clinics where I could get "the procedure." No matter what happened, I was the principal, and Ryan was merely the coconspirator. Just as in pregnancy, labor, birth, and postpartum recovery, I'd have to face the music entirely alone, relinquishing, even, my dormant companion inside. How did I even convince myself to dial those numbers? I told myself, *At least get a consultation. You have plenty of time to decide.* I wondered about a pseudonym but decided I was not a character caught in the web of my own plot. Like the Velveteen Rabbit, I was palpable, mother incarnate, very real, even if this pregnancy seemed imagined, conjured up by that same godlike warden who'd summoned Ryan and me back to Oshkosh years earlier.

Judges were rarely interested in Ryan's clients' stories. Aren't stories just excuses, anyway, long-winded justifications for the crimes we commit? How would Annie Jungwirth or Lucy Vasquez explain their breaches in protection for their sons, after all? And the Morality Squad didn't waste time on stories either, so what could I possibly say to them, or to my neighbors and friends? The answer, obviously, was nothing, and so I didn't. Not a single party to the crime entered our as yet undecided plan, but we talked endlessly, between ourselves, until my brain went blue and numb.

Ryan believed we were doomed by age, especially after the scare over Gustav's kidneys. Our midwife, who delivered Fern, Francis, and Gustav, had even urged us to stop, offering testimonials about fetal abnormalities, late miscarriages, and stillbirth. Of course, Ryan also worried over money; he always would. He'd continue to "check our finances" ten times a day. What if we lost our new house? I worried myself sick over Irie. If Gustav was driving her to regular anxiety attacks, what might another fragile creature do to the stress level in our house? Our support network was limited. If it takes a village, ours was sadly a ghost town. My mom had moved to Colorado; my dad was eighty years old, entirely deaf in one ear, winding down. Ryan's parents, just a mile away, responded to emergencies and hosted get-togethers for all major holidays, but otherwise kept to themselves. We wondered, why had we returned home to Oshkosh? I agonized about the short term: could I sustain another twenty weeks of lethargy and sickness? Ryan lamented the long term, a sixth child in day care. If straw could break a camel's back, could babies break a mother's or father's body too?

"I'm afraid you'll blame me," Ryan said. "You'll wake up in twenty years and wonder where your sixth baby went." True, I'd fought, lobbied, and advocated for more babies, and now I felt nearly incapable of nullifying this one. But I'd go to the appointment. State-mandated counseling might help me decide. Maybe the ultrasound technician would confirm some anomaly, liberating me from the freedom of choice.

I drove to Milwaukee alone. Outside the clinic, which was hidden away in an old building on the east side of the city, a handful of protesters marched. My heart dropped like a yo-yo on a tight string. With some luck, I found a parking spot on another block, approached the clinic through an alley, and emerged a couple hundred feet from the entrance. "Don't kill your baby today," a man whooped, a fiery and scripted greeting. His sign depicted the word MURDER in thick letters like it was a trademark.

Was this, finally, my coup de grâce? Tina Last—my alter ego, my deepest fear—had come to roost. She remained confused when the state of Wisconsin charged her with child neglect. Love and negligence were incompatible, right? For Tina Last, crime was a matter of perspective. Wisconsin statutes define murder, or "first-degree intentional homicide," in part, as causing "the death of an unborn child with the intent to kill that unborn child," even if the Supreme Court has ruled otherwise. In the eyes of this man—one of the "nut jobs," as he'd be referred to inside the clinic—I was a premeditated killer, but was I really? In my mind, I was intercepting an egg; but he probably would have pegged me far below the likes of Allison Shaffer, Alyssa Brandt, or Lucy Vasquez. Perhaps Brenda Lund, plunging that scissors into her baby's skull, was the only mother figure one step closer to hell.

Months later, at a grocery store in Oshkosh, an old man in a motorized shopping cart would stop me in the coffee aisle. "Hey, hey," he said. "Can I give you this?" He offered me a plastic silver cross embossed with the words GOD LOVES YOU. "Sure," I said, "of course." What would my protester in Milwaukee have to say about that? I wondered. In life, everybody is a judge, everybody serves on a jury, or so they believe.

Outside the clinic, the protester jockeyed for eye contact and tried handing me a tract or Bible, but I'd wired my arms to my torso, my legs miraculously still moving. A tall man in an orange vest and rainbow sash said, "You don't need to listen to them." Completely unprepared, in the blitz of assaults and crowding, I couldn't divide up the camps—pro-life, anti-abortion, pro-choice,

God's choice, no choice—comingled into a furious and baffling cluster. When I hit the silence beyond the clinic doors, I felt as if I'd slipped underwater into a muted version of the world.

Apparently fifty-six million women worldwide get abortions each year, and about one-fifth of all pregnancies are electively terminated. These numbers seemed impossible until that day. Women were coming and going, separately but in droves. As if entering some secret underground nightclub, I grasped for my bearings, my eyes adjusting to flashes of light. Did I dissociate, rising above my body, in that moment? Nothing seemed real. The doorman welcomed women and their boyfriends, lovers, parents, and siblings to this moment in women's reproductive rights. Tall, short, slim, rotund, white, black, brown, young, and middle-aged, wearing everything from booty shorts to button-up blouses, every woman on earth seemed to be there with me, a blessing, as Ryan was home with our children, and nobody in my life knew. We could not think of a single babysitter to ask for help at a time like this, and we needed the money for gas and to pay the clinic.

After filling out paperwork, getting a finger prick—a dot of pain that would linger for days—and waiting indefinitely, clinic personnel called me for my ultrasound. According to law, the technician was required to aim the screen at my eyes. "You don't need to look," she said, squeezing jelly onto my flat stomach from a tube the size of travel toothpaste, but my whirling black uterus was like a crystal ball that drew my gaze with secrets of my future. Neither of us discerned anything significant, not even the tiniest speck of life. "Are you sure you're pregnant?" she asked. "Yes, but only about five weeks," I told her, though now I doubted myself. She sent me to the bathroom for a urine sample; then I waited longer. Bad daytime TV elicited sarcastic comments from a rowdy redheaded woman and her boyfriend, as if they were impersonating Siskel and Ebert. Loud and indiscreet, this woman was either in denial or seizing her rights without shame. When a staff member confirmed my positive test, I was called to meet a nurse.

"Are you sure you want to do this?" she asked. Her wearied voice was acerbic, devastatingly cynical, dead as deadpan could be.

"That's what I'm trying to decide," I said, ready to talk and share my misgivings. Not so long ago, I'd have paid a pretty penny to be pregnant, and part of me secretly still would. If a recovering junkie unearths a forgotten bindle of heroin in an old jeans pocket, does she shoot up? I could already smell my new baby's scalp, yeast and uterine water. Part of me was already high, and this was counseling, or so I mistakenly guessed, waiting for the nurse to guide me in some definitive direction.

"I already have five kids at home," I said.

"I've only got two, and they drive me mad," she said. "You're a saint." In the same day, only moments apart, I'd been condemned then exalted; I was me and not me.

"Well, there's no rush, but our schedule fills quickly," she said. "You might as well schedule something and then call and cancel if you'd like." And that was the extent of the counseling, hardly sage or illuminating.

Then, the doctor: young, beautiful, but equally wearied. Abortionist—yet another example of a job that induces empathy fatigue, I thought. She handed me a pamphlet, again required by law, detailing the so-called risks of abortion, but I already knew vacuum aspiration was one of the safest procedures in medicine—far safer than natural childbirth. "You can either take this with you or deposit it inside the waste bin right there," she said, pointing to a receptacle filled to the brim. When I dropped mine in there, adding to the abundance of propaganda, she said, "Good choice."

"Even if the decision feels painful, that doesn't make it wrong," she continued. Her job was to counteract the emotional warfare on the front sidewalk. Everybody outside was fired up; everybody inside was cool, calm, and fully collected, even if nobody sang me a lullaby. Perhaps I was disappointed, furtively waiting for a health care professional to talk me out of this, to send me home, where I'd announce my pregnancy.

On my way to the front entrance, I stopped at the sliding glass window, deciding to make an appointment I could later cancel, and when I finally reemerged on the street, a new escort was waiting. A sleeveless T-shirt beneath his orange vest revealed tattooed biceps, bulging and oily. He walked alongside me in bodybuilder stance, eclipsing the protesters with every step, a barricade between me and a public flogging. Through the scruff around his mouth, he muttered, "They're just ignorant. Don't let it bother you."

And in that moment, for the first time since learning of this, my sixth potentially viable pregnancy, I began weeping uncontrollably. Although he never touched me, I could swear he gave me a swift but gentle push into the alley as if sending me like a small rowboat from shore into the big, wide lake. When I called Ryan, I cried so incoherently that we had to hang up.

On the drive home, I passed a pickup truck hauling a motor home. The jokester in charge had propped an inflatable woman behind the camper's steering wheel. Her plastic cone-shaped head bobbled up and down, her red lips puckered to blow kisses, if only her synthetic hands moved. My bad habit was to take every oddity as a sign—from the universe, from myself to myself. This hollowed-out female body: was she me? I hated to think of that sinkhole inside me, my defunct uterus growing cobwebs instead of babies, if, in fact, I ended this pregnancy. I'd become a caricature of what feminists I knew rallied against, a woman defined by reproductive function, a pathetic, washed-up beauty queen refusing to abdicate her throne. I'd been in favor of women's reproductive rights—I'll say it, *abortion*—since girlhood, but paradoxically, I was also singing the blues. Mine was not a song of guilt, regret, or relief. Predisposed all those years to depression, I felt my sadness entirely usurping everything else. I could not win. From baby maker to baby killer, and nothing in between, I felt the solid footing of the middle ground slip away.

For three days, between my initial consultation and *the* appointment, I ran endless miles, my little blastocyst becoming a gastrula, just barely an embryo. They said time was on my side, but I kept thinking, *It's now or never.* I needed to be soothed, but I was a mother to my own five children. Nobody remained to comfort me. I wanted more than anything to rock, to read, and to be lulled to sleep. Whenever I read *Goodnight Moon*, a personal favorite, I wondered about the quiet old lady whispering "hush." Did Margaret Wise Brown mean for her to represent comfort or rigidity, and why isn't she referred to as the bunny's mother or grandmother? After all, Rob McNally was the only person I knew who referred to his mother in this fashion, as in, "My old lady was such an addict she was all collapsed veins and track lines and shit."

Less than a year later, released from prison on the meth charges, McNally would materialize in Ryan's office as only a magician can. *Poof*, and there he loomed like a genie from a lamp Ryan hadn't even rubbed. He'd fattened up again, a little extra plumpness smoothing out the hard lines. Ryan snapped a photo and sent it to me: "Look who just paid me a visit." My heart ballooned up with emotion and almost popped. This was how guys like McNally discharged their old debts.

Say cheese (from bottom to top): faded jeans, a nickel-plated wallet chain, a black T-shirt with a sexed-up zombie lady walking a pit bull, and a real smile, sweet as punch. Our favorite criminal was living in a Podunk town west of Oshkosh now.

"And guess what, bro?" he said. "I'm getting hitched." The gal at his side was recently widowed when her husband died of a heroin overdose. Naturally, Ryan had represented the guy who sold it to him, and back in 2008, he had also represented that guy's son. That was just the way these things worked in Oshkosh—by three degrees of separation. Before leaving, McNally loitered at Ryan's desk, trying to spit out something important—it would be a courthouse wedding followed by a reception in a tent on his future father-in-law's land.

"If you want to swing by or something," he said, nearly asphyxiating on emotion, "that would be cool."

The ambiguity of the quiet old lady in *Goodnight Moon* is also the story's magic. We are bewitched by the matriarchal rabbit, rocking back and forth across the orange and green pages. This book was first published in 1947, the year my mom was born, such that it has endured the test of time, seven long decades.

Maybe the old lady in the antique mustard-colored rocking chair, knitting with green yarn, is my own mom, or maybe she's yours. In the form of a rabbit, that quiet old lady might be all mothers, maybe even me—but if she is, I am not whispering "hush" to my children. I'm shushing myself. Goodnight Mama. It's time we lay that starry-eyed, fullest-moon phase of your life to rest.

On my return to the Milwaukee clinic, the rain was formidable, descending upon Highway 41 in liquiform curtains. When thunderstorms rev up to seventy miles per hour, windshields are whited out. The downpour generated a great blinding hole, a void I'd known only in blizzards. So many cars had stowed themselves away beneath overpasses that no room remained for me. The torrent had not subsided as I continued to seek an oasis, but when I finally exited at a rest station, the rain slowed with me. As I decelerated, so did the velocity of the raindrops, reminiscent of some lesson I'd learned junior year in physics.

Was this *the* sign I'd been seeking? On the wayside of Highway 41, was I fated to look at myself in the rearview mirror? I could easily have turned my compass north back toward Oshkosh. I called Ryan on the phone, and he said, "You can turn around." But I didn't. Feeling more alone than I'd felt in what seemed like a lifetime, I continued along my forward trajectory. Limbo was not a place I could afford to reside.

I felt apprehensive, skittish. I worried about the so-called nut jobs. Today might be their day to plant a bomb, so the clinic, its providers, and all the patients would burst into flame. In middle school, I'd read about the supposed phenomenon of spontaneous human combustion, long having imagined my burning flesh. What would I smell like, melting to ash, if murdered by zealots at the tables of damnation? We'd be heaped together, a momentous human pyre, covered on the evening news. Inside, I paid the receptionist $550—dirty money for a dirty cause—in cash, then stepped to a side window to receive my paper cup filled with lukewarm water. To my right, a young woman paid for hers using her father's credit card. "Just pop that pill," the attendant said. As I swigged the doxycycline, to prevent the unlikely event of infection, I felt like Susanna in *Girl Interrupted*, being monitored so as not to hide my antipsychotic. Upstairs, in the site for medical procedures, I was the only woman alone, so I grabbed *Shape* magazine and read about new trends in exercise such as "puppy Pilates" till they called me.

A nurse named Tia guided me into an examination room. "You gonna be all right," she kept saying, a mantra or a hymn. She laid me back, guiding my legs into a tent, making overtures toward the ceiling tiles with her hands and soft voice. Postcards from the founding doctor's extensive travels were pasted in neat rows—Bali, the Serengeti, Bangladesh, Ireland, Mexico—photos seemingly ripped from books of fairy tales. She held my hand, and I wrung hers, my only lifeline. When the doctor arrived, I began to tremble. In this lonely world, McNally had paid for Ryan, and I for Tia, in some cockeyed economy of moral support.

"Remember," I said, "I'd like to see the egg afterward." Not a problem, she reassured me, warmer and more gentle upstairs, in clinic, than she'd been in counseling mode, days earlier. When she numbed and levered open my cervix, wide enough for the vacuum tube, I'd reached some threatening final frontier. I was no victim; I was strong and self-possessed enough to call it off, but as with labor and delivery, I closed my eyes, and breathed long and deep, drawing strength from all the women who'd lain there before me—thousands of them, waiting for their bodies to be penetrated by some man-made machine.

I expected to hear the vacuum's roar, but instead I heard slurping, like jelly being suctioned from a jar. Tia kept counting down but then would start the clock over. The procedure lasted four to five minutes, after a three-minute promise. I didn't feel pain so much as waves of agony, my insides deflating, like maybe I was an inflatable woman, after all. When the doctor left the room with my petri dish, I called out, "Can you bring that back?"

Needing something tangible, even corporeal, I sat upright too fast and nearly vomited, just as she emerged again, through the scrubs-colored curtain. I should have been relieved rather than disappointed. My pregnancy looked like nothing—one speck of blood, scant fluid, and a corroded-looking egg the size of caviar, or rather, like a single Skittle Gustav had sucked to its soft candy core before depositing it in my palm.

The state of Texas had recently approved new rules requiring abortion providers to properly bury fetal remains, separate from other biomedical waste—just one of many efforts to sabotage abortion rights. Mothers, of course, buried their placentas, postpartum, under trees to celebrate closure or to call blessings upon their families. What would happen, I wondered, if I buried that egg, nearly dissolved though it was, in my yard? If this were a Dr. Seuss story, perhaps a baby tree would grow—a preposterous notion that gave me a dotty flicker of hope. "Let's go pluck a baby from the tree," I'd say to Ryan, and we'd collect an entire bushel. They'd be free and nutritious, enough to keep me happy till the day I died.

"It's so tiny," I said. "It doesn't look like much."

"Amazing how something so small can cause so much trouble, isn't it?" the doctor said.

Tia told me to dress slowly, but I slipped into my underwear and leggings swiftly, suddenly feeling like I needed to get home. Ryan was alone with all five kids for the second time in a week. We'd told them I was visiting an old friend in Madison, but eventually, one at a time, I'd tell them the truth. I hoped Ryan would beam with pride, praise himself: "I didn't scream once." Later that evening, I'd escape to bed and bawl—deliverance from some black hole in my personal universe, feel-good, life-sustaining hormones beginning to drain from my body like water from a bathtub—but for now, I vowed not to cry. As Tia guided me to the recovery room, light-headedness blew a fuse in my brain. My blood pressure dropped, and I collapsed on my knees in the hallway. "You OK, baby," she said, squatting beside me. She eased me into a reclining chair, between two other women, and pulled over a fan, cranking up the dial. The propellers whipped, fast and dizzying.

The young woman to my right turned to me, and I to her, several times before I initiated conversation. I asked how she felt; she returned the favor. She confessed that, with her parents' moral and financial support, she was getting the abortion behind her boyfriend's back. She planned to tell him she miscarried. "He'd never forgive me," she said. When the young woman—better yet, girl—to my left joined our conversation, she said her parents blamed her boyfriend for demanding the abortion; they were shunning her now and might fully disown her later.

Despite their pain, I envied them both, their reproductive lives unfurling in front of them, full of color and streaming like ribbons from a maypole. "You have plenty of time, when you're ready," I said, flanked by youthful promise, old enough, just about, to be their mother. Another young woman joined us in recovery, obviously having elected sedation, entering the room like a sleepwalker, eyelids drooping, adrift on some faraway ocean.

A nurse sent me twice into a bathroom to monitor my bleeding: one streak, and nothing more. After an hour, I felt startlingly strong, as if I could run the ninety miles back to Oshkosh, my body a well-calibrated system, a scientific wonder to which I owed the gratitude of five beautiful children waiting for me at home.

Out in the lobby, one of the young women's parents looked up at me expectantly. "She's doing well," I said. "She just needs a little more recovery time, and then she'll be out." With our faces, we tried to convert angst to tenderness, bracing ourselves against shared secrets. Downstairs, I stopped at the receptionist's window to make sure an escort awaited me outside.

"Actually, no, our last volunteer just went home," she said.

The eldest woman at the clinic, she wore her silver hair long, with children's plastic barrettes, and holey jeans. A woman in her sixties who'd come of age in the 1960s, she'd preserved herself, still riding those old waves of feminism.

"I'll tell you what," she said. "I'm not supposed to do this, but come with me." We voyaged through the tangle of hallways and time, a snarl of decades, even centuries, it seemed, to a staff-only exit, where she vented the door and peered beyond. "All clear," she said and nudged me toward the daylight. I squinted in all directions and then dashed for my getaway car, a van with a SWIM MOM bumper sticker and upholstery kid-stained beyond detail, except that I wasn't getting away. I was going home.

ACKNOWLEDGMENTS

My son Leo says I use too many exclamation points in my personal notes. Why do I insist on such over-the-top punctuation?

Simply put: one of my greatest anxieties is that I will fail in adequately expressing my gratitude to people who most deserve it.

But herein, I shall try, without a single dagger of typographical joy, to thank my most essential partners in publishing this book.

Infinite gratitude goes to:

My wise, tenacious, and unwaveringly loyal agent, Nat Sobel, and the Sobel Weber team, especially Siobhan McBride, Sara Henry, and Adia Wright.

Anna Bliss, my editor, whose faith in *The Motherhood Affidavits* and whose supernatural gifts, one of which is mind reading, made me a believer in the spiritual process of collaboration.

Matthew Lore, who is a kinetic wonder of creativity, tirelessness, and generosity. I would not want to publish this memoir anywhere but with you.

The entire staff at The Experiment, including Karen Giangreco, who helped to brainstorm more than fifty title options; Sarah Smith, who designed the book's jacket; Jennifer Hergenroeder, whose matter-of-fact lessons on publicity prepared me for the real world; and Dan O'Connor, who gave the pages a last look before printing.

Anne Horowitz, who carefully straightened every paragraph with her fine-tooth comb.

Suzanne Williams, my publicist, who championed my story.

Elizabeth Johnson, who mapped my Midwestern debut.

Kim Thiel, who captured my genuine laughter during the author photo shoot, and Ken Koenig, who designed my colorful website just as I imagined it.

Staff at the UW Oshkosh Women's Center, who hosted an event to celebrate my book's release.

Readers who endured early chapters of the manuscript: Alex Albertson, Stewart Cole, Peter Geye, Shelley Puhak, and finally, Jenna Rindo, who inspired me to log my sanity miles and baked me plenty of treats to earn back those calories.

Heidi Wheaton, Laura Sandberg, Kelsey Maples, Jamie Lynn Buehner, Betty Wegehaupt, Angie Mich, Shannon Berg, and Paul Klemp: additional names I find soothing in the event of an emotional emergency.

All my writing teachers over the years, notably Judith Claire Mitchell, Ron Kuka, Eileen Pollack, Peter Ho Davies, Nancy Reisman, Charles Baxter, Stuart Dybek, Reginald McKnight, and Nicholas Delbanco.

My mentor and dear friend, Pamela Gemin.

The Office of Faculty Development at UW Oshkosh for funding my sabbatical during the fall 2015 semester and the Children's Learning and Care Center for loving our children and keeping them safe so that I could write.

Gabby Bird, our babysitter and beloved family friend, for nurturing our children, often in times of crisis.

My mom, my dad, and my stepmom Nancy, for teaching me empathy and for being eccentric enough to make life interesting. You raised this daughter to think (and live) outside the box.

Irie, Leo, Fern, Franco, and Gussie: one-fifth each of my whole happiness.

And Ryan, who supplied me with everything essential—from facts and stories to babies, laughter, and love—for my mental wellness and joy.

(Now on to the next book!)

ABOUT THE AUTHOR

LAURA JEAN BAKER teaches at the University of Wisconsin Oshkosh, specializing in memoir, women's stories, crime narratives, and literature for children. She earned her MFA in creative writing from the University of Michigan, where she was a Colby Fellow. Her poetry and essays have appeared in *Alaska Quarterly Review*, *War, Literature, and the Arts: An International Journal of the Humanities*, and *Calyx*, among others, and she has been twice nominated for a Pushcart Prize. Her essay "The Year of the Tiger" was named a Notable Essay in *Best American Essays 2013*. She lives in Oshkosh, Wisconsin.